DARK TWINS

IMPOSTURE AND IDENTITY IN
MARK TWAIN'S AMERICA

SUSAN GILLMAN

THE UNIVERSITY OF CHICAGO PRESS

CHICAGO AND LONDON

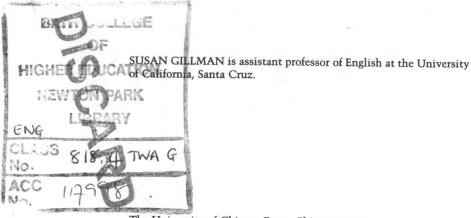
SUSAN GILLMAN is assistant professor of English at the University of California, Santa Cruz.

The University of Chicago Press, Chicago 60637
The University of Chicago Press, Ltd., London
© 1989 by The University of Chicago
All rights reserved. Published 1989
Printed in the United States of America
98 97 96 95 94 93 92 91 90 89   5 4 3 2 1

Library of Congress Cataloging-in-Publication Data

Gillman, Susan Kay.
    Dark twins : Imposture and identity in Mark Twain's America / Susan Gillman.
        p.   cm.
    Bibliography.
    Includes index.
    ISBN 0–226–29386–6.   ISBN 0–226–29387–4 (pbk.)
    1. Twain, Mark, 1835–1910—Criticism and interpretation.
2. Doubles in literature.   3. Split self in literature.
4. Impostors and imposture in literature.   5. Identity (Psychology) in literature.   6. United States in literature.   7. Psychoanalysis and literature.   I. Title.
PS1342.D64G55   1989
818'.409—dc19   88–21802
                                                     CIP

To my father and to the
memory of my mother

A book is the writer's secret life,
the dark twin of a man.
                    Faulkner, *Mosquitoes*

CONTENTS

ACKNOWLEDGMENTS

For their support and encouragement at various stages of this book, I would like to thank the following: Richard Bridgman, rigorous critic of my prose, trusted adversary, and only incidentally the director of the dissertation that formed the basis of this study; Michael Rogin, for his attentive reading of the whole manuscript in an earlier form and for his ongoing enthusiastic conversation; Wendy Lesser, Robert L. Patten, Edward Snow, George Marcus, and the members of the Rice University Critical Circle, who read a portion of chapter five at a crucial stage in my thinking; Forrest Robinson, for his shared interest in Twain generally and in *Pudd'n-head Wilson* in particular; and finally, the late Henry Nash Smith, whose seminar on nineteenth-century popular culture originally inspired my interest in Twain and whose scholarship continues to be an inspiration. Robert H. Hirst and the staff of the Mark Twain Papers at the University of California, Berkeley, have helped me since the first stages of research by encouraging me with a friendly scepticism, by sharpening my awareness of textual matters, and by employing me.

I wish to thank the Regents of the University of California for the Bancroft Library Fellowship at the start of my research and the American Council of Learned Societies for the fellowship that enabled me to finish.

I owe the most to my husband John Kadvany, best and most rigorous of all critics.

CHAPTER ONE

INTRODUCTION:
MARK TWAIN IN CONTEXT

Ever since William Dean Howells insisted in his memoir *My Mark Twain* on defying his own title and calling his friend "Clemens . . . instead of Mark Twain, which seemed always somehow to mask him," the peculiarly double personality Samuel Clemens/Mark Twain has continued both to elude and to fascinate.[1] A critical language of twinning, doubling, and impersonation has subsequently developed around this writer, in part fostered by what James Cox calls "the primal creative act of inventing Mark Twain."[2] There is also all the fascination with alternate selves in his writing: the paired and disguised characters, the mistaken, switched, and assumed identities, the confidence men and frauds that everyone remembers as part of Twain's fictional world, even if they have read only *Tom Sawyer* and *Huckleberry Finn.* Gender and genetic twins seem especially to proliferate: lookalikes (*The Prince and the Pauper*), putative half-brothers (*Pudd'nhead Wilson*), Siamese twins (*Those Extraordinary Twins*), and characters such as Huck and Tom Driscoll who through imposture become twin selves of both genders. The writer also doubles himself through autobiographical projections within the fictions and by his pseudonym. As Howells recognized, though, the problem with these writerly doubles (as with the treatment of doubles/twins) is that they tend not only to multiply confusingly but to entangle one another in complex ways. Mark Twain presses his investigations of twinness to the point where coherent individual identity collapses: it ceases to be possible to separate one brother from the other, or to punish one-half of a a pair of Siamese twins, or even to determine whether a housemaid is female and pregnant or male and larcenous.[3] Similarly, Samuel Clemens himself invents a persona that not only becomes a second self but after a time enslaves the first, so that the twin Twain eclipses Clemens. "Mark the Double

Twain," Dreiser once entitled a short critical piece on Samuel Clemens.[4]

The proliferating doubles therefore seem frustratingly as much to mask as to reveal the self they also project. No wonder that the language of doubling used by Howells and others since has sought to identify the overlapping series of masks that constitute the writer's invented personae—funny man, satirist, public performer/reformer—and to situate these roles in the context of his life and times. The primacy of his biography was of course encouraged by Mark Twain himself as a writer of autobiographical fiction. Certain biographical explanations are repeatedly, almost ritualistically cited as evidence that Twain felt himself to be a man divided: he was a southerner living in the North; a frontier bohemian transplanted to urban life in genteel Hartford; an American who lived in Europe for at least ten years of his life; a rebel who criticized, inhabited, and even named the world of the Gilded Age.

The most insightful of Mark Twain's biographers, Justin Kaplan, recognizes that these biographical versions of dividedness were inflated by Mark Twain himself into the kind of legend that hides its subject by flaunting only a spectacular composite of his personality. In the suggestively titled *Mr. Clemens and Mark Twain*, Kaplan argues that even before the pseudonym Mark Twain had become an identity in itself and "swallowed up" Samuel Clemens, he was "already a double creature. He wanted to belong, but he also wanted to laugh from the outside. The Hartford literary gentleman lived inside the sagebrush bohemian." At the center of the Kaplan biography, the whole issue of duality is represented as Clemens's "wrestling" "with the enigma of dual personality"—by which Kaplan means personal, psychological problems often worked out in, or placed in parallel relationship to, Twain's writing.[5] This broad biographical approach has provided powerful accounts of, and explanations for, the problematic authorial identity summed up in the *nom de plume* that Mark Twain sometimes called a *nom de guerre*.[6] Or as Leslie Fiedler once described the particular dilemma that Kaplan addresses so perceptively: "From the moment he gave himself the telltale pseudonym Mark Twain, Samuel L. Clemens was haunted by that second self, and his last words were inchoate murmurings about Jekyll and Hyde and dual personality."[7]

No one would deny that the figure "Mr. Clemens and Mark Twain" of the Kaplan biography has his own idiosyncratic and urgently personal claims on problems of identity. But as his reference to Robert Louis Stevenson's popular novel *Dr. Jekyll and Mr. Hyde* suggests, Mark Twain is also very much of a representative man, given to thinking and speaking in nineteenth-century colloquialisms. Thus to pick only two examples from contemporary popular culture, Twain's allusions to Jekyll and Hyde and to Siamese twins bespeak a fascination, beyond Twain's personal predicament, with things that in themselves embody questions about the boundaries of human identity. My approach to the subject that might be called by its nineteenth-century name of "duality" is to (re)create the dialogue between Twain's language of identity and the cultural vocabularies available to him.[8] Such a dialogue would reflect the complex interplay between personal insights and cultural tradition. My own method also depends on the dialogue of cultural history informed by and emerging from literary analysis, or literary analysis of cultural history. This kind of "historical criticism," Jane Tompkins points out, is not merely "backdrop" for the writer's individual genius. Instead, literary texts are read for the "cultural work" they do as "agents of cultural formation," "a means of stating and proposing solutions for social and political predicaments."[9]

Such contextualizing allows us to broaden our conception of the subject beyond the conventions of literary dualities traceable to Mark Twain's own unstable personal identity. The problem of identity and imposture—that is, of a unitary, responsible self—led Twain to become interested in potential solutions embodied in the processes of identification and legitimation, primarily legal and scientific, that were available in the world around him. Thus we will see how Twain's most apparently unique and idiosyncratic representations of problematic identity engage with late-nineteenth-century efforts to classify human behavior within biological, sexual, racial, and psychological parameters. At the same time, Mark Twain's America is also representative in its denials and silences, in what he, like his culture, dismissed as trivial, disguised, or concealed, or simply did not acknowledge. By reading Twain, for example, in the context of writings (his own and that of others, journalistic, scientific, legal) that have been considered, then and now, as "nonliterary," we may open up the canon in terms of how we understand both Mark Twain and late-nineteenth-century questions of identity.

In identifying the predicament and its solutions, of course, it will be *my* Mark Twain and *my* nineteenth century that emerge, but they share both the features and the non-canonical sources of what several cultural historians have already recounted of the man's class and his time. Drawing on a heterogeneous set of texts, both public and private utterances, Peter Gay premises his first volume of *The Bourgeois Experience: Victoria to Freud* on "a broad band of far-reaching cultural shifts between, for the most part, the 1850s and the 1890s." Mark Twain's writing career, from 1865–1910, not only happens to span those critical decades, but as I will argue, registers intimately their cultural transformations. Among the heady and anxiety-producing changes, Gay focuses in this volume on sexuality: patterns of courtship and marriage, fears about masturbation, concepts of childbirth, and the psychological images of "offensive women and defensive men" generated by feminist movements. Although Mark Twain is generally seen as a writer reluctant or unable to address issues of adult sexuality, I will show, through a number of Twain's little-known or unpublished writings, mostly from the 1890s and concerning the subjects of pregnancy and legal paternity, that he was indeed a child of the "Age of Nervousness"—the time, as Gay points out, christened at the end of the century at a meeting of physicians, psychologists, and sociologists.[10]

The period has also been characterized as an age of "weightlessness," "marked by hazy moral distinctions and vague spiritual commitments, . . . [such that] personal identity itself came to seem problematic." "Weightlessness" is Nietzsche's term, here mediated through Jackson Lears's reinterpretation in his penetrating analysis of a broad "anti-modernist" impulse at the turn of the century.[11] Mark Twain's late, so-called "dream writings" of the 1890s and after—science fiction and fantasy tales—reflect some of the kinds of reaction formations Lears identifies in Henry Adams and others: paradoxical efforts to master, through repeated flights into nostalgia and other regressive fantasies, what is perceived as the increasingly uncontrollable social and natural world. Among the changing nineteenth-century realities that induced the sensation of weightlessness in Mark Twain, the most important centered around man's often contradictory efforts to ground his environment through technological and corresponding social inventions: the creation of a culture industry through massive increases in book and journal output, paralleled by increases in population and literacy; the twin movements of immigration and imperialism that, along with civilization's "triple curse" of railroad, telegraph, and newspapers, made the world seem simultaneously smaller and more alien;[12] and, finally, the curves of scientific thought, especially the proliferation of conceptual systems, such as Darwin's, Marx's, and Freud's, that applied self-consciously and self-critically the scientific, classificatory analysis in which so much modern faith was put. Out of all of this, a nineteenth-century "culture" constructs itself as a time, in Peter Gay's words, "of progress and for confidence, but also one for doubt, for second thoughts, for bouts of pessimism, for questions about identity."[13] It is those questions of identity, framed in terms of their economic, legal, social, psychological, and metaphysical dimensions, that I will address in Mark Twain.

Although Mark Twain writes obsessively about twinness, doubling for him was always less a literary than a social issue. Whether these lookalikes are random and contingent (such accused innocents as Muff Potter; the prince mistaken for a pauper; Huck Finn "born again" as Tom Sawyer) or willful and exploitative (the unexposed criminal Injun Joe; all Twain's confidence men), they raise a fundamental question: whether one can tell people apart, differentiate among them. Without such differentiation, social order, predicated as it is on division—of class, race, gender—is threatened. Thus Mark Twain, champion of the subversive, also championed the law as one agent of control that resolves confusions about identity, restoring and enforcing the fundamental distinctions of society. A number of legal premises particularly fascinated him: that innocence and guilt are two distinct categories; that proofs in the form of legal evidence exist to back up that distinction; and that legal evidence is so rigorously defined as to constitute nearly "absolute" knowledge.

In Mark Twain's fiction throughout the seventies and eighties, the law solves problems of identity by sorting out the captor/captive confusions in "Personal Habits of the Siamese Twins" (1869); by exonerating the falsely accused Muff Potter in *Tom Sawyer* (1876); and by rectifying the exchange of social identities in *The Prince and the Pauper* (1882). The problem, at once literary, social, economic, and legal, might better be called imposture than twinning or doubling, for by 1890 Twain is replacing the more legitimately confused, switched, or mistaken identities, which spill over in his fiction of the seventies and eighties, with the impostor, a figure of potentially illegitimate, indeterminate identity.

Yet imposture is a slippery term. Whereas twinning or doubling suggests merely mathematical division, imposture leads to a kind of logical vicious circle. Since "posture" already implies posing or faking, "imposture" is the pose of a pose, the fake of a fake: the word implies no possible return to any point of origin. Synonyms for imposture complicate this ambiguity by distinguishing degrees of intentionality on the part of the impostor. "Deceit," for example, is "strongly condemnatory" because it refers to "purposeful" deceiving or misleading, whereas "counterfeit" and "fake" may or may not condemn "depending on culpable intent to deceive."[14] Thus imposture raises but does not resolve complex connections between morality and intentionality. Its multiple confusions leave room for lawyers, confidence men, and, ultimately, the writer himself to erase boundaries and circumvent the law, making suspect the premise that knowledge is possible—by legal or any other means.

P. T. Barnum, an artist at turning humbug into big business, recognized the difficulties in confining imposture to clear-cut boundaries. "Many persons have such a horror of being taken in," he noted shrewdly, "that they believe themselves to be a sham, and in this way are continually humbugging themselves."[15] Mark Twain began his career by trading humorously on that horror, representing for entertainment the fictional impostors, including the deadpan narrators of frontier humor, that he observed in the world around him; he ended by getting entangled in the process of representation and convicting himself and his writing of imposture. In short, Twain initially assumed that imposture is a social problem that he could expose through the neutral lens of the writer's eye, but ended by turning that eye inward on himself and his own art. In the art of humor he discovered the same capacity for deception that he sought to expose in life. For imposture is intimately related to his art: the early journalistic hoaxes, the humor of the tall tale, even the humor of irony that works by making language itself duplicitous.

Clemens's extraordinarily successful self-creation as the humorist "Mark Twain" testifies both to his grasp of showmanship and to his exposure of all the attendant "anxieties of entertainment."[16] In nineteenth-century America humor was perceived as a "popular" rather than a "serious" mode, and fame as a humorist was not easy to transcend. Still worse, the role of humorist, which Mark Twain alternately exploited and railed against, put him in the ambiguous position of being lionized by his own targets of derision. Telling tales about people being duped, Mark Twain reflects his own ambivalent relationship to his audience, those he entertained quite literally at their own expense. Kenneth Burke's comment on irony helps to discriminate the tangled boundaries among Twain, his art, and his audience: "True irony is based upon a sense of fundamental kinship with the enemy, as one *needs* him, is *indebted* to him, is not merely outside him as an observer but contains him *within*, being consubstantial with him."[17] Mark Twain, wearing the mask of the ironic stranger observing the human race of "cowards," ultimately unmasks himself and discovers that he is "not only marching in that procession but carrying the banner."[18]

The term "imposture" with all its inherent ambiguities thus captures not only the problem of identity that Twain both observed and embodied, but also the problem of his representing that problem: the tendency of conscious intentions to entangle and expose unconscious ones and of public voices and vocabularies to emerge from and merge with the private. Some of these particular cultural vocabularies are clearly articulated by Twain himself. He was bitterly aware, for example, of the double bind of his success as an artist. "Playing professional humorist before the public" gave him a voice and an audience, he reflected late in life in his autobiography, but it was to the exclusion of other, more serious voices and at the cost of other, more serious audiences (*MTE*, 201). Even as early as 1874, he wrote to William Dean Howells that his preferred audience was that of the highbrow *Atlantic Monthly*, "for the simple reason that it don't require a 'humorist' to paint himself striped & stand on his head every fifteen minutes."[19] It was in part the ambiguities of his status as an artist—humorist or serious writer? master of audiences or their slave?—that led Twain to his most explicit formulation of what he called in a January 1898 notebook entry the "haunting mystery" of "our duality."[20]

This long and complex notebook entry, to which I will return in detail in the next chapter, demonstrates how Mark Twain's own awareness of problems of identity, or duality, to use his word, tended to shift radically, according in part to the cultural vocabularies available to him. In the entry he identifies, explicitly or implicitly, several particular vocabularies and contexts that helped to give voice to his various "new 'solutions' of a haunting mystery." Yet the notebook also confirms that Twain's omissions, silences, and elisions can be traced to cultural as well as to personal blind spots. While he drew quite self-consciously on the findings and language of psychology, for example, the metaphors of the law and criminality, conventionalized through actual trials and in detective fiction, were appropriated more unintentionally, as part of the world around him. And the entry alludes to a link between racial identity and sexuality that is, in the explicit theory of duality formulated in the notebook, not acknowledged at all.

Using the 1898 notebook entry's rough outline, I have followed suit in the shape and sequence of my own argument, mapping out Mark Twain's "solutions" to the "haunting mystery" of human identity and tracing their complex, shifting relationships to the culture whose vocabularies he alternately appropriated and quibbled with, exploited and subverted, inhabited and ironized, but which were always enabling. Reading his whole career in the light of what he self-consciously articulated only in the 1890s and after, I argue that Twain's early reliance on literal, literary conventions of external, consciously divided identity becomes entangled with a social conception that treats identity as culturally controlled and then gives way to an imposture that is increasingly internal, unconscious, and therefore uncontrollable: a psychological as opposed to social condition. Finally, though, even these distinctions—external/internal, conscious/unconscious, waking/dreaming—collapse into an undifferentiated darkness, as Mark Twain, during the much-debated dark period of "pessimism" and artistic "failure," confronted the impossibility of his arriving at any foundation of self and other—and yet continued to produce a poignant series of half-finished writings, his effort to create an abstract, ahistorical metaphysics of identity.

Each chapter in this book identifies a group of diverse Mark Twain materials—newspaper and magazine pieces, fiction, journals, letters, speeches—which I believe bear on the different rough stages I have outlined and which I situate in dialogue with a specific cultural context. The second chapter begins by exploring Twain's attitudes toward authorship, his own authorial control, and the authority of the humorist, since the whole issue of identity for Twain always involved his art, even as it broadened out to include social, legal, and psychological dimensions. The increasing professionalization of authorship in the nineteenth century, especially the role of machinery and technology in making literature a consumable product and the role of the lecture platform in making the writer a public performer and property, generated deep conflicts that Mark Twain both sprang from and helped to shape.

The third chapter, centered on the bifurcated stories *Pudd'nhead Wilson* and *Those Extraordinary Twins* (1893–94), argues that those novels draw on Twain's earliest literary conceptions of twinning and mistaken identity in order to explore the historical actualities of slavery. Thus Mark Twain was led to the serious social, psychological, and moral issue of racial identity, a genealogy that I argue must be understood against the context of turn-of-the-century racism: legal discourse on issues of blood, race and sex, miscegenation; Jim Crow laws and Negrophobic mob violence; the ideologies of imperialism and racial Darwinism. There are also barely articulated implications here about sexual identity that I pursue in the following chapter, through materials that I alluded to earlier, a series of largely unknown writings on the law and sexuality. Although some of these pieces date from Mark Twain's early period—*A Medieval Romance*, for example, from 1870—most were written during the last two decades of his life—1890–1910—when popular Darwinian debates over heredity and environment informed Twain's representations of both racial and sexual difference. In the trials that culminate (but often without concluding) many of these tales as well as *Pudd'nhead Wilson*, legal determination of identity becomes a metaphor for questioning to what extent difference, both of race and of gender, is as much culturally as biologically constituted. Thus Mark Twain discovered in a very graphic context, rooted in the historical actualities of race slavery, how social fictions assume not the pose but the power of unalterable realities; he exposed human bondage to cultural categories and historical circumstances.

Once these concepts had been called into question, Twain began questioning his own basic assumptions about selfhood and reality. *Pudd'nhead Wilson* directly initiated the confused and confusing writings of 1895–1910, the dream narratives and science-fiction fantasies that are frequently incoherent, some only half-finished. Chapter five argues that these formless, inchoate works—it is hard to tell where one begins and another ends—express poignantly Twain's late struggle to find a new form, emptied of history and divorced from social reality, whose only referent is to itself, and whose only subject is the dreamer and the problem of his artistic imagination. The tales begin with narrators dreaming themselves into a nightmarish reality from which neither they nor the story ever emerges. Even these fantasies of escape from history, however, bear explicit cultural marks. As the author himself recognized in his January 1898 notebook entry and elsewhere in the notebooks and letters, his conception of the unconscious dream-self crystallized only in the context of turn-of-the-century psychology: not only Freud's dream analysis, but Charcot's experiments with hypnosis and William James's with spiritualism and psychical research. So, too, did Twain's late, rather crude, philosophical essays on human nature—*What Is Man?*, for example—take full shape (for they were variations on earlier themes) in the context of popular debates about the "pseudoscience" of spiritualism and the "science" of psychology. Thus Mark Twain turned ironically to the popular sciences in writing his late dream narratives, which repeatedly turn on inversions of scale, time, and space to create their fantasies of disorientation and escape from reality.

The teleology outlined here is somewhat too neat, since Mark Twain was fascinated not just at the end of his life but throughout by the vocation of the artist and the sources of his creativity. Even in his early writings there is a kind of duplicity in the narrative strategy. The deadpan mask of the narrator derived from frontier humor is a complex convention, difficult to penetrate. Simon Wheeler's appearance of unconscious artistry, for example, is never exposed as either genuine or fraudulent. The audiences of the "Jumping Frog" (1865) cannot tell if Wheeler is only posing, consciously assuming the mask of innocence, or if his innocence extends inward, part of his unconscious personality. Similarly, Mark Twain's letters and notebooks strike different poses at different times toward contemporary scientific and pseudoscientific research in the human imagination, ranging from the stance of the would-be believer in his eldest daughter Susy's faith in "mind cure," to that of the sceptic *malgré lui* during séances when he and his wife Livy tried futilely to contact the dead Susy's spirit, to the analytical sceptic in his polemic on Mary Baker Eddy, *Christian Science* (1907). The rough chronological progression of my argument is thus only rough, not meant to be enshrined, as the curve of Twain's life, from humorist to nihilist, optimist to pessimist, has tended by now to be rigidified in Mark Twain studies. Although the book moves forward in time, within each chapter I draw on materials from various periods of Twain's life, because that is how his own investigation proceeded: erratically, in fits and starts, gaining new terrain by retracing old ground.

My argument also follows the overall drift of Mark Twain's writing toward incompleteness. Much of the material I discuss in the second half of the book remains unfinished, and because of their aesthetic incoherence, some manuscripts have not yet been published, or even if available, have not received much sustained, sympathetic attention.[21] But in spite of this, I argue that they are an important, perhaps essential, part of the picture. The incoherent, fragmentary state of both the sexual manuscripts and the dream writings makes them resistant, even inaccessible, to conventional literary analysis; an interdisciplinary approach helps to make their silences speak, in part because it is receptive to the cultural realities on which these works so ostentatiously turn their backs. Indeed, even grouping the pieces as I have done itself constitutes the beginning of my argument. No single one of the tales of sexual identity makes much sense in isolation; only putting all of that material together defines it as belonging among Twain's "solutions" to the "haunting mystery" of "duality." He himself never speaks directly or indirectly of the "sexual writings" in these terms at all, and surely would have disavowed any role to sexuality in his various solutions to the problem of establishing a criterion of the self. It is I who argue that such a context enables otherwise apparently incoherent, vestigial, and even rather silly texts to begin to articulate themselves. Mark Twain's views of sexuality were never formulated as consciously or self consciously as they were on the (for him) closely allied subject of race, certainly in part reflecting the cultural vocabularies available and the collective denial in force. But when sex was wedded to race, as in antebellum legal regulation of miscegenation and in turn-of-the-century popular fiction justifying Negrophobia on the grounds of uncontrollable black sexuality, the pair was obsessively returned to, in a kind of cultural return of the repressed. In this context, Mark Twain was very much a representative man.

Given these multiple voices and glaring silences, my approach is to speak both *through* Mark Twain as a conscious, articulate critic of and spokesman for his culture, and *for* Mark Twain when he is less aware and more disguising, displacing, or denying of his own subject. At times this means permitting oneself to be constrained by one's materials. I have tried to adhere to the usual convention of using "Clemens" to refer to Samuel L. Clemens in his extra-authorial identity and "Twain" to refer to the authorial self. Unfortunately, the two selves do not remain fixed in their proper categories, making it difficult to maintain the linguistic distinction consistently. But, then, that is the problem with all the dual taxonomies that might be used to label Mark Twain, by himself or others—and, indeed, that conflict is the theme of this book. In addition, it is not I but Mark Twain who takes the term "fraud" as a *locus classicus*. He relies astonishingly often on the language of "fraud" and its cognates—swindle, humbug, sham, pretense—

to convey a vision of the broadest array of social beings, events, and conventions, thus ironically giving unintentional voice to the wish that a world without fraud is either possible or desirable.

Just the reverse, however, seems to apply to Mark Twain's America. As he saw it, nothing and no one were immune from charges of imposture. Individuals could be frauds: George Carleton, a publisher who rejected a collection of early Mark Twain pieces, including the "Jumping Frog," was, the author wrote a friend, "a Son of a Bitch who will swindle him." The old European masters whose art Mark Twain observed in 1867 on the *Quaker City* excursion are "dilapidated, antediluvian humbugs," but so, too, are some American masters, such as the three "impostors" posing in Mark Twain's "Whittier Birthday Dinner Speech" as the "littery" men "Mr. Longfellow, Mr. Emerson, and Mr. Holmes." Even a whole geographical and cultural region, the South, for example, may fall "in love with . . . the sham grandeurs, sham gauds, and sham chivalries of a brainless and worthless long-vanished society," also known as "the Walter Scott Middle-Age sham civilization." In sum, anyone who, like Mark Twain, has been through the "mill" of the world must know it "through and through and from back to back—its follies, its frauds and its vanities—all by personal *experience* and not through dainty *theories* culled from nice moral books in luxurious parlors where temptation never comes."[22]

But finally, perhaps precisely because Mark Twain, by his own admission, has so intimately and personally known the frauds of the world, he sets out to expose fraudulence through the art of humor. "Ours is a useful trade," he said of humor in 1888 when he accepted an honorary M.A. from Yale:

> With all its lightness and frivolity it has one serious purpose, one aim, one specialty, and it is constant to it—the deriding of shams, the exposure of pretentious falsities, . . . and whoso is by instinct engaged in this sort of warfare is the natural enemy of royalties, nobilities, privileges and all kindred swindles, and the natural friend of human rights and human liberties.[23]

The problem, of course, as Kenneth Burke's comment on irony suggests, is that such a war of exposure may expose the self in "fundamental kinship with the enemy," and thus end by confusing the distinctions between friend and enemy, self and other, the authentic and the fraudulent, the observer of sham and the participant in it. It is exactly these risks that Mark Twain ran throughout his life, alternately succumbing to and resisting them. And it is that process of continual self-construction and destruction by someone who is both critic and child of his culture that I hope to represent in this book.

CHAPTER TWO

IMPOSTURE AND THE "LITTERY MAN"

Yes, this is a swindling shop and a swindling show, and you
don't do nothing but swindle people.
Mark Twain, "Historical Exhibition
—A No. 1 Ruse" (1852)

From the very beginning of Mark Twain's career as a writer, simply
practicing his own craft embroiled him quite literally in imposture. In the early 1860s, he first made a reputation in the
western press with journalistic hoaxes, the most infamous of
which were "Petrified Man" and "A Bloody Massacre near Car-
son" (better known as "The Empire City Massacre"). Both pieces,
published in the Virginia City *Territorial Enterprise*, matter-of-
factly report totally imaginary, sensational discoveries—one a fos-
silized corpse, the other the slaughtering of a whole family by their
deranged father—hoaxes that apparently (at first) hoodwinked
newspaper readers accustomed to such gory fare. In a letter to the
Enterprise in 1868, some six years after the hoaxes appeared, Mark
Twain listed the "feats and calamities" which, he said, "*we* never
hesitated about devising when the public needed matters of thrill-
ing interest for breakfast. The seemingly tranquil *Enterprise* office
was a ghastly factory of slaughter, mutilation and general destruction in those days."[1]

Like other artists and entertainers in mid-nineteenth-century
America, Mark Twain was responding to an insatiable appetite,
both on popular and literary levels of culture, for the hoax and the
stunt, often in the form of the sensational "true science" or "true
crime" report. "Scientific discoveries"—P. T. Barnum's "natural
curiosities" at his "American Museum" or the *New York Sun*'s
"moon hoax" or probably the most famous dramatic stunt, staged
by the *New York Herald*, of Henry Stanley's African search for the
missing Dr. Livingston—appealed to a mass audience, while more
sophisticated journalistic and literary frauds also found their audience.[2] In the 1830s and 1840s, Poe's hoaxes simultaneously
pandered to and lampooned the public mania for sensation. During
the same period, southwestern humorists experimented with a
literary form that created the illusion of telling an oral tale, often
the tall tale characteristic of frontier humor. The pleasure com-

mon to these various "swindling shows" comes only just before they close, somewhat like the very last exhibit that Barnum's patrons paid to see, the sign "Egress" posted on the way to the exit. The punch line is always in the knowing that one has been deceived, and so not until the "egress" is one finally "taken in." In this way the swindle's sweetness must be inherently fleeting, taking place in the moment when victimization turns itself into realization. By thus exhausting its pleasures the hoax paradoxically renews them.

P. T. Barnum exploited the national appetite for fraud by extending the moment at the egress. As Neil Harris has shown, Barnum created an audience for the exhibits in his American Museum (the name itself another appeal to the true-science claim) partly by casting doubt on their authenticity and inviting public suspicion, thus making the issue of fraud one of the attractions that drew customers in. Writing to Moses Kimball, owner of the "Feejee Mermaid," one of Barnum's more transparent frauds, Barnum proposed an advertising campaign that would flaunt rather than hide the mermaid's problematic status. "Who is to decide," a proposed advertisement asked, "when *doctors* disagree? If it is artificial then senses of sight and touch are ineffectual—if it is natural then all concur in declaring it *the greatest Curiosity in the World*."[3] Capitalizing on the scientific community's charges of fraud, as he did with the mermaid, proved to be as successful a publicity device as Barnum's own self-created image of the showman/humbug—an image nurtured in the numerous editions of Barnum's autobiography. In "Advice to Others," the chapter that sums up his self-styled business philosophy, Barnum attributes his success not merely to the public's blind enthusiasm for even a probable hoax, but, more shrewdly and convincingly, to their desire to uncover the process of the hoax, to know *how* the fraud has been worked.[4] As one of the legendary but unattributed Barnum sayings goes, "First he humbugs them, and then they pay to hear him tell how he did it. I believe if he should swindle a man out of twenty dollars, the man would give a quarter to hear him tell about it."[5]

While public enthusiasm for Barnum's hoaxes indicates enjoyment more than fear of duplicity, both responses were clearly essential to the Barnum show. The process of deceiving and that of exposing deception—both almost simultaneously enacted by exhibits in the American Museum—work by inducing the same double vision, half of which sees appearances only, the other half of which sees through them. In both cases, the viewer is balanced uneasily between pleasure and fear as the acts of deceiving and exposing tend to merge together. As David Brion Davis puts it, "In the era of P. T. Barnum, whom could you trust?"[6]

Mark Twain's era, we might say, began with Barnum and ended with a different kind of "trust-buster," Teddy Roosevelt. Always a representative man, Twain used the Barnum idiom to dismiss "the President's ferocious attacks" on big business (such as that of Twain's friend H. H. Rogers's Standard Oil) as "merely a sham and a pretense." But still, we know, the humorist cast himself in a similar role to Roosevelt as "enemy" of "privileges and all kindred swindles."[7] Yet of course neither for Roosevelt nor for Twain was the impulse to expose fraudulence in the American scene simply a matter of imagined devils—nor was it always possible to identify, and hold accountable, the responsible individuals.

Bedeviled throughout his life by foreign publishers pirating his books, by unauthorized use of his name in print, and sometimes even by "deadbeats" lecturing as "Mark Twain,"[8] the writer at first saw these instances of imposture as a simple and straightforward, if irritating, problem. Typical of the misappropriation of his name, and his initial response to it, was a piece in the *New York Tribune* during January 1875, purportedly written by Twain, favorably reviewing Kate Field's performance as Laura Hawkins in the dramatized version of *The Gilded Age*. (An unauthorized stage version of the novel had already played in San Francisco in late 1874 until Twain managed to close it.) He was "trying to circumvent a deadbeat," Twain wrote to the managing editor of the *New York World*, requesting a public printing of his letter of protest against the author of the *Tribune* article:

> This woman is the most inveterate sham and fraud and manipulator of newspapers I know of; and I didn't think she would ever be smart enough to get a chance to use me as a lying bulletin board to help her deceive the public, but by cutting down and printing a *private* note . . . she really has got the best of me, after all.[9]

The authoritative tone of rage deflating to impotent protest partially accounts for Mark Twain's increasing reliance on legal authorities as the only reliable means of redress for such infringements. He appealed to the law in another case, this one a matter of the so-called "Dubuque swindler" taking Twain's person as well as his name in vain. Hopeful about unmasking this "specimen of villainy," Twain described how "a man pretends to be my brother and my lecture agent—gathers a great audience together . . . and then pockets the money and elopes, leaving the audience to wait for the imaginary lecturer! I am after him with the law."[10] A few weeks later, however, writing to his brother Orion "in a petulant state," Twain complained that "a loafing vagabond swindles Dubuque in my name and that spiritless and dirty community let him go. I employ a lawyer here [Elmira] to plan the rascal's capture, and the first move he makes proves him a fool. A sheriff starts after the culprit and *he* turns fool—and rascal, [too] I judge."[11]

The law in this case found no proof to incriminate the swindler; it merely demonstrated its own resemblance to the "fools" and "rascals" it pursues. Yet the possibility that the law would prove to be a definitive means of resolving doubt about imposture continued to appear promising. Even here, when Twain expresses disappointment at the outcome of his legal manoeuvering, his language reflects an untouched belief in basic legal processes: the lawyer "proves" himself a fool and the sheriff turns fool, "I judge."

Notwithstanding legal failures to circumvent deadbeats, then, Mark Twain remained fascinated all his life by the spectacle of the law at work. Unsuccessful lawsuits in fact stimulated rather than quenched Twain's litigious appetites.[12] Like his contemporaries he also avidly followed newspaper reports of celebrated trials. Extensive coverage of sensational murder trials, including daily transcriptions of testimony, was an innovation gradually introduced after the 1830s, a result of the increasing circulation and broadened audience of the cheap dailies.[13] But even as it became a fixed feature in the dailies, "trial by newspaper" was attacked on moral grounds. As early as 1830, charges of sensation mongering forced one editor to defend the press as "the living Jury of the Nation."[14]

Mark Twain's attitudes reflect the ambiguous status of "trial by newspaper." Although he would attack the New York newspapers in 1907 for violating the right to privacy in their excessive coverage of the Harry K. Thaw murder trial, in 1873 he hired a secretary who collected six scrapbooks of newspaper clippings from the English press on the celebrated perjury trial of the Tichborne claimant— the prolonged effort of Arthur Orton to be recognized as Sir Roger Charles Tichborne. Drawing directly on life, as Twain's fictional preoccupations so frequently did, his focus on spectacular fictional trials reflected contemporary interest in a number of other well-known legal cases: the Laura D. Fair murder trials in 1871–1872, the Beecher-Tilton adultery trial in 1874–1875, and the Dreyfus case in France in 1893.

The law exerted a much deeper intellectual fascination on Twain, however, than either personal need for legal redress or increased public awareness of legal cases would suggest. As we will see, it held out the promise of a systematic differentiation of the legitimate from the illegitimate in almost every sphere of life, as well as a system of evidence and proof to shore up that process of identification. Twain's complex response to his problems with fraud during the 1870s not only demonstrates his initial assumption that imposture can be exposed by legalistic proofs but also sets the stage for his eventual disillusionment with both the law and the very idea of proof—or knowledge—of identity.

Legal proofs of identity appeal to external authority for verification of an inner state, embodying a confusion of boundaries that characterizes Mark Twain's approach to problems of confused or uncertain identity. By posing the issue as one that existed entirely outside himself, Twain projected onto the outside world what was partly a psychological problem. Ultimately, however, the process of projection also ironically reversed itself; Twain's suspicions of the external world were internalized, making him doubt his own sense of authenticity. Far more than these examples from the 1870s imply, his fears of fraud would center at least as much on himself as on others. Fearing exposure himself, he saw impostors everywhere. Like Barnum's victims of humbug who end by humbugging themselves, Mark Twain had "such a horror of being taken in" that he "believed himself to be a sham."[15] The volatile and convoluted circumstances of Twain's early years as a successful writer—and his literary capacity both to grasp in writing and to mask the significance of his own actions—are epitomized by a culminating event of the 1870s, the occasion of the Whittier birthday dinner speech, to which we now turn.

II

On the evening of 17 December 1877, Mark Twain delivered a postprandial speech at a dinner given by the publishers of the *Atlantic Monthly* to commemorate John Greenleaf Whittier's seventieth birthday.[16] Invited by the new editor, William Dean Howells, to speak to an audience that included Emerson, Lowell, and Oliver Wendell Holmes, as well as other members of the Boston literary establishment, Twain was put in a peculiar position. The role of the Wild Humorist of the Pacific Slope, certainly a reputation that helped bring him to such an honor, represented a new and different literature from that of the "men of letters" in his honorable audience. If the dinner celebrated the passing of that old order, then Twain—and his fellow westerner Howells from Ohio—represented part of the newer age that was in the process of supplanting the old. The obvious intention of the speech delivered on this charged occasion was to communicate gracefully and humorously Twain's sense of unworthiness to his Boston audience, but a latent antagonism broke free from his control to make him mock and subvert their authority.[17]

Told in the form of a literary burlesque, the Whittier dinner speech exploits the linguistic confrontation in southwestern humor between perceptions of western vernacular and eastern genteel cultures. Twain pretends to reminisce about a time once during his own early "callow and conceited" days as a young writer when he "resolved to try the virtue of his *nom de plume*." While on "an inspection-tramp" through the Sierra foothills, Twain happens upon a miner's lonely cabin, announces his pen name, and hears a dejected response. He is "the fourth littery man that's been here in twenty-four hours," the miner complains, the others being Mr. Longfellow, Mr. Emerson, and Mr. Holmes (*SSW*, 151). The three men, however, did not behave at all like the great writers whose names they use; after eating the miner's food and drinking his whiskey, they cheated him at cards. The impostors amuse the reader (if not the miner) primarily because they offer farcical misquotations from the writings of the authors they claim to be.

Mark Twain, now no longer the teller of the tale but the listener, also takes on the role of the straight man in the frontier tale. Speaking in the typically elevated language and supercilious tones of such characters, he condescends to explain the deception to the naive westerner who has been taken in by such unmistakable frauds: "Why, my dear sir, *these* were not the gracious singers to whom we and the world pay loving reverence and homage; these were impostors." The miner replies, "Ah—impostors, were they?—are *you?*" His deadpan response deflates Twain's "callow conceit" by challenging his assumption that, unlike the miner, he can distinguish between three tramps posing as "gracious singers" and the genuine articles (*SSW*, 154). The miner's parting shot—the "nub" of the joke—is a humorously sly reminder that Twain, himself a poseur with a *nom de plume*, is not one to be exposing frauds when as a "littery man" it is his business to create them.

But turning the tables directly on Twain, the punch line also turns the tables on us, the audience, because like him we have assumed that the joke is on the humorless miner, who can neither recognize bad literature when he hears it nor see the humor when great literature is misquoted. As in so many of Twain's humorous sketches, the apparently witless vernacular character gets the best of his cultured listener in the end, reversing their roles and, in the process, implicating the audience as well. We are deceived by not one but two poses: Twain's pose of the superior visitor and the miner's pose of fool, both built into the literary conventions of frontier humor and reinforced by the values of the dominant culture.

If Mark Twain miscalculated, thinking that he had humorously expressed his genuine sense of being a fraud aspiring to the august *Atlantic*, virtually no one else missed the implication that the three "gracious singers" were also somehow fraudulent. The problem, though, was that public response was mixed. Accounts published in Boston newspapers the following day were generally favorable, but the speech was received with some hostility in the press outside Boston. It was particularly criticized in many quarters as "irreverent"—a notion to which Twain had himself subscribed in asserting that "we and the world pay loving reverence and homage" to these venerable figures.[18] He wrote Howells afterwards that he "must have been insane" when he wrote the speech "& saw no harm in it, no disrespect toward those men whom I reverenced so much."[19] Echoing both the term reverence and its corollary, the lack of responsibility (invoked by "insane") to account for the irreverence, Howells defended his friend in a letter to Charles Eliot Norton: "I pitied him; for he *has* a good and reverent nature for good things, and his performance was like an effect of demoniacal possession."[20]

The opposition between the reverent and the insane or between the reverent and the demoniacal implies the same rigid moral code so often comically exploited by Twain—this time apparently at his peril—to define himself and his relationship to his culture. One unsigned letter to the *Springfield Republican* perfectly expressed the twin poles of the dilemma in which Twain caught himself at the Whittier dinner: it accuses him of being "a wild Californian bull" bursting into the "China shop" of American letters and trampling underfoot a most "precious possession— reverence for that which is truly high."[21] Such outrage is generated by the peculiar double status cultivated at times by Twain himself: he is not simply an outsider but an outsider with one foot in the door, a bull *in* the china shop. At the moment of the Whittier dinner, he was suspended between two roles: the California humorist mocking the institution of Men of Letters while being accepted as a member of that institution. The metaphor of imposture central to the speech captures the sense of disruption that occurs when Twain, who presents himself as the unmasker of sham and pretense, is himself unmasked as one of "them."

But Twain was not, of course, just another gracious singer. Howells's metaphor of demoniacal possession had unknowingly apt cultural resonance, for Mark Twain had already begun to trade, as a writer and as a personality, upon the role of impudent demon. The public eventually lionized him as the eccentric humorist, the token subversive, parts that he willingly, even eagerly played, dressing flamboyantly and becoming known first for his red hair and flaming mustache, later for the white suits. Howells judged such "relish for personal effect" to be "not vanity but a keen feeling for costume . . . ; yet he also enjoyed the shock, the offence, the pang which it gave the sensibilities of others."22

In short, Mark Twain gave back to the world the images he saw reflected in its eyes. But at the same time, he chaffed against the role of humorist and his own complicity in creating it. While his humor was often rooted in the impulse to subvert authority, he lived out the most extravagant of Gilded Age social and economic fantasies. And this champion of the subversive also championed the law as one agent of control that resolves problems of identity. Concerning his vocation as an artist, this ambiguity continued to torment Twain, suspended as he would remain throughout his life between the roles of humorist and serious writer—roles that were culturally constituted.

The Whittier speech, of course, represents a comic moment in Twain's career as a writer. The tale's humor, like that of the hoax, lies in the unexpected exposure, the reversal of expectations, those both of Twain and of the audience. Twain liked to tell what he called in 1852 "double jokes,"23 those that aimed at deceiving the listener but also at making him pleasurably conscious of his own deception. Precisely the same reversal of expectations, we know, disturbed Twain in his actual experiences with fraud. But transmuted into fiction, the kind of double take he found so unnerving in his own life fed directly into the tradition of southwestern humor, which frequently took as its subject the process of gullibility duping itself. Like the miner in the Whittier sketch, many of the dialect characters in frontier humor assume poses of inferiority that are comic precisely because the poseurs never reveal whether they are themselves fooled by their own falsity.

In Twain's "The Notorious Jumping Frog of Calaveras County," for example, the gentle narrator Simon Wheeler appears to have taken in his cultured, eastern listener with his tale of Jim Smiley, the confidence man, and his well-trained frog with few "visible p'ints," both men duped in turn by a poker-faced stranger.[24] But because Simon Wheeler never breaks his own deadpan presentation, we never know exactly who is the duper and who is the duped. The whole notion of imposture, then, essential to Twain's humor, exploits the same enjoyment of duplicity that Barnum's humbugs assume—and that Twain's hostility toward fraud in his own life seems to belie. The confidence man presides over the comic tale as hero, not villain. Simon Suggs, a character created by Johnson J. Hooper, another humorist, proclaims in his favorite motto, "It is good to be shifty in a new country."[25] Twain was manipulated in life by frauds perpetrated by the Simon Suggses of this world—the very frauds he had called forth in his fiction.

Being a "littery man," then, provided the central impetus to Mark Twain's conception of himself and, ultimately, to his conception of selfhood. Throughout his career as a writer, the profession of authorship in America was dramatically reshaped by events in the culture at large, especially by developments in law, science, and technology. All of these changes directly affected the situation of the professional writer, and Mark Twain in particular. We have briefly seen how the literary scene of the 1860s and 1870s impelled him toward confrontation with the problem of imposture on different fronts: in the courts, in the press, and in his own writing. Culminating in December 1877 with the "Whittier Birthday Dinner Speech," this early period sets the stage for the rest of this chapter, which will move forward in time to explore the developing interaction between the profession of writing and Twain's conception of the self. We will first look at the business side of authorship in the nineteenth-century literary marketplace, and then at how this environment, and Twain's response to it, shaped the metaphors he consistently used to refer to his own process of composition. Finally, we will see how those metaphors of literary creativity were themselves applied in wide-ranging ways to Clemens's personal life, particularly in his responses to family deaths and to his own dreams, culminating in one long dream that I will argue helps us to relocate his ongoing conception of identity back in the context of American culture at the turn of the century.

III

The Whittier dinner speech combines fiction and autobiography to suggest more eloquently than evidence from either Twain's life or art alone how resonant the notion of imposture became for him, how entangled it was with literature and literary creation, and how difficult he found it to articulate such resonance. But the text of the speech, paired with and read in the context of its aftermath, points clearly to a constellation of metaphors, some apparently contradictory yet central to Twain's conception of authorship: the artist as willful impostor, imposing his (illegitimate) control on a gullible audience, and the artist as will-less impostor, possessed by controlling spirits in the form of his art and his audience.

However idiosyncratic these figures may seem, they emerge from a particular historical moment, coalescing in a number of actual conditions associated with the industrialization of literature and the corresponding professionalization of authorship in the late nineteenth century. Increases in population and literacy, combined with advances in technology and transport, were the enabling conditions for a massive increase in book and journal output following the Civil War. The rapidly expanding business of producing and marketing literary products created what was in some ways a boom for writers. There were not only more readers but also more kinds of publishers, reviewers, and modes of publication, as well as a plethora of contemporary commentary on the growth of this new literary culture industry. Speculation focused particularly on its visible or potential effects on the book-product, the reader-consumer, and the publisher-advertiser.[26] As to its effects on the author, Howells coined the phrase "the Man of Letters as a Man of Business" to acknowledge the hybrid "class" of writers he saw coming into existence. Musing in *Literature and Life* (1902) on the origins of this hybrid, Howells sees the Civil War as a watershed:

> It is only since [then] that literature has become a business with us. Before that time we had authors, and very good ones; . . . but I do not remember any of them who lived by literature except Edgar A. Poe, perhaps; and we all know how he lived; it was largely upon loans . . . But many authors live now, and live prettily enough, by the sale of the serial publication of their writings to the magazines.[27]

Howells could speak with some authority of such historical transition, having himself been novelist, magazine editor, and critic in both the Brahmin literary center of Boston and the more commercial New York environment that replaced it. In spite of the undeniable benefits of such commercialization to "a whole class" of authors "wholly unknown among us before the Civil War," Howells argues, still certain "drawbacks"—some of the traditional unpredictable "muse" type, others the product of the new literary business—"reduce the earning capacity of . . . the high-cost man of letters." Now "the higher class of novelists" may have a "steady market" for its "literary wares," but this new consciousness of "market prices" produces new contours in the literary landscape. The very conditions that expand the market for literature also dictate what "brands" of art and "kinds" of artists sell to what audiences. "The sort of fiction which corresponds in literature to the circus and the variety in the show-business seems essential to the spiritual health of the masses, but the most cultivated of the classes can get on, from time to time, without an artistic novel" (LL, 5, 31–32). Thus the price of literature's entry into the marketplace, according to Howells, is a series of divisions in audiences—the "masses" and the "cultivated classes"—in writers—"higher class" and "inferior" novelists—and in literature itself.

The net result was an implied paradox: as the man of letters' name grew more and more widely known and his books were more and more popularly consumed, he became less and less in control of his book/product, his audience/consumer, and his own image. He was subject not only to readerly "fashions" but also to the vagaries of the general climate of social and political opinion—and the most obvious potential solution, the law, was not yet available to him:

> There is, indeed, as yet no conspiracy law which will avenge the attempt to injure him in his business. A critic, or a dark conjuration of critics, may damage him at will and to the extent of their power, and he has no recourse . . . The law will do nothing for him, and a boycott of his books might be preached with immunity by any class of men not liking his opinions on the question of industrial slavery or anti-paedobaptism. (LL, 30–31)

The writer's authorial freedom, then, is fatally compromised by the success of his own writings; the more his work is read, the more he himself becomes a celebrity, a public figure to be admired or reviled on his own, apart from his books, almost as a public property. Finally, these issues of ownership and control over literary properties make Howells doubt even whether authors, "the makers of literature," have any legal power over the thing they make: "It is true that we now have an international copyright law at last" (something that writers' organizations in both America and England had fought for since the early nineteenth century), "but literary property has only forty-two years of life under our unjust statutes, and if it is attacked by robbers the law does not seek out the aggressors and punish them. . . . The Constitution guarantees us all equality before the law, but the law-makers seem to have forgotten this in the case of our literary industry" (*LL*, 6).

Mark Twain, the quintessential Man of Letters as a Man of Business, experienced with particular intensity the anomalous inflation and fragmentation of the post–Civil War literary marketplace. An author who owned his own publishing house, Charles L. Webster and Company (named for its manager, Clemens's nephew by marriage), established in 1884 to publish *Huckleberry Finn*, Twain was also engaged throughout his life in business ventures that included but did not give precedence to his writing. Investments in inventions, foremost the Paige typesetter but also including his own patented self-pasting scrapbook and "Mark Twain's Memory-Builder," a history board game, ranked equally for Twain with the investments, financial and emotional, he made in literary inventions and ventures.[28] So intertwined, in fact, were these various investments in various inventions that in 1894 his publishing house was finally mined all the way to bankruptcy, drained as much by the escalating costs of the Paige typesetter as by an over-expanded list of titles. Because Clemens's wife Livy was a preferred creditor with the largest single claim on the firm, all of her husband's literary copyrights were transferred to her possession—a legal arrangement that suggests how compromised were the writer's own authority and control over the business side of authorship.

Clemens's double commitments as inventor/writer and entrepreneur/publisher fostered the kind of untenable conflicts that Howells implicitly identified as the lot of the hybrid class of post–Civil War authors. For spectacularity, his financial failures matched his literary successes; the record of obsessively poor judgment in investment balanced against the fact that through writing and lecturing he was able to repay his debts after 1895. But however proud of having paid back his creditors "one hundred cents on the dollar" as Livy insisted they do, Clemens was disturbed by the swings from extravagant Gilded Age living to periods of frugality, specifically because they embodied the precarious control he exerted over his literary creations—in the business both of creating them and, afterward, of publishing and marketing them. Nothing in his literary career, however, fit the definition of public failure quite like his investments did.

One striking response to this lack of control was Clemens's self-styled divided relationship to the world of money. Although the bankruptcy in 1894 culminated at least eight years of draining investment in the Paige typesetter and poor management of Charles L. Webster & Co., he represented his bankruptcy as an overnight reversal. Three months before filing for bankruptcy, on 15 January 1894, "a great day in my history," he exulted in his notebook about a possible new typesetter contract: "Yesterday we were but paupers with but three months' ration of cash left and $160,000 in debt, my wife & I, but this telegram makes us wealthy" (MTN, 235). More than mere financial success, money represented a source of personal identity that could transform Clemens's sense of himself from pauper to millionaire. He comprehended his bankruptcy, then, as a process more far-reaching than a temporary financial reversal. It became an image central to his experience and to his writing, a graphic symbol of the reversibility of identity and of the instability of the boundaries that define the self's outer and inner worlds.

So powerful was the spectre of the pauper self that it compressed all the most devastating reversals of fortune Clemens suffered, emotional as well as financial. He repeats the word "pauper" in two letters to his lifelong friend the Reverend Joseph H. Twichell, one written after his oldest daughter Susy's death, the other after his wife Livy's. Each reveals how emotional loss was framed and measured in terms of financial standards. Susy is "treasure in the bank," never precisely counted, but "now that I would do it, it is too late; they tell me it is not there, has vanished away in a night, the bank is broken, my fortune is gone, I am a pauper."[29] Livy's death makes him feel similarly bankrupt, like "a man worth a hundred millions who finds himself suddenly penniless and fifty million in debt in his old age. I was richer than any other person in the world, and now I am that pauper without peer" (MTL, vol. 2, 760). The repetition of "I am a/that pauper" suggests how bound up with the language of money were not only his experience of loss but also his own sense of self. Clemens's images of double destiny—the opposite extremes of pauper and millionaire, for example—were in part a response to external events, a poignant attempt to control those events by imaging only two possible outcomes.

But even when the facts do not support him, he represented sudden reversals, as in the letter about Livy, who had been seriously ill and bedridden for two years before her death. In an odd way, then, the constructions of dual selves and of reversible fortunes, both of which organize experience into two extreme but categorizable opposites, compensated for an increasingly debilitating loss of control.

Even after repaying all his debts in full, Clemens wrote himself into another scenario of financial doubleness, this one rather playful, in a notebook entry entitled "The Prophecy":

> In 1895 Cheiro, the palmist, examined my hand & said that in my 68th year (1903), I would become suddenly rich. I was a bankrupt and $94,000 in debt at the time . . . I am superstitious. I kept the prediction in mind and often thought of it. When at last it came true, Oct. 22, 1903, there was but a month and nine days to spare. (*MTN*, 381)

Clemens dwells mockingly on the conjunction of prediction with "sudden" wealth, again representing as uncontrollable the caprices of even good fortune. The only role he concedes to himself is the comic and passive one of the superstitious mind. As a means of evading his own responsibility, such comically deflated self-conceptions provided some relief, but at the same time further undermined a wavering sense of control over his own actions. As a result, these letters and notebook entries translate Clemens's unstable financial condition into a figurative double identity which is literally embodied in the fictional prince and pauper. We cannot dismiss this imagery merely as a product of Clemens's distorted self-perception. For not only did he recover from bankruptcy, but with the help of Henry Huttleston Rogers, the Standard Oil millionaire (and as some observed even at the time, an odd bedfellow for the enemy of privilege and "kindred swindles"), he became a rich man again. He lived a divided life as much in financial as in literary terms; the prince and the pauper are a kind of economic analogue to the divisions and connections between Samuel Clemens and Mark Twain.

Clemens's representation of his personal financial crises must also be framed by the particular late-nineteenth-century context of the profession of authorship, whose anomalous expansion impinged directly on Mark Twain as one of its most celebrated figures. As we have seen, a growing mass market, particularly in fiction, gave authors new status and in some cases an increased income, yet, as Howells complained, the correspondingly increased complexity of marketing literary property worked paradoxically to deprive the individual author of substantial creative and economic control over his own work. The technological changes that occurred in book production, for example, as a result of nineteenth-century industrialization and of specific inventions, particularly in automatic typesetting (Ottmar Mergenthaler's Linotype in 1884 and Tolbert Lanston's Monotype in 1887), made possible the enormous flood of cheap books and paperbacks, the "fiction factories," the profitable pirating of foreign editions—all of which threatened the livelihood of high-cost men of letters like Mark Twain. In spite of this, we know, Twain expressed his enthusiasm for the machine side of the book business through his ultimately disastrous involvement with James W. Paige's typesetter, that "awful mechanical marvel" which made "all the other wonderful inventions of the human brain . . . sink pretty nearly into commonplace."[30] The paradoxes eventuated by such an attraction to machine culture bore fruit in *Connecticut Yankee*'s final paean of praise to nineteenth-century civilization's automated capacity for self-destruction. Nevertheless, writing the *Yankee* at the end of the 1880s did not prevent its author from further entanglement with the contradictions of the "awful mechanical marvel."

Intertwined with these technological developments was a subset of the problems of the Man of Letters as a Man of Business: an increasingly adversarial relationship between author and publisher, especially in contractual matters such as advances, royalties, and copyright infringement.[31] Twain attempted to circumvent the author-publisher problem (somewhat as he did with the Paige typesetter) by becoming his own publisher, but also, along with Howells and others, by joining in authors' efforts to organize themselves into societies dedicated to the protection of literary property and to the passage of an international copyright. Even after the International Copyright Law of 1891, Twain continued to testify before copyright committees in Congress and Parliament, arguing that, as both author and publisher "experienced in the scorching griefs and trials of both industries," he was uniquely situated to state the case for perpetual copyright—the extension to literary property of the rights and controls accorded to any other property. "Then it would be recognized that an author's children are fairly entitled to the results of his ideas as are the children of any brewer in England, or of any owner of houses and lands and perpetual copyright Bibles" (*MTE*, 374, 380). The impetus behind this argument, like that motivating the rest of

Clemens's ventures into the business of literary ownership (the Paige typesetter, Charles L. Webster & Co.), was to assert some control, even if only rhetorical, over the alternately inflated and fragmented environment of the professional author.

In such an age of mechanical reproduction, to use Walter Benjamin's phrase, the author may suffer a fate similar to the one that Benjamin ascribes to the work of art: "what is really jeopardized" by technical reproduction is "the authority of the object," its "authenticity," its "unique existence."[32] In Twain's case, though, the threat is not so subtle as a diminution of aesthetic response; it is loss of literal authenticity, that is, of the *author's* control over the work. At the same time that books were mass-produced, imitated, and pirated, so in some cases did the writer himself become a commodity, marketed as platform artist, lecturer, reader, and personality. The problems of an emerging technology of mass reproduction were thus intertwined with analogous concerns with artistic identity.

The late-nineteenth-century lecture circuit, for example, had originated in the earlier lyceum system and such "educational" lecturers as Emerson, Thoreau, and Bronson Alcott, but it shifted to entertainment as it experienced a vogue for dramatic "author's readings" following Dickens's American tour in 1867. Not only Mark Twain but also Henry James, Sr., Bret Harte, George Washington Cable, and Henry Ward Beecher all courted a public that paid as much to see an author in person as to read his books. The flamboyant personalities associated with Twain's fellow leading platform humorists of the day—Artemus Ward, Josh Billings, Petroleum V. Nasby—were as essential to the platform art of oral storytelling as were their pseudonyms, derived from the tradition of southwestern humor, whose form required the tale-teller to adopt a persona. The humorist's pseudonymous personality inflated as it also masked the author, an anomaly that Howells recognized in "most American humorists,"

> who have all found some sort of dramatization of their personality desirable if not necessary. Charles F. Browne, "delicious" as he was when he dealt with us directly, preferred the disguise of "Artemus Ward" the showman; Mr. Locke likes to figure as "Petroleum V. Nasby," the crossroads politician; Mr. Shaw chooses to masquerade as the saturnine philosopher "Josh Billings."[33]

In contrast to the more-or-less unidentifiable pen names of British authors such as George Eliot or Ellis, Acton, and Currer Bell or

the Danish Isak Dinesen,[34] the "dramatization" of the pseudonymous personality in American humor fostered something like the
"cult of personality" that Benjamin later criticized in the film
industry: "The cult of the movie star . . . preserves not the unique
aura of the person but the 'spell of the personality,' the phony spell
of a commodity."[35] Indeed, Mark Twain, a writer almost better
known as a platform artist and public personality, found his celebrity status as problematic as the business side of book production.
In particular, the consumers who constituted his market—the
audiences on the lecture circuit who paid to see him read from his
books—focused the conflicts, both social and psychological, of a
writer constrained by his early image as the Wild Humorist of the
Pacific Slope.

Although Twain hated the lecture circuit (alternately "crucifying myself nightly on the platform" and "robbing the public from
the platform"), he was forced (by "pecuniary compulsions") to
depend on it for most of his writing career, culminating in the
emotionally draining but financially rewarding round-the-world
tour in 1895.[36] This particular tour Howells assessed equivocally
as "not purely perdition for [Clemens], or rather, it was perdition
for only one-half of him, the author-half; for the actor-half it was
paradise . . . Clemens was victorious on the platform from the
beginning. . . . But I suppose, with the wearing nerves of middle
life, he hated more and more the personal swarming of interest
upon him."[37] Howells's language confirms the divisiveness of
Twain's lecturing experience; not only are there the perdi-
tion/paradise, author/actor divisions, but also the battle-like
tension between the "victor" of the platform and the "swarming
interest" upon him.

Twain's own numerous analyses of his astounding success on
the platform all similarly assume that the speaker's relationship to
his audience is essentially adversarial. In 1870, for example, only
his second lecture season, he boasted to his fiancée Livy about his
daring to use silence, the extended pause to mesmerize his lis-
teners. Standing "patient and silent, minute after minute," he
"conquered their reserve, swept their self-possession to the
winds." Underscoring his need to seek absolute control of the
audience, Twain concluded, "An audience captured in that way
belongs to the speaker, body and soul, for the rest of the evening.
Therefore, isn't it worth the taking of some perilous chances
on?"[38] But like the perils that Twain would later ascribe, in similar
language but different context, to both master and slave in the

system of race slavery that permitted blacks to "belong" to whites "body and soul," neither participant in such an intimately opposi-tional relationship escapes unscathed. Each is utterly dependent, though in very different ways, on the other for a sense of identity. If the performer Mark Twain, for example, "used to play with the pause," he remembered in 1907, "as other children play with a toy," it was the audience who determined the length of the pause and therefore controlled his play. And different audiences can be so precise in their differing measurements that they may be com-pared to Twain's *bête noir*, the machine: "An audience is that machine's twin; it can measure a pause down to that vanishing fraction" (*MTE*, 226). For Twain, one unanticipated result of pur-suing that vanishing fraction during so many years of performing onstage was a self-image almost as hollow and yet confining as efforts, satirized in *Pudd'nhead Wilson*, to measure racial black-ness down to a fraction of a drop of black blood. "I am demeaning myself," Clemens commented in 1885 during a six-week lecture tour with George Washington Cable. "I am allowing myself to be a mere buffoon. It's ghastly. I can't endure it any longer."[39] Al-though he and Cable were billed as "Twins of Genius," the very concept of creative genius, either in terms of his art or himself, was undermined by Twain's particular experience as an artist in the age of mechanical reproduction.[40]

IV

The process of literary creation confronted Mark Twain in busi-ness, in the law, in publishing, and in performing, with graphic divisions between authorship and control. Although never a par-ticularly programmatic or self-conscious theorist, Twain responded to the pressures of the literary marketplace by address-ing the broad issue of authorial control through a series of related tropes: the artist as passive amanuensis/unconscious plagiarist, as unwilling midwife/proprietor/father, and finally as the uncon-scious.[41] These scattered metaphors suggest that, unlike some literary men, Twain experienced creativity not through the model of the pen-penis disseminating its writings on the virgin page, but rather as illegitimately sexualized, a threateningly un-controllable power.[42] Amanuensis to plagiarist to midwife to father: the relationship of author to text is envisioned as in-creasingly intimate, entangled, complicit.

The first set of metaphors figures the author as distant from and as passively related to his literary creations as possible. Sometimes the "books would go gaily along and complete themselves if I would hold the pen," Twain reminisced in 1906, and "as long as a book would write itself I was a faithful and interested amanuensis." But in practice the process of composition, like childbirth, often proved to be laborious, and so the pen-holding amanuensis resorted to a more mechanistic turn of phrase. The Mark Twain "literary shipyard" almost always had "two or more half-finished ships on the ways, neglected and baking in the sun," because "the minute that the book tried to shift to *my* head the labor of contriving its situations, inventing its adventures, and conducting its conversations, I put it away . . . [until it] was ready to take me on again as amanuensis." By accident, he says, during the year-long lull (in the mid-1870s) in producing *Tom Sawyer*, he discovered the reason—and new imagery—for his own fitful process of composition:

> My tank had run dry; it was empty; the stock of materials in it was exhausted . . . It was then that I made the great discovery that when the tank runs dry you've only to leave it alone and it will fill up again in time, while you are . . . quite unaware that this unconscious and profitable cerebration is going on. There was plenty of material now, and the book went on and finished itself without any trouble.[43]

As Justin Kaplan argues, this "basic tenet of Mark Twain's faith in himself as a writer" is framed in metaphors which reflect "both his mechanistic turn of mind and his frontier assumption of endless forests and numberless buffaloes."[44] But I would add that this is an oddly self-compromising tenet of faith. The tank will fill up again, but the writer, "unaware" and "unconscious," denies himself any control over the process. For Twain to authorize his art means, it seems, to qualify his authority over it. What is jeopardized, then, by the process of artistic production is, to extend Benjamin's terms, not simply the "authority" of the "object," but the "authenticity" of the self that produces the object.

Just how problematic this conception of creativity is may be gauged from a related metaphor: the author as plagiarist. Unlike the Walt Whitman poet, an "original," "the Me myself," Twain rejected the possibility of originality in art. Even thoughts are not self-generated, he argued in a letter to Helen Keller on St. Patrick's Day, 1903:

> As if there was much of anything in any human utterance, oral or written, *except* plagiarism! The kernal, the soul—let

us go further and say the substance, the bulk, the actual and valuable material of *all* human utterances—is plagiarism. For substantially all ideas are second-hand, consciously and unconsciously drawn from a million outside sources, and daily used by the garnerer with a pride and satisfaction born of the superstition that he originated them. (*MTL*, 2:731)

More than consciously drawing on sources, the notion of *unconscious* plagiarism, like the "unconscious cerebration" of the tank filling up, becomes a major trope in Twain's theorizing about creativity.

Both Twain's letter to Helen Keller and his *Autobiography* recall one striking case of unconscious authorial borrowing from the 1860s. So influenced was Twain (according to his own account) by reading a book of Oliver Wendell Holmes's poetry, *Songs in Many Keys*, that three years later Twain "stole" Holmes's dedication to the book when dedicating his own *Innocents Abroad*. Although Twain was later mortified that the gist of the dedication "was promptly mistaken by me as a child of my own happy fancy," Holmes assured the culprit (in Twain's paraphrase) that "there was no crime in unconscious plagiarism." "No happy phrase of ours is ever quite original with us," but rather "all our phrasings are spiritualized shadows cast multitudinously from our readings."[45] If no originality is possible, still here *some* more intimate relationship than that of mere amanuensis is postulated between the writer and his "phrasings." Together the images of a child and spiritualized shadow, which conjure up writing for Twain in the case of the Holmes plagiarism, lead us to his most extended metaphors for creativity, those that link books to childbirth and to the shadows of the unconscious cast by dreams.

Responding in 1889 to George Bainton's request for a few words on authorial methods for a book to be called *The Art of Authorship*, Twain underscored the unconscious nature of his own creative process:

If I have subjected myself to any training processes, and no doubt I have, it must have been in this unconscious or half-conscious fashion . . . This unconscious sort . . . is guided and governed and made by-and-by unconsciously systematic, by an automatically-working taste—a taste which selects and rejects without asking you for any help . . . Yes, and likely enough when the structure is at last pretty well up, and attracts attention, *you* feel complimented, whereas you didn't build it, and didn't even consciously superintend . . . So I seem to have arrived at this: doubtless I have

methods, but they begot themselves, in which case I am only
their proprietor, not their father.[46]

This theory of creativity should be read first in the context of
Twain's general doctrine of determinism and the particular text
What Is Man? (written 1898, published 1906), which Twain called
his "gospel" and De Voto called "a plea for pardon."[47] *What Is
Man?*'s mind-as-machine thesis explicitly formulates what the
Bainton letter implies, that rejecting the notion of conscious taste
(and hence of personal merit) is a prerequisite to abrogating any
question of personal responsibility. But the letter addresses itself
specifically to literary responsibility, disavowing any credit or
blame for authorial "methods" that "begot themselves." The
birth metaphor must strike us as odd, since it actually affirms
some tie in the act of denying others, just as the distinction between proprietor and father begs the critical question of whether
even a proprietary relationship does not entail significant claims
and responsibilities.

The metaphor reflects, then, a paradoxical double desire with
striking affinities to the contradictory divisions many have perceived in the Mark Twain-Samuel Clemens relationship. From
Van Wyck Brooks's thesis that the writer was emasculated by the
conflict between the forces of Puritanism and the frontier ("Mark
Twain was an unworthy double of Samuel Langhorne Clemens")[48]
to James Cox's contradictory view that Samuel Clemens chan-
neled his aggressions and found a literary identity in the comic
personality of "Mark Twain," critics have been themselves divided over how Samuel Clemens relates to Mark Twain: in creative or
destructive opposition? The critical division goes all the way back
to the divided subject himself, who regarded his literary methods
with similar ambivalence. No one, including the writer himself,
can decide whether "Mark Twain" was a blessing or a curse for
Samuel Clemens.

The cultural components of Clemens's self-creation as "Mark
Twain" further remind us that the role of humorist evoked a popular image fraught with contradictions.[49] As "Mark Twain," he was
indeed trapped by the split perceived in nineteenth-century America between the roles of humorist and litterateur, humor defined as
part of "vernacular" or "low" culture and literature assigned to
"high" culture. As early as the 1860s, purportedly the heyday of
humor on the San Francisco "literary frontier," Twain exhibited a
reluctance to accept his vocation as a humorist. Indeed, he appeared to share his contemporaries' low opinion of the humorist's

calling—the opinion not merely of his later, genteel Hartford contemporaries but also of his fellow writers in the West. "Funny
fellows are all right and good in their place," cautioned one California journalist, but "the sole supreme taste of the public ought not
to be in that direction."[50] At the other end of the continent and of
Twain's career, a similarly qualified "good" was similarly equivocally extended to humor. At a ceremonial banquet at
Delmonico's on 5 December 1905, in honor of Twain's seventieth
birthday, Professor Brander Matthews of Columbia University
spoke of "the proper praise" to be paid him: "With Mark Twain,
the humorist, his humor is always good, his humor is never irreverent, never making for things of ill repute."[51] While asserting the
"good"-ness of Twain's humor, Matthews clearly felt obliged to
distinguish Twain from those who indulged in "irreverent"
humor, just as earlier the California journalist had praised "funny
fellows" as "good in their place." When even praise for the art of
humor betrays such unintended slights, and when those slights
appear to be ubiquitous, part of western culture of the 1860s and of
the eastern literary establishment at the turn of the century, we get
a full sense of the deeply ambivalent treatment accorded the funny
man throughout Twain's lifetime.

Given this cultural ambivalence, it is no wonder that in the
letter to George Bainton, Mark Twain would rather envision himself as proprietor than father of his art, wanting to separate himself
from the bulk of his writing, associated as it was—and as he was—
with the taint of humor. He did not, however, want to repudiate all
of his literary offspring; such birth imagery as that of the Bainton
letter crops up apparently only in relation to his fiction. The non-
fiction—political articles, satiric pieces—and the fiction based on
long distant fact—historical novels like *The Prince and the Pauper*
or *Joan of Arc*—constituted a different, less revealing, more distanced and controlled kind of writing. Only imaginative writing
was sufficiently threatening to be envisioned in images of unnatural or abortive or violent birth.

Literary creation is most strikingly associated with freakish
birth in the preface to *Those Extraordinary Twins*, itself a farce
about Siamese twins that evoked, if not gave birth to, the tragedy
Pudd'nhead Wilson. Twain's flippant account of the composition
of his twin novels unmasks how a "jackleg" novelist works: much
like that of the amanuensis, his writing "goes along telling itself"
until "it spreads itself into a book." A "tragedy" that first mas-
queraded as a "farce" during the long and tortuous composition,
the finished novel exposed unwanted truths linking black and

white genealogies through the institution of slavery—truths so unwanted that their author refused to acknowledge his own creation. His "original intention," he protests in the preface and afterword published with the two books, was to write an "extravagantly fantastic little story" about a "monstrous 'freak'"—a pair of Siamese twins. But when "it changed itself from a farce to a tragedy" and other new characters, among them "a stranger named Pudd'nhead Wilson," began "working the whole tale as a private venture of their own," Twain turned into a powerless bystander at an event beyond his control, with not one "but two stories tangled together." Moreover, between the "two stories in one" there was now "no connection . . . no interdependence, no kinship." The solution was violently to reassert his authorial control: "I pulled one of the stories out by the roots, and left the other one—a kind of literary Caesarean operation."[52]

Twain assists at this twin birth, more midwife than mother, attempting to sever himself from his progeny, whom he also severs from one another. Not only does he characterize the entire tragedy as an unwilled creation "intruding" into his authorial consciousness and "superseding" the farce that nurtured it, but also his chief character is a "stranger" in terms of the plot and perhaps to the author himself. Earlier, in the 1889 Bainton letter, the grudging admission of paternity ("Doubtless I have methods, but . . . I am only their proprietor, not their father") raises the spectre of the suspicious father, forced to assume paternal responsibility but unsure that the child is really his. The preface to *Pudd'nhead Wilson* retreats behind a similar veiled accusation of loose behavior in its suggestion that two such different siblings could not possibly share the same paternity. The midwife image, too, repudiates authorial responsibility. If, it implies apologetically, the tragedy seems as "monstrous" as the "grotesque" farce out of which it grew, the author is not implicated, for, like all his literary creations, "they begot themselves." The *Pudd'nhead Wilson* preface thus conflates acknowledgment of the paternal responsibilities of authorship with denial. The question Twain begs in this literary family history, consisting almost entirely of denials of kinship, is whether the tragedy of the part-black Tom Driscoll is not as preposterous as the grotesquerie of *Those Extraordinary Twins*, so preposterous that it had to be representd as the unwilled product of the author's creative unconscious.[53]

With this literary genealogy based on division rather than connection, Mark Twain tried to separate himself from possible charges of poor taste (in the "extravagant farce") and of immorality (in the racial tragedy). But at the same time the theory of unwilled creativity shook his confidence in his ability to "consciously superintend" his own art—a phrase, we remember, that appears, along with "proprietor," in the Bainton letter. The Whittier dinner speech and its aftermath raised similar fears. Howells's metaphor of "demoniacal possession" for Twain's performance at the dinner conjured an extreme image of the creator who cannot control his own creations, his demons. So, too, we remember, did Twain's own confession to Howells that he must have been "insane" when he wrote that speech. Echoing that confession, in Twain's formal letter of apology to Emerson, Longfellow, and Holmes he similarly castigates himself for not having exercised better control over his crude, but unconscious, impulses. "I ask you to believe that I am only heedlessly a savage, not premeditatedly," he wrote on December 27, 1877:

> I come before you, now, with the mien & posture of the guilty . . . If a man with a fine nature had done that thing which I did, it would have been a crime . . . but I did it innocently & unwarned . . . But when I perceived what it was that I had done, I . . . suffered as sharp a mortification as if I had done it with a guilty intent.[54]

If the real author of this crime is some savage, the logic goes, then Twain is paradoxically savage but guiltless, an innocent criminal. Ironically, each of these attempts, both Howells's and Twain's, to distinguish between willful and unintentional artistry, and thereby relieve the artist of any criminal complicity, envisions some kind of guilty association between artist and art: he is either demoniacally possessed or insane or savage. No matter what the metaphor, Twain's art seems fatefully conjoined to the illicit or the illegitimate.

In this context, Twain's choice of procreative metaphors for literary creation becomes particularly revealing, for he persistently associated creativity not with conventional, communally sanctioned sexuality but with violation of sexual taboos. In 1872 Twain thanked Howells for his favorable review of Roughing It: "I am as uplifted and reassured by it as a mother who has given birth to a white baby when she was awfully afraid it was going to be a mulatto" (MTHL, 1:10–11).[55] This casually off-color joke more radically confuses boundaries than the Pudd'nhead Wilson preface; literary conception not only threatens sexual taboos, it also crosses racial barriers. Twain fantasizes not merely that he is a woman but an adulterous woman who may be disgraced by bearing racially mixed offspring. We can see the perverse logic of the joke emerging if we remember that humor was indeed regarded as a kind of "mongrel" literature violating social and linguistic conventions. Humor also generates a crossbreeding of modes (farce, burlesque, satire), of purposes (serious, entertaining), of audiences (mass and elite), and it even, in the case of southwestern humor, generates a cross between oral and written traditions. In addition, Twain's humorous writings traversed the formal boundaries of journalism, travelogue, autobiography, and fiction. As a writer permanently confused over what category his work belonged to, divided over whether to write farce or tragedy, Twain imagined himself violating literary, racial, and sexual taboos.

The relationship of an author to his books thus did not so much convey to Twain an image of dividedness where there should be unity as it undermined the very notion of division itself. That is, the categorical divisions (between races, sexes, between self and other) on which definitions of identity depend seemed not to hold up in the context of Twain's creative process. The act of creation results in an intimate relation, yes, but a contaminated intimacy that blurs boundaries between self and other. Hence the increasing closeness and complicity of Twain's metaphors for creativity. His language suggests that a book is part of the self but also an alien other—in Faulkner's words the writer's "dark twin"[56] revealing unacceptable or forbidden knowledge—including self-knowledge of which even the self is unconscious. Any absolute separation between self and creation thus proves unstable as the control creator wields over creature breaks down—and the unconscious dimly emerges as the tie that binds the two.

V

It is clear how Mark Twain's particular metaphors for authorship portray the act of writing in ways that would have led to speculation about selfhood, control, and responsibility. So fundamental for him was the issue of creativity that the main figures through which the writer conceived his own creative process were themselves metaphorized and broadly applied to his personal life. In particular, we will see, Twain's view of writing, summed up in the Bainton letter as an "unconscious or half-conscious process" that he does not "even consciously superintend," was reconceived as a means of understanding similarly unconscious or uncontrollable aspects of his emotional life.

Writing, always a stressful activity for an author whose "inspiration tank" so frequently and inexplicably ran dry, proved nevertheless to be a nearly obligatory defense during times of personal loss—an unwilled yet effective source of consolation. "We are dead people who go through the motions of life," he wrote to Howells from London just six months after Susy's sudden death from spinal meningitis:

> Indeed I am a mud-image, & it puzzles me to know what it is in me that writes, & that has comedy-fancies & finds pleasure in phrasing them. It is the law of our nature, of course, or it wouldn't happen; the thing in me forgets the presence of the mud-image, goes its own way wholly unconscious of it & apparently of no kinship with it. (*MTHL*, 2:664)

A paradoxical relation between death and creation—"apparently of no kinship"—is reluctantly acknowledged here. Barely alive, the "mud-image" seems to go through only the motions of life, yet the term also recalls the biblical moment when man was created from dust in God's own image ("mud" being all the more degraded). As a writer, Mark Twain is similarly both creator and created. Ordinarily an opposed pair, these overlapping images both betray and create tension when, as here, they tend to blur together in confusing opposition. To clarify the opposition and reaffirm the categories of difference that make possible a sense of control,[57] Twain divides himself in two but identifies consciously only with the mud-image ("I *am* a mud-image"). He thus separates himself from the alien "thing *in* me" that writes, that dominates, and "forgets the presence of the mud-image, goes its own way wholly unconscious of it." The fact that he can write at all at such a time arouses guilt, projected onto "the thing in me," but the guilt is also projected as a sense of lost control, of a writerly self that is involuntary, uncontrollable, unknowable. If it were not for "the thing in me," however, he would simply be dead, a "mud-image." The father's guilt that he should live while his daughter dies thus projects itself onto anything connected with creation as opposed to death. And artistic creativity, associated with life itself, constitutes the ultimate betrayal, since it is also a process of self-creation.

The disparity between death and creation, between mourning and creating humor evoked images of dividedness, but so, in a visual rather than linguistic context, did the inability to create. At times the grieving father could not bring his imagination to bear to help him picture the faces of the dead. In the one case, he created something he did not consciously will; in the other, he could not create what he desperately desired. But the element common to both links creativity with loss of control over the self. A month after Livy's death in June 1904, Clemens lamented in his notebook that he "was never in my life able to reproduce a face. It is a curious infirmity—and now at last I realize that it is a calamity" (*MTN*, 388). But even more curious, if he cannot deliberately will this act of imagination, it does occur, apparently of its own accord, in his dreams:

> How is it that I, who cannot draw or paint, can sometimes shut my eyes and see faces . . . most delicate and perfect miniatures and can note and admire the details. How is it? They are not familiar faces, they are new—how can I invent them? And what is it that makes perfect images in my dreams? I cannot *form* a face of any kind by deliberate effort of imagination. (*MTN*, 322)

Because dreams are not subject to conscious controls and because they are so often the repository of "perfect images," they promised knowledge both of unconscious creativity and of the unconscious self responsible for that creativity.

Dream analysis fascinated Mark Twain most of his life, and from early on he cultivated the habit of recording his own dreams. Probably the best-known example is a notebook entry in the late fall of 1884 containing the germ for *Connecticut Yankee:* "Dream of being a knight errant in armor in the middle ages. Have the notions & habits of thought of the present day mixed with the necessities of that" (*MTN*, 171). A less well known experiment with translating into writing the peculiar disjunctions of time experienced in dreams is "My Platonic Sweetheart," a short story written in 1898, published in the 1912 *Harper's Magazine* Christmas issue, and based on a recurrent dream of over forty-four years.[58] The dream is always the same: the narrator loves and loses his "Dreamland sweetheart," but each time his loss of her is mitigated by his knowledge that she will appear in another dream. The "platonic" nature of this unconsummated fantasy, like its transitory and elusive female figure, seems both to protect and to titillate the male dreamer/narrator. Indeed, the dream sequence is far less sexual than it is mournful, a recurrently rehearsed sensation of loss—loss of unsublimated, prelapsarian energies, whether sexual or artistic.

The story's structure underscores the plot of recurrent loss by moving back and forth in time between the unchanged dream-self and the aging dreamer, whose experiences exactly match Clemens's own. We are told, for example, that one version of the dream took place in a San Francisco newspaper office in 1864 when the narrator was twenty-nine years old, another on a snowy New York street when he was thirty-one, which would be just after Clemens first returned from the West in October 1866. In the dreams themselves, set in exotic locations such as Athens and Bombay, the narrator's age is always seventeen, that of his "Dreamland sweetheart" fifteen. By constructing parallels between the time and place of each dream and the events of the author's actual life, the story emphasizes the disjunction between "dream-time" that does not move at all and "waking-time," measured to fractions of seconds by calendar and clock. "It would not cost me very much of a strain," the narrator asserts, "to believe in Mahomet's seventy-year dream, which began when he knocked his glass over and ended in time for him to catch it before the water was spilt" (*MPS*, 22–23).

Chronological dislocation within dreams themselves can translate into analogous difficulties in the dreamer's reconstruction of his own dream. Dream analysis for Mark Twain began as a process of narrative construction that explicitly harnessed the "dream-memory" by cultivating "the habit of writing down my dreams of all sorts while they were fresh in my mind, and then studying them and rehearsing them and trying to find out what the source of dreams is, and which of the two or three separate persons inhabiting us is their architect . . . (*MPS*, 11). Reminiscent of the Bainton letter on authorial methods and of Clemens's bewilderment over his "comedy-fancies" following Susy's death, his dreams—ostensibly his own creations—led to the postulate of alternate selves responsible for those creations. The Bainton letter, we remember, confesses that although the author inevitably "feels complimented" at the completion of one of his literary "structures," it must be admitted that he "didn't even consciously superintend." Exactly who does the superintending, or who the superintendent is, he does not say in the letter, but in this whimsical short story published for the Christmas trade, the superintendent's or architect's identity begins to emerge.

As Clemens did after Susy's death, "My Platonic Sweetheart"

imagines a divided self, again envisioned in terms of artistic creation, only this time the selves are named not "mud-image" and
"the thing in me" but "dream-artist" and "day-thought architect." Both pairs of names take as their reference point the comparative ability to create. According to a passage not published in the
abridged *Harper's* version, "the day-thought architect in us is comparable to the dream-artist in us as you and I are comparable to
Shakespeare" (*MPS*, 12). Their relationship, clearly that of inferior
to superior, begins to sketch how pervasively Twain conceptualized selfhood, in defiance of his views on social and political
equality, as itself dependent on a hierarchized opposition between
the self and some other. A vocabulary of dominance and submission even more explicitly informs the analysis in "My Platonic
Sweetheart" of a dream-vision of a spectacular Greek monument.
The dream forces the dreamer to acknowledge

> what a master in taste and drawing and color and arrange-
> ment is the dream-artist who resides in us. In my waking
> hours, when the inferior artist in me is in command, I cannot
> draw even the simplest picture with a pencil . . . But my
> dream-artist can place before me vivid images of palaces,
> cities, hamlets, hovels, . . . and people who are intensely
> alive (*MPS*, 25–26).

The poignant similarity of this passage to Clemens's grieving
response to Susy's death recorded two years earlier shows how
deeply creativity engendered in him a sense of powerlessness.
More than he was able to during his bereavement, however, in
"My Platonic Sweetheart" he directly addresses the issue of who
controls or "superintends" or "architects" his art and ends by
broadly questioning the validity, even the reality, of both himself
and his world. Emotional pain, for example, suffered in this recurrent dream of loss, transcends and therefore seems to question the
validity of waking suffering,

> for everything in a dream is more deep and strong and sharp
> and real than is ever its pale imitation in the unreal life which
> is ours when we go about awake and clothed with our *ar-
> tificial selves* in this vague and dull-tinted artificial world.
> When we die we shall slough off this cheap intellect, perhaps,
> and go abroad into Dreamland clothed in our *real selves*, and
> aggrandized and enriched by the command over the myste-
> rious mental magician who is here not our slave, but only our
> guest. (Twain's emphasis; *MPS*, 37)

Structured in opposed pairs—dreaming/waking, real/unreal, cheap/rich, artificial selves/real selves—this passage confirms Twain's habit of articulating perception in binary terms. Dreams articulate themselves structurally through oppositions between various selves and various layers of experience. Furthermore, these dichotomies privilege dream over waking life. Twain's inverted hierarchy defines the "real selves" of "Dreamland" by their contrast to and precedence over the "artificial selves" in "this vague and dull-tinted artificial world." But the lines of authority are not so clearly drawn for the "mysterious mental magician," a commanding figure with an ambiguous relation to the dreamer. His authority seems to shift with the fine distinctions in his status, for he is defined equally as a guest to be hosted with courtesy and as a part of the self to be commanded but not enslaved. Or to use another image from "My Platonic Sweetheart" of this ambiguous relationship, we are both "landlords and victims" to him (MPS, 27). His power is unquestionably a source of "aggrandizement" and "enrichment," but the question still remains, who commands such power?

The mysterious mental magician or dream-artist in this story prefigures other mysterious strangers in Twain's later fiction, whom I will discuss in chapter five: Satan and 44, who both create and destroy dream-visions in The Mysterious Stranger manuscripts, and the "Superintendent of Dreams," architect and stage manager of a nightmare voyage in an unfinished story De Voto entitled "The Great Dark." These arch-manipulators are also, of course, fictional progeny of the "superintendent" Twain dimly identified in himself in the Bainton letter. The superior visual faculties of virtually all of these artist figures also call up another of Twain's important figures of the artist, this one representing him as seer and visionary. Howells's "literature," for example, "all such truth—truth to the life," has such a visual quality that Twain tells his friend, "Everywhere your pen falls it leaves a photograph . . ."

> and only you see people & their ways & their insides & outsides as they *are*, & make them talk as they *do* talk. I think you are the very greatest artist in these tremendous mysteries that ever lived. There doesn't seem to be anything that can be concealed from your awful all-seeing eye.[59]

Like all Twain's artist figures, this one uneasily associates authoring with controlling through its ambivalence toward the omniscient authorial eye that creates and controls the textual environment. Twain distances himself as always from the controlling artist (in this case, Howells his peer), identifying with the victim under the penetrative scrutiny of Howells's "awful all-seeing eye." If all of these overlapping versions of the artist—amanuensis/plagiarist, midwife/proprietor, seer/superintendent, the unconscious/dream-self—represent the creative power of the imagination, then this power is ambiguous, wielded by shadowy agents with an uneasy relationship to the artist. Twain's ambivalence toward his own art frames itself particularly as a problem of power, of who assumes the dominant and who the submissive role—the artist or his superintendent.

In the sense, then, of our being agents of forces we do not control, literary creativity posed for Twain problems of mastery similar to those posed by sexuality. More important, though, both creativity and procreativity in some fundamental way violate the social and psychological boundaries they also help to enforce—boundaries between creator and creature, between maleness and femaleness, between dominance and submission. As Twain revealed in his comparison of himself, the male artist, to a white woman who fears her child may be a mulatto, the author may be betrayed by his own intentions, much as the social world divides itself along sharp racial and sexual lines that are readily, if covertly, crossed. And once the concept of authorial intentionality had thus been called into question, Twain began questioning the very nature, even the possibility, of a "self" in control of "reality." The late dream narratives repeatedly interrogate reality: "Which Was the Dream?"

VI

All of these issues came together during 1898 in Twain's most sustained effort to work out a theory of the mind. What he called "the duality idea" framed his hypothesis, summarized in unpublished sections of "My Platonic Sweetheart" (written August 1898), but first and most fully formulated in a long notebook entry, to which I have already alluded, written a few months earlier, in January 1898.[60] This extended entry, actually a short essay of about 1,500 words, goes a long way toward filling out what seem sometimes merely to be incoherent fragments of thought in his fiction—epitomized by that figure of indeterminate identity, the writer/impostor in the Whittier dinner speech. For the long and complex January 1898 entry acknowledges explicitly that Twain himself recognized as his own lifelong project the inquiry into identity and that a cluster of apparently disparate issues and languages was continually brought to bear on the subject. Finally, this entry documents for us how the unconscious was not only a personal territory to which Twain lit out during the 1890s and afterwards, but also a late-nineteenth-century cultural terrain.

Playing the detective, Twain begins the entry, "Last Sunday I struck upon a new 'solution' of a haunting mystery." Like the detective fiction whose ratiocinative structure Twain draws upon here, the mystery of "our seeming duality" is conceived almost immediately as posing a threat to social order and control. The mystery of divided selves is for Twain a problem of divided control, the same mystery that resisted solution in his various metaphors for the artist. The relationship between detective and mystery meant more to Twain, though, than simply a representation of external social control; it also stood as a model for an internalized power struggle in which the criminal, antisocial self is constantly threatening the control of selfhood willed by the socialized self. As far back as 1877, Twain remembers, he had experimented with this detective-criminal model of the doubled psyche in "Facts Concerning the Recent Carnival of Crime in Connecticut":

> That was an attempt to account for our seeming *duality*—the presence in us of another *person*; not a slave of ours, but free and independent and with a character distinctly its own. I made my conscience that other person and it came before me in the form of a malignant dwarf and told me plain things about myself and shamed me and scoffed at me and derided me. This creature was so much its own master that it would leave the premises . . . and go off on a spree with other irresponsible consciences—and discuss their masters (no—their slaves) (*MTN*, 348).

Like Huck's "deformed conscience" internally berating him in the linguistic pieties of the dominant culture,[61] Twain's dwarf serves as no ethical guide but instead dominates as an alien "creature" invading from without, as "master" to Twain's "slave." But the precise structure of roles in this internal power struggle eludes Twain, just as the division of power between the dreamer and his dream-artist ("the mysterious mental magician who is here not our slave, but only our guest") does in "My Platonic Sweetheart."

The conception of duality in "Carnival of Crime" as a conscious power struggle was "a crude attempt to work out the duality idea,"

Twain asserted later in 1898, in both his notebook and the "Sweet-heart" story. By this time "Carnival" appeared lacking, especially in comparison to Robert Louis Stevenson's version of a similar duality (presented with "genius and power") in *Dr. Jekyll and Mr. Hyde* (1886) (*MPS*, 9). Stevenson's book was "nearer, yes, but not near enough" to Twain's own developing theory, he explained in his notebook: "J. & H. were the dual persons in one body, quite distinct in nature and character . . . the falsity being the ability of the one person to step into the other person's place, *at will*" (*MTN*, 348). Stevenson was wrong, Twain says, just as he himself was wrong "in the beginning" to theorize the conscience as man's conscious tormentor. On the contrary, "distinct duality" is unconscious: "The two persons in a man do not even *know* each other and . . . have never even suspected each other's existence." Twain's "*new* notion" of duality, then, led away from literary conceptions derived from popular fiction and toward contemporary experimentation in America and Europe with hypnosis, hysteria, thought transference, and dream analysis—all apparent avenues to the unconscious.[62]

Of these various bodies of research, Twain singles out "the French experiments in hypnotism ten or twelve years ago, and the investigations made by our Professor William James" (*MPS*, 9) as both shaping and confirming his own theory of personality:

> The French have lately shown (apparently) that that other person is in command during the somnambulic sleep; that it has a memory of its own and can recall its acts when hypnotized and thrown again into that sleep, but that *you* have no memory of its acts. (*MTN*, 349)

The fine points of this hierarchy are clarified in "My Platonic Sweetheart": "The subordinate person is always in command during somnambulic (not the common) sleep, therefore his chief is ignorant of what is happening and will have no recollection of it; but the somnambulic sleep can be reproduced by hypnotism" (*MPS*, 10). What "the French" have clearly contributed is an experimental vocabulary amenable to Twain's own earlier language of control, the dualisms of masters and slaves, power and subordination.

To identify briefly, at this point, *which* French experiments Twain might have had in mind: Until the 1880s (roughly the period Twain refers to) research in hypnosis as a therapeutic tool was dismissed by medical science as the quackery of mesmerists and animal magnetists, who had been theorizing about the psychological origins of mental illness since Anton Mesmer's work in the late eighteenth century. But beginning in the 1880s, hypnotism acquired new scientific status through the work, and well-publicized rivalry, of two competing schools, one at Nancy associated with Auguste Liebault and Hippolyte Bernheim, the other at the Salpêtrière in Paris led by Jean-Martin Charcot and his collaborator Pierre Janet. Their widely circulated theories on the separate personalities that seemed to emerge under hypnosis, as well as on the status of hypnotism as a discipline within medical science, constituted perhaps *the* body of knowledge crucial to Twain's later years. From continental psychology and from its counterpart, the field of psychical research in England and America, Twain drew his explicit formulation of an unconscious that controls from within the self, emerging only through the techniques of hypnosis and dream analysis or in art itself.[63]

In part, then, because hypnosis suggests the possibility of multiple levels of communication within the self, Twain's notebook entry postulates a triadic theory of personality. The third self, variously called a "spiritualized self" or a "dream self" or, in "My Platonic Sweetheart," "the dream-artist," "can detach itself and go wandering off upon affairs of its own" in what we take to be "unreality" and call "dreams, for want of a truthfuler name" (*MTN*, 349–50). A counterpart to the Superintendent of Dreams and the other unconscious artists in Twain's writing, the dream-self is further defined in terms close to the amoral energies of the id. In dreams,

> I do actually make immense excursions in my spiritualized person. I go into awful dangers; I am in battles and trying to hide from the bullets; I fall over cliffs (and my *un*spiritualized body starts). I get lost in caves and in the corridors of monstrous hotels; I appear before company in my shirt; I come on the platform with no subject to talk about, and not a note; I go to unnameable places, I do unprincipled things. (*MTN*, 351).

As dreamer, Twain transgresses boundaries and taboos of all kinds, some of course very much like his own perceived violations in the role of humorist. But he never makes such connections. Although he shares shadowy memories in common with his transgressing dream-self, he is separated from its antisocial energies (and from its imaginative powers) by the "No.2" self "in command during the somnambulic sleep":

> I am not acquainted with my double, my partner in duality, the other and wholly independent personage who resides in me—and whom I will call Watson, for I don't know his name, although he most certainly has one, and signs it in a hand which has no resemblance to mine when he takes possession of our partnership body and goes off on mysterious trips. (*MTN*, 349–50)

The sheer proliferation of terms for the multiple self provides striking evidence both of Twain's obsession with identity and of how fragmentary and confused were the manifestations of that obsession. The "other person in us" is variously named the conscience, the dream-self, the spiritualized self, and finally even Watson. To take the latter as a reference to Sherlock Holmes's Watson would certainly be consistent with the notebook's earlier language of mystery, detection, and criminality, although Twain's relationship to his "partner in duality" reverses that of the pre-possessing Holmes to his partner in (solving) crime, Watson.

Moreover, the possible literary and cultural associations of these resonant names do not stop here but continue to multiply somewhat dizzyingly. The handwriting of the self called Watson ("which has no resemblance to mine") reminds us of one area of psychical research, cases of automatic writing, in which the subject's hand produces communication and expresses a character quite different from those of the hand's owner. In addition, Watson's ability to "take possession of our partnership body" echoes Twain's own frequent jokes about Siamese twins squabbling over their shared body, jokes that finally issued in the severed body of the once-joined farce/tragedy *Pudd'nhead Wilson and Those Extraordinary Twins*. The notion of a body possessed also speaks to the generalized metaphor of possession that we have seen Twain (and Howells) apply to the relationship between the artist and his art. And these echoes resonate even further to take in a whole cluster of late-nineteenth-century intellectual concerns centering on psychical research and the new domain of experimental and theoretical psychology, but also including claims like Mary Baker Eddy's Christian Science for the self-healing powers of the mind.

These complex, half-formed interrelations within and without Twain's own terminology tend to contradict the retrospective view the notebook offers of an orderly chronological progression from the "crude" Connecticut conscience to the more elaborate theory of a tripartite self. Yet the entry remains an accurate guide to Twain's wide-ranging formulations of the personality and their equally various literary and cultural analogues, accurate even in its omissions. What Twain neglects entirely here—the twins, pairs, and doubles that have so interested his critics—I would argue actually comprise his earliest depictions of "distinct duality," some even antedating "Carnival of Crime." But in omitting them, the entry also silently accounts for why Twain would not himself consider such literary devices as part of his theorizing. All the variations on the motif of exchanged or mistaken identity that regularly figure throughout Twain's fiction are, like the repudiated conscience, externalized versions of doubleness. Just as he argues that he had mistakenly personified his conscience as a dwarfish creature outside of himself, we may argue that he made similarly crude attempts to embody duality in the diametrically opposed personalities of that freakish creature, the Siamese twins; in the exchange of social roles by the prince and the pauper; in the other claimants and pretenders who usurp noble identity; in the assumption of false identities by frauds and confidence men. Such graphically visible symbols of more or less self-conscious doubling did little to articulate "distinct duality" as Twain ultimately formulated it, an internal psychological condition that raises questions about degrees of consciousness and of control.

The 1898 notebook entry indicates in small, then, what I want to argue is the characteristic development of Mark Twain's inquiry into identity: away from literal, external, and conscious forms toward the increasingly metaphysical, abstract, and speculative. That is, as we will see, the double conceived as a character or characters gives way to a structural conception of narrative doubling. In addition, the entry acknowledges how the curve of the whole enterprise took its shape from contemporary culture. Not until the 1880s and 1890s did contemporary interest in the "pseudoscience" of spiritualism and the "science" of psychology finally provide Twain with a body of knowledge through which he could directly address issues that had long, but elusively, concerned him. The many theories of the unconscious that entered the public domain—through debates over the insanity plea in criminal law or through controversial new conceptions of and treatments for mental illness or through efforts to authenticate psychic phenomena such as thought transference—focused attention on the structure of the personality and on the relationship between conscious behavior and unconscious motivation. For Twain, long restricted to modes of externalizing problems of identity, the result of this climate of thought was a frantic outpouring of a distinctly different kind of writing during the last two decades of his life. Whether one characterizes these late works as dream tales, science fiction, or fantasy, collectively they experiment with a new narrative structure that could articulate the instabilities of a divided psyche via an unstable relationship of author to text to reader.

If there is a cultural explanation for why dreams became such a presence only in Twain's late writing, similar explanations account for the other vocabularies and concepts in the 1898 notebook entry. I have noted how the terms "master" and "slave" and hierarchies of control pervade every aspect of the entry. These psychological issues of power have a social and political analogue in the institution of slavery, whose historical realities provided the major cultural context instrumental in forming Twain's views. "The skin of every human being," Twain wrote in his notebook, "contains a slave" (MTN, 393). In part this reflects his much-discussed (and often maligned) determinism, the view that the individual is enslaved by some combination of external forces and the internalized version of those forces. More particularly, though, Twain saw the institution of race slavery as an arena of subtle power reversals in which the ideology of white supremacy so dominated both groups, masters and slaves, that, for example, many whites were driven to deny that their skin did in fact mask some "black blood." Slavery thus engendered for both whites and blacks a problematic heredity that could not be legislated away.

The contradictions historically associated with slavery—its overt policies of racial classification and strict separation of the races subverted by covert crossing of racial and sexual lines— anticipated Twain's own unacknowledged link between race and sex as part of his otherwise deliberate theorizing about the self. The January 1898 notebook entry ends with a description—not an analysis—of one of Twain's own dreams that betrays unintentionally, through its presence in this entry, how the conjunction of race and sex is somehow conjoined with the rest of the meditation on the self. Twain dreams of "a negro wench," "not at all bad-looking," who made a proposition to him, one that was "disgusting" yet "seemed quite natural." She sold him an apple pie—"a mushy apple pie—hot"—but neglected to provide a spoon, and Twain recounts his revulsion at her offer of her own tin teaspoon. "She took it out of her mouth, in a quite matter-of-course way, and offered it to me. My stomach rose—there everything vanished" (MTN, 352).

Twain's dream of black female sexuality merges with his perception of his conscience, his dream-self, and his unconscious. Aside from the fact that all of these figures appear together in one notebook entry, linked in a sort of free association that Twain called "the methodless method of the human mind,"[64] what does this amalgamation imply? To the notebook writer, each figure is marked by a paradoxically strange familiarity, somehow known, intimate, even a part of himself, yet at the same time distinctly other. The young black female's "disgusting" proposition, for example, does not surprise the dreamer, for in the dream he is also young "and it seemed quite natural that it should come from her." The alien intimacy of something disgusting yet natural repeats itself in the other figures in the entry, an intimacy further enforced by possessive pronouns: "my" conscience is a malignant dwarf; "my" dream-self is "my" other self "with the ordinary powers of both [body and mind] enlarged in all particulars" (MTN, 350–52). Throughout the entry this configuration of recognition and otherness constantly promises (or threatens) to dissolve so that the boundaries between the self and his other may be crossed, freeing (or forcing) him to confront his own desires for the forbidden. But none of the scenarios in the entry goes so far; instead each remains suspended on the border between promise and threat.

First, communication is thwarted in the case of the conscience, which Twain dismisses as an inauthentic representation of the other self ("It is not a separate person . . . merely a *thing* . . . whatever one's mother and Bible and comrades and laws . . . have made it"). Next, communication with the dream-self is also frustratingly incomplete. The waking dreamer, "dimly acquainted" with his dream-self, only partially remembers the dreams whose occasional "vividness" serve to remind him merely of his own distance from such powerful experiences ("Waking, I cannot create in my mind a picture of a room . . . but my dream self can do all this with the accuracy and vividness of a camera" [MTN, 350]).

And finally, Twain's dream ends similarly, just at the moment when he and the black woman are on the verge of eating together from the same spoon—that is, after the acceptable transaction of buying a pie from her (purchasing a suggestively sexual offering?), followed by the less acceptable "disgusting" proposition (the sexual suggestion is overtly offered?), the white male's fantasy of an undifferentiated sexualized nourishment from the "negro wench"/wet-nurse breaks off just before consummation. The dream's long moment of suspension between male self and female other is epitomized in the way he sees and the way she is clothed. He visualizes her body despite its being hidden from view: "She was about 22, and plump—not fleshy, not fat, merely rounded and plump; and . . . not at all bad-looking. She had but one garment on—a coarse tow-linen shirt that reached from her neck to her ankles without a break" (*MTN*, 350–52). That shirt marks the boundary that trembles, but remains unbroken, in the dream as in the rest of the entry.

Both the dream and the whole entry that contains it thus verge on the edge of violating a number of boundaries that are carefully maintained. Something illicit threatens in all of the figures—the Connecticut conscience, the dream-self, and the dreamer Mark Twain. But the notebook entry, structured around the rather finely calibrated hierarchy of waking, dream, and somnambulic selves, contains those threatening figures by bounding the illicit pleasures of dreams from the safe but dull waking world. Twain's hierarchy of selves is so confused and confusing, though, that while ordering the personality through division and classification, it calls attention to the possible weaknesses in its own foundation as an ordering system. Similarly, his fictional dream tales question such epistemological order by deliberately confusing the boundaries between dream and reality. They leave open the question posed by the title of one of them, "Which Was the Dream?" Just before beginning this body of speculative writing, and perhaps before he *could* begin, Twain wrote *Pudd'nhead Wilson and Those Extraordinary Twins*. These twin novels, like the notebook entry composed within only a few years of their publication, experiment with hierarchies of difference, but unlike the more theoretical entry, the novels center on racial and (to a lesser extent) sexual difference, only obliquely present in the notebook. Anchored in Twain's earlier "crude" twinnings, the novels pressed further into farcical trials and deeper into the historical actualities of slavery. But they also revealed, in Faulkner's words, echoing Twain's on the unconscious, that "a book is the writer's secret life, the dark twin of a man."

CHAPTER THREE

RACIAL IDENTITY IN
PUDD'NHEAD WILSON AND
THOSE EXTRAORDINARY TWINS

Soon after *Pudd'nhead Wilson* was published in late November 1894, the well-known contemporary critic and novelist Hjalmar Hjorth Boyesen reviewed the novel with the kind of qualified praise it has received ever since. Puzzled particularly by Mark Twain's "stock" treatment of the highly charged issue of race relations, Boyesen struck a typically bemused tone at this "novel of the ante-bellum days in Missouri, rather melodramatic in plot." "If anybody but Mark Twain had undertaken to tell that kind of story," the review begins,

> with exchanges of infants in the cradle, a hero with negro taint in his blood substituted for the legitimate white heir, midnight encounters in a haunted house between the false heir and his colored mother, murder by the villain of his supposed uncle and benefactor, accusation of an innocent foreigner, and final sensational acquittal and general unraveling of the tangled skein—if, I say, anybody else had had the hardihood to utilize afresh this venerable stage machinery of fiction, we should have been tempted to class his work with such cheap stuff as that of . . . the dime novelists. But Mark Twain, somehow, has lifted it all into the region of literature.

Part of the "somehow," Boyesen suggests, is a certain historical verisimilitude in *Pudd'nhead Wilson*—the "credible and authentic" "local atmosphere"—that makes us "swallow the melodrama without a qualm—exchange of heirs, haunted house, murder, and all—and scarcely dream that we have been duped, until we wake up with a start at the end of the last chapter."[1]

Readers since Boyesen have continued to invoke similar terms. Like him, many have felt "duped" by *Pudd'nhead Wilson*'s "tangle" of the "authentic" and the "melodramatic," the historical texture embedded in (and sometimes suppressed by) the most conventional of sensation plots. So many difficult questions about the social construction of racial identity surface partially in the narrative, only to be arbitrarily closed off by the formulaic clarity of the conclusion to the murder/detective plot, where there seems to be no room for racial loose ends. Even the history of the composition of the manuscript itself bears out this reading, given that the text, which began as a farcical literary sideshow about Siamese twins, became entangled with a racial "tragedy" of the antebellum South. As Hershel Parker points out, the manuscript in the Morgan Library, consisting of both the Siamese twins story and the race/murder plot, raises questions primarily about race and how Mark Twain represented—and submerged—racial issues in the process of composition and revision. After conceiving of the idea of switched racial identities, for example, roughly midway during the compositional process, why did Twain proceed to write—and then cut out—much new and explicit material on Tom Driscoll's agonizing discovery of his racial patrimony?[2]

Perhaps even more telling, why would Twain himself construct a literary family history in the Preface to *Those Extraordinary Twins* that, as we have already seen, is literally situated between the two works and yet consists mainly of denials of their kinship? What of the "literary Caesarean operation" which, we recall, the author asserted had successfully separated the seemingly outré and often tasteless lore of Siamese twins from the racial issues of *Pudd'nhead Wilson*—only to be followed by Twain's publishing the two texts together in 1894 in a single volume entitled *The Tragedy of "Pudd'nhead Wilson" and the Comedy "Those Extraordinary Twins"*?

Defying their author's protestations of severed ties, the books are connected, we will see, by a number of important shared issues, none of which emerges as fully or as clearly in either work alone: the anomalous connections between bond and bondage in the relationships of Siamese twins and of blacks and whites under slavery; the legal classifications that seek to determine individual responsibility by defining the status of Siamese twins and of racially mixed offspring; and finally, a self-conscious demonstration of the problems of authorship that joins the two works quite literally through the bridge passages (prefatory and final remarks) in which the author reveals their process of composition.

The novels are also joined by their specific connections to the cultural circumstances that produced them. Both condense what may strike us now as an incongruous combination of fads, vocabularies, and concepts, all of which were then part of the debates over whether and how biological differences determine the natural capacities of racial groups. *Those Extraordinary Twins*, for example, was based on the Tocci brothers, the Italian (rather than Siamese) twins whom Mark Twain had seen on exhibit in 1891,[3] and it was also inspired by the power of the cultural mythology that arose around Siamese twins at the time. *Pudd'nhead Wilson* drew similarly on popular culture, incorporating fictional forms (the detective plot, the changeling plot), factual sources (Francis Galton's pioneering monograph *Finger Prints*), and most important, historical circumstance. The novel's satire of racial classification by fractions of blood mirrors problems in American race relations during both the antebellum period in which the novel is set and the 1890s when it was written.

In this sense, Twain's novel implicitly reminds readers that racial codes regulating miscegenation and classifying its mixed offspring did not disappear after Emancipation but rather were reenacted or reaffirmed, with even more rigorous definitions of whiteness, during the nineties, when anti-black repression took multiple forms, legal and extralegal.[4] *Pudd'nhead Wilson* was serialized in *Century Magazine* in the middle of a decade that saw not only an epidemic of lynchings but also the beginnings of newly enacted Jim Crow laws defining the "Negro's place" in a segregated society, laws paralleled in the political sphere by a variety of voting restrictions to disenfranchise most blacks. The novel may thus speak even more pointedly to the growing racism of its own era of the 1890s than to the race slavery abolished thirty years earlier. At the very least, the connection between the times of the book's setting and of its writing acknowledges silently an unwelcome tie between race slavery of the past and racism in the present, just as the link between *Pudd'nhead Wilson* and *Those Extraordinary Twins* acknowledges an unspoken kinship between those defined as other, freakish, monstrous, whether Siamese twins or mulattoes.

These twin novels must thus be read together, despite the fact that the farce makes a mockery of the Siamese twins' grotesque attachment, whereas the tragedy, obsessed with genealogy, race, and miscegenation, offers a critique of an American historical actuality.[5] My own reading of the two begins in 1869, long before either the "farce" or the "tragedy," with the mythology of Siamese twins propagated by Twain and others.

II

The twentieth-century reader may well find Mark Twain's jokes about Siamese twins the crudest of what he remembered, in the long January 1898 notebook entry on duality, as his crude twin-ning devices. Ridiculing "freaks of nature" disturbs our sensibili-ties, so that today circus sideshows have been mostly dismantled and their exhibits accorded the status of the handicapped who are to be specially protected, not exploited, by society. In the nine-teenth century, though, "living curiosities" were routinely exhibited, not even relegated to the vaguely sordid sideshow, but openly displayed at multi-purpose museum-theaters advertising themselves as places of family entertainment. A puff for Barnum's new Wood's Museum and Metropolitan Theatre opened in the fall of 1868 read, "Everybody Delighted. The long want of A Family Resort now most satisfactorily supplied."[6] During the new estab-lishment's opening week, every advertisement also touted, in prominent capital letters, the Siamese Twins as feature attraction. Chang and Eng, the original Siamese twins, born of predominantly Chinese ancestry in Siam in 1811, toured America and Europe widely before marrying sisters and settling in North Carolina in houses about two miles apart—none of which facts was lost on newspaper humorists with columns devoted to factual oddities or "wonders of nature."[7]

In short, Mark Twain was not alone in his easy acceptance of Siamese twins as objects of both fascination and humor. Most popular lore assumed, however, that they could be unambiguously differentiated, whereas Twain, consciously switching back and forth from singular to plural in describing his extraordinary twins—a " 'freak'—or 'freaks'—which was—or which were—on exhibition in our cities"—saw them as occupying some inter-mediate status, in part one and in part two individuals (*PW*, 119). The real question was whether one believed in a "harmonious sympathy" or an adversarial duality connecting the two. The newspaper articles that advocated what one journalist sceptically called "the doctrine of supposed sympathy" invariably offered as evidence the well-known fact that the twins lived alternately three days at their two homes; some articles speculated further that their self-control alternated equally smoothly. As the *Alta California* reassuringly put it, "Each twin is boss of his own man-sion, the other becoming for the time merely a silent partner."[8] About the same time, in July 1864, the *San Jose Mercury* reprinted a piece from the *Macon* (Georgia) *Telegraph* that expands on the *Alta*'s theme of distinctly separable yet harmonious relations.

> Though united by a ligament, as strong as life itself, they live a mile apart—spend alternately three days at one and the

other's house . . . The one at whose house you visit them
leads the conversation and acts as master of ceremonies,
while the other speaks only as occasion or politeness may
require . . . They are, to all appearances, two separate and
different men, with very little social resemblance, and a
marked contrast of character . . . They are seldom both sick
at the same time. Why should death result from a separation
of persons so unlike, and so little subject to be afflicted by
each other's infirmity![9]

But as if in response to the oddity of such a sanguine view of
union expounded during the Civil War, some journalists stressed
the conflicts caused by the possibility of the twins' taking opposite
sides in the war. The 1864 *Alta* article that begins by being so
positive that each twin is "boss of his own mansion" ends by
inquiring "what General Sherman would do if one [of the twins]
were disloyal and had to be sent South, while the other remained
loyal." In 1866 the *Downieville* (California) *Mountain Messenger*
became expansively and punningly humorous about the idea of the
twins' Civil War service:

The real trouble was, that from long habit they took opposite
sides and adhered to them, declaring that they would not give
them up except with life itself . . . Whether the Chang part
was for the North, or the Eng part for the South, or *vice versa*,
is not yet made public . . . I believe, however, that Chang is
on the right side, and was therefore for the North . . . The Lee
side lost, and the windward side scorning to take advantage of
the wind raised in this manner, gave all the stakes to Southern martyrs, and this raised a breeze among the wives. To
pacify them, the twins now promised to appear in public
again, and renew the cash celebrity of their early days . . . If
they have got any more twins of the same sort, it would be
doubly interesting.[10]

The extended pun, starting with "the Lee side," is a reassuring
witticism: we can now joke about our Civil War, it says, even
about brothers taking opposite sides and not giving them up "except with life itself."

Mark Twain drew on both of these approaches to Siamese twinhood, the portrayals of freakish harmony and of comic disharmony
between the twins. But his own adaptation of Siamese twin lore
localized the joking, focusing on the law's problems with the
twins' identity (one person or two?) and, more abstractly, on the
relationship between determinism—the twins' physical bond—
and individual responsibility. In addition, contrasting with what

we will see is *Pudd'nhead Wilson's* denial of the socially and legal-
ly complicated sexual relations between the races, sex among
Siamese twins is acknowledged, if disguised as an object of humor.
Twain's "People and Things" column in the *Buffalo Express* con-
tains one of his earliest pieces on twins, an item about Millie and
Christine, a "wonderful two-headed girl" then on exhibit in New
England:

> She has a lover, and this lover is in a quandry, because at one
> and the same moment she accepted him with one mouth and
> rejected him with the other . . . He wishes to sue for breach
> of promise, but this is a hopeless experiment, because only
> half of the girl has been guilty of the breach.[11]

Combining sexual and legal entanglements, as this early sketch
does, would later provide the basis for Twain's most explicit medi-
tations on sexuality; the transvestite tales of the 1890s substitute
the legal predicament of the female Siamese twins with that of
women, disguised as men, who are repeatedly (and of course mistakenly) accused of fathering illegitimate children. Both early and
late tales use the law to question our cultural conceptions of sexual identity.

Just a few months before the *Buffalo Express* item on the "double girl," the uncertain legal status of Siamese twins had moti-
vated Twain to write another piece, this one more complicated and
better known. "Personal Habits of the Siamese Twins" (1869)
elaborates certain widely circulated facts about the real Chang and
Eng into a sketch that also incorporates popular mythology of the
twins.[12] Set against a Civil War backdrop, like so many of the
humorous newspaper accounts, Twain's sketch is clearly the pre-
cursor of *Those Extraordinary Twins,* but also, less obviously, of
Pudd'nhead Wilson. The common denominator among these
three works is their exploration of a paradoxical connection between union and division; all three question both when division is
destructive and union desirable (as in the cases of the divided
country, the attached Siamese twins, and the mulatto's divided
racial patrimony), and when division is not only desirable but
essential to social order.

"Personal Habits" initiates this questioning by playing on the
effects of the recently concluded Civil War and humorously insist-
ing on Chang and Eng's admirable loyalty to their "bond"—this in
spite of their opposite and conflicting temperaments (like the later
Luigi and Angelo of *Pudd'nhead Wilson and Those Extraordinary
Twins*): "What a withering rebuke is this to our boasted civiliza-

tion, with its quarrelings, its wranglings, and its separation of brothers!" (*DE*, 7: 248). The voice of the funny man, ostensibly unaware of the twins' lack of volition in their "perfect accord" ("there has always been a bond between them which made them unwilling to go away from each other and dwell apart"), does not disguise or mitigate the intended rebuke. Very little play on words is needed to make "bond" read "bondage," thus forging a linguistic link between the Siamese twins' paradoxical bond(age) to one another and the war fought not just to free the slaves from their bonds, but also to restore the national bond that had been divided by the South's secession from the Union. In their permanent but not always amicable attachment, the Siamese twins were, for Twain and others, a powerful representation of all these causes.

In Twain's sketch, however, images of bondage, imprisonment, and captivity multiply so that, as both a figure of speech and an historical actuality, "bondage" vibrates with an intensity unmatched by any of the other journalistic pieces:

> During the war they . . . both fought gallantly—Eng on the Union side and Chang on the Confederate. They took each other prisoners at Seven Oaks, but the proofs of capture were so evenly balanced in favor of each, that a general army court had to be assembled to determine which one was properly the captor and which the captive. The jury was unable to agree for a long time; but the vexed question was finally decided by agreeing to consider them both prisoners, and then exchanging them. At one time Chang was convicted of disobedience of orders, and sentenced to ten days in the guard house; but Eng . . . felt obliged to share his imprisonment, notwithstanding he himself was entirely innocent; and so, to save the blameless brother from suffering, they had to discharge both from custody—the just reward of faithfulness. (*DE*, 7: 249–50)

The puzzle of the twins' dual-yet-singular identity, here represented by the "vexed question" of their mutual self-capturing and mutual imprisonment, must be taken to a court of law to be resolved. Legal power to determine identity does not prove entirely satisfactory, though, since the jury's decision in the first case that Chang and Eng are "both prisoners" apparently collapses any meaningful distinction between captor and captive. Similarly, in the second case of legal sentencing in the passage, the distinction between the blameless and the guilty is thwarted by the brothers' shared imprisonment—a state, we note, that can refer either to their temporary incarceration or to their permanently conjoined condition. Twain's twins can escape neither one another nor the law's determination to resolve the dilemma of individuality they present. Is Chang/Eng one person or two? Should we admire or recoil from what Twain burlesques as the "sympathy existing between these two brothers," a sympathy "so close and so refined that the feelings, the impulses, the emotions of the one are instantly experienced by the other"? (*DE*, 7:252).

Not until the early 1890s does Twain again address these questions, again in farcical form, in *Those Extraordinary Twins*. This time it was not Chang and Eng (who died in 1874) but, as I indicated earlier, the Italian brothers Giacomo and Giovanni Tocci who provided the factual basis for Twain's Luigi and Angelo Capello. The physiological differences between how the two pairs of twins were attached are telling. The Toccis shared one body, unlike Chang and Eng, whose separate bodies, complete in themselves, were joined by a ligature. The crucial distinction is the shared body, which heightens the dilemma of whether the twins should be accorded individual or collective status. An article on the Tocci twins in the December 1891 *Scientific American* describes, in great technical detail, their physiological condition, but it also devotes surprising attention to the metaphysics of Siamese twinhood, speculating seriously rather than comically on whether and to what degree they are joined or separate, collective or individual—exactly the questions Mark Twain was asking. However, while his 1894 farce plays both on the twins' differences to make their inescapable attachment more disturbing and on their correspondences to challenge the notion of individuality, the article tries to reassure readers about the stability of these categories:

> Their lives are distinct. They have regions of common sensibility, and of purely individual sensation . . . Giovanni drinks beer in considerable quantities. The other one, Giacomo, not liking beer, drinks mineral water in its place. Giovanni is quite fond of sketching and draws with some spirit. He rests the book or paper on his knee. Sometimes his brother, who is more of a talker and more volatile in disposition, finding some fault with the drawing, will kick the drawing off his knee. All this in good part, for they live on excellent terms with each other, and seem unconscious of any misfortune in their condition.[13]

The last sentence, especially, defuses the spectre of excessive discord in their union raised by the text's own descriptions of their opposing natures, an opposition needed to maintain dramatically the opening premise of "distinct lives." That premise assures readers, in similarly circular fashion, that the distinction between individual and communal identity can be verified by the freakishly combined physiology of Siamese twins.

It was not only popular journals like *Scientific American* that thus sought to resolve the dilemma of individuality posed by Siamese twins. The great medical anatomist Etienne Serres, for example, concluded in his 1833 monograph *Théoris des formations et des déformations organiques, appliqué à l'anatomie de Ritta Christina, et de la duplicité monstreuse* (Theory of organic development and deformation, applied to the anatomy of Ritta Christina, and to duplicate monsters in general) that a verdict of unified duality is the most embryologically consistent solution to the problem. Of a pair of conjoined males with four legs and a single head, he argued:

> There is a perfect unity produced by two distinct individualities. There are sense organs and cerebral hemispheres for a single individual, adapted to the service of two, since it is evident that there are two *me*'s in this single head.[14]

Both the scholarly and popular stances insist on the lack of ambiguity in the status of Siamese twins. In contrast, Mark Twain's jokes keep his twins in permanent intermediate limbo, neither unambiguously one nor two.

III

The "conglomerate twins" of *Those Extraordinary Twins* cannot even claim the most fundamental self-control over their own body. They share what Twain calls "authority over their mutual legs": "leg power" alternates between the brothers by week, their system being to trade control at midnight Saturday. Most of the humor in the farce is similarly generated by how freakish ordinary activities like walking seem when carried out by Siamese twins. Grammatical conventions, especially, become stumbling blocks when the twins are (is?) the referent. Twain's Preface, we know, plays on his linguistic uncertainty about whether the twins should take the singular or the plural: "I had seen a picture of a youthful Italian 'freak'—or 'freaks'—which was—or which were—on exhibition in our cities . . . and I thought I would write an extravagantly fantastic little story with this freak of nature for hero—or heroes" (*PW*, 119). Similarly, in the story itself, when the twins take off their hats ("just a wormy squirming of arms in the air") or when they eat breakfast ("the commingling arms feed potatoes into one mouth and coffee into the other at the same time"), acts and expressions which are ordinarily taken for granted themselves come to seem bizarre. To their small-town southern landlady and her family, the twins are, somewhat like the mulatto who was sometimes viewed as a monstrous hybrid, an "uncanny apparition . . . a weird strange thing that . . . had shaken them up like an earthquake with the shock of its gruesome aspect" (PW, 125).

Twain's burlesque account of this uncanny sensation has something in common with Freud's comments on the ambiguous meaning of the German word *heimlich* (home-like) in his essay "The Uncanny."[15] Freud remarks that the uncanny is frightening because it taps an experience or fantasy that has been forgotten or repressed; thus *das Heimliche* is easily extended into its opposite, *das Unheimliche*. On the one hand, it means what is familiar and agreeable, and on the other, what is concealed and kept out of sight, or unfamiliar. The paradoxical linguistic connection between *heimlich* and its opposite is echoed in Mark Twain's switching back and forth from singular to plural in describing Luigi and Angelo, as well as in the juxtapositions insistently drawn between the exotic freak and the homely details of their daily life. Pictured preparing for bed, "each buttoned [into] his own share of the nightshirt," Luigi reading Paine's "Age of Reason" and smoking, Angelo reading "Whole Duty of Man" and coughing, the twins appear uncanny precisely because they combine the familiar with the unfamiliar, simultaneously arousing sensations of both recognition and otherness.

Those Extraordinary Twins burlesques the twins' uncanniness. Responding to Aunt Patsy's mystification about how one twin is able to nap when the other would rather be active, Angelo notes the "extraordinary fact" that one "prime essential"—their body—does not belong to both at the same time: "If our legs tried to obey two wills, how could we ever get anywhere?" (PW, 138). The solution is a mechanism operating invisibly, "by a mysterious law of our being," giving "'each of us . . . utter and indisputable command of our body a week at a time, turn and turn about' . . . The week ends . . . and in that instant the one brother's power over the body vanishes and the other brother takes possession, asleep or awake" (PW, 139). This alternating mechanism bears a comic resemblance to Clemens's own experience with his "double," his "partner in duality," which, we remember, he describes in the

January 1898 notebook entry as a "wholly independent personage who resides in me" and occasionally "takes possession of our partnership body and goes off on mysterious trips" (*MTN*, 349–50). Even when joking about Siamese twins in 1892, then, Twain plays on the same puzzle he later noted in relation to himself: a sense of one's own body being possessed and controlled by some rival other.

All of the comic references here to possession, power, control, and command make the twins' conjoined body a visible metaphor for the peculiar enslavement they experience. Although their division of control over the legs appears to be well regulated (so much so, Twain jokes, that clocks around the world are set by the twins' "supernatural chronometry"), the system of power sharing between the twins generates ambiguity rather than a clear relationship of dominance and submission. Alternately occupying master and slave roles, the twins themselves know at any given moment who controls the legs, but no outward sign makes visible the inner distribution of power (and responsibility) between the two. Thus, in the eyes of the world, possession of the legs cannot mean total mastery since the twins must be held jointly responsible for individually controlled actions.

The twins' problematic leg power must surely seem an absurd joke unless we also see in it an analogue to Twain's view of the equally problematic power relations in the institution of slavery. When Twain imagined "the rigid and beautiful impartiality with which the possession of power had been distributed between the Twins" (*PW*, 140), he approximated but oversimplified the role reversals he would very soon discover at the heart of the slavery system and would then embody in the changeling plot of what became *Pudd'nhead Wilson*. In neither system—that of the twins in the "comedy" or that of slavery in the "tragedy"—is there one single, clear agent of power; instead, authority is split neatly and regularly between the twins, erratically and almost untraceably with slavery.

The twins' interchangeable master-slave roles conform at least to some predictable movement. As we will see, Roxana's exchange of her baby for her master's, on the other hand, is paradoxically and unpredictably set in motion by the very system it violates, for the threat of being sold "down the river" makes her search for ways to avoid that fate, a process that in turn reminds her that unclothed babies look identical, and thus that the slave might be exchanged for the master. In a peculiar way, Twain suggests, the master is responsible for enslaving his own child. In much the same way, the historian Joel Williamson has argued that the increase during the 1850s in mulattoes who were slaves meant "white people were enslaving themselves, as it were, in the form of their children and their children's children."[16]

If the Siamese twins, with their comically alternating leg power, initiated such implicit social analysis in *Pudd'nhead Wilson*, they also functioned as comic censors, suppressing a more explicit critique of race slavery. While writing the manuscript, even after conceiving of the race/changeling plot, Twain repeatedly invented new farcical interludes involving the Siamese twins, not only because they offered comic relief, but also because he could imagine a readily controlled power structure between them. It was more difficult to untangle the lines of authority among masters, slaves, and the legal and social structures underlying slavery. The twins' conflicts with the law are the best example of how far Twain was able to go with what might be called social criticism in the farcical mode. The "rigid and beautiful impartiality with which the possession of power had been distributed between the Twins" comes into conflict with what Twain sees as an equally rigid and perhaps even more arbitrary locus of social power: the law.

Not one but two legal cases take place in the ten short chapters of *Those Extraordinary Twins*. Both set forth the legal challenge inherent in the twins' ambiguous individuality. The first is the "kick trial": the twins are charged with assault and battery as a result of kicking Tom Driscoll in retaliation for his "human philopena" insult at the Sons of Liberty anti-temperance meeting. The second is actually a series of court cases to resolve the difficulty created when Luigi is elected alderman but unable to take his seat on the board because he would have to bring along an unauthorized person—his twin. In both instances the law seeks to treat the twins as separate legal entities by convicting the guilty twin and exonerating the innocent one of crimes—or civic stalemates—of which they are, as a unit, wrongfully accused. But as Twain's 1869 story of Chang and Eng had already demonstrated, separating the innocent from the guilty proves a problematic task when "the accused" are Siamese twins. One of the villagers is unwittingly right, then, to see in the twins' alternating or dualistic authority "a far finer justice than human law exhibits in related cases" (*PW*, 140).

When Tom Driscoll brings the charge of assault and battery

against the twins, there is no doubt that a crime has been committed, since Tom was kicked with such "unprecedented violence" that "he was lifted entirely off his feet and discharged into the midst of the audience." Yet legal complications ensue because Pudd'nhead Wilson (in the first case he has ever been given) succeeds in establishing that, although there is no way of knowing which individual committed the act, this was legally an "individual" and not a "mutual" kick. Such a distinction, Twain emphasizes, adheres strictly to legal logic. But Wilson uses legal logic against itself while cross-examining a witness about the proper numerical classification of the kick. The witness asserts that only one kick was delivered; Wilson argues syllogistically that "if two men kick, the result should be two kicks," and asks what happened to the other kick. This argument, which ultimately earns David Wilson his first success as a lawyer since coming to Dawson's Landing and ruining his reputation with his fatal "half-dog" remark, is strikingly similar to the illogical logic of that very remark. But in the case of Siamese twins rather than dogs, reasoning from halves turns out to be what the public and the law want. Taking Wilson's mathematical proposition to its logical extreme, the witness reckons that "one of them did half of the kick and the other one did the other half" (*PW*, 144, 147).

The patent absurdity of his conclusion indicts not just the witless witness, Twain wants to show, but also the apparently logical way of thinking that produced his answer: the law's reliance on strict bifurcation as the basis of its determination of innocence or guilt. For once the court accepts the argument that the assault was the act of an individual, as it must to be consistent with its own premises, Twain shows, it becomes stymied by the epistemological, rather than purely legal, problem of knowing which twin possessed the leg-power at the time of the assault. Here is the point, then, of Twain's elaborate jokes about the twins' physiology. At issue in the trial is who controlled the single pair of legs and therefore is legally identifiable as guilty: "Which of them was in possession of the legs . . . would of course indicate where the guilt of the assault belongs" (*PW*, 150).

This presumption, almost a burlesque of the truism "possession is nine-tenths of the law," leads to explicit questions about what the law can know. Wilson continually badgers the witnesses by harping on the issue of knowledge, what they "absolutely *know*" (Twain's emphasis). His speeches repeatedly give rhetorical evidentiary weight to "knowledge which can be of the utmost value just at this moment—knowledge which would at once dispose of what everyone must see is a very difficult question in this case." The reader, of course, sees the point of Wilson's strategy long before the villagers do. For since it has already been established that only the twins know the facts of their alternating leg power, no eyewitness testimony can be allowed by the judge. Other than the accused themselves, no witness can meet the basic legal requirement that evidence must consist of what we know as fact, not mere hearsay. As final witness, Aunt Patsy Cooper bristles when the judge questions whether she can "absolutely *know*, independently of anything these gentlemen [the twins] have told you—that the power over their legs passes from the one to the other regularly every week." And when he questions how she knows, she explodes in what is surely Twain's burlesque of his own epistemological concerns: "How do I know, indeed! How do *you* know what you know? . . . You didn't invent it out of your own head, did you?" (*PW*, 145, 152).

Thus Wilson wins his case and the twins are acquitted in a comic miscarriage of justice. The jury summarizes the dilemma posed by the trial in a three-part argument that again parodies legal dependence on quantification.

> 1, an assault was committed, as charged; 2, it was committed by one of the persons accused, he having been seen to do it by several credible witnesses; 3, but his identity is so merged in his brother's that we have not been able to tell which was him. We cannot convict both, for only one is guilty. We cannot acquit both, for only one is innocent. (*PW*, 153)

The unusual insight apparent particularly in the jury's third finding is canceled out by its final verdict that "justice has been defeated by the dispensation of God." Actually, justice has been defeated, Twain wants to emphasize, by the premises of the legal system itself, premises which rest on rigid and sometimes unverifiable distinctions. The Siamese twins baffle the system because they defy legal mathematics, lying somewhere in the middle of a continuum between individual and collective responsibility, between singular and plural status. Precisely because the questions Twain wants to ask about identity require such ambiguous status as that of the Siamese twins, the revised version of the kick trial in *Pudd'nhead Wilson* is only reported, not shown. Once the twins were separated, the trial lost its power to expose the inadequacy of legal codification of identity and so merited only a

summary reference. No mere "vestige" of Twain's inadequate revising job (as some would have it), the continued, although
truncated presence of the twins' trial for assault and battery in
Pudd'nhead Wilson reminds us that the law and its potential as a
reliable classificatory tool remained a central, still unresolved,
issue for the author.[17]

Those Extraordinary Twins approaches the issue comically
through the judge's frustration at his court's inability to get its
man—or men. The third point of the jury's summary establishes
that the guilty twin's "identity is so merged in his brother's that
we have not been able to tell which was him." The judge then
places the blame squarely on "the fickle forms of law":

> I was confronted by a law made in the interest of crime,
> which protects the criminal from testifying against him-
> self . . . You have set adrift, unadmonished, in this
> community, two men endowed with . . . a power by which
> each in his turn may commit crime after crime of the most
> heinous character, and no man be able to tell which is the
> guilty or which the innocent party in any case of them all.
> (*PW*, p. 154)

The judge's warning about the twins' "power" implicitly admits
both the law's lack of power and its lack of knowledge ("we have
not been able to tell which was him"; "no man able to tell which is
guilty or innocent"). However, the hollow but threatening war cry
with which the speech ends— "Look to your homes—look to your
property—look to your lives—for you have need!"—suggests an
inverse relationship between power and knowledge. Increasingly
complex systems of knowledge that divide and quantify experience compensate for a lack of control over experience, just as
power—in the form of harsh and excessive punishment—is asserted to mask what we lack in knowledge.

The grotesque end of *Those Extraordinary Twins* acts out this
inverse relationship as it fulfills the judge's inflammatory rhetoric.
During the election campaign leading up to the conclusion, the
"double performances" of the twins—Luigi's possession of the
legs forces Angelo, running on a temperance platform, to frequent
rum shops and horse races, and Angelo's possession puts Luigi in
the role of pious moralist at religious gatherings—arouse in
Dawson's Landing "a storm of frantic criticism . . . and rage over
their extravagant and incomprehensible conduct" (*PW*, 167). Even
after Luigi had won his alderman's seat, the "incomprehensible"

continued to multiply, as a legal stalemate is created when the courts decided that non-member Angelo could not sit on the board with Luigi,

> and at the same time forbade the board to deny admission to Luigi, a fairly and legally chosen alderman. The case was carried up and up from court to court, yet still the same old original decision was confirmed every time. As a result, the city government not only stood still, . . . but everything it was created to protect . . . went a steady gait toward rack and ruin. (*PW*, 169)

The townspeople, responding to this irrational situation created by their own rational system of law, decide to hang Luigi. As for the innocent Angelo: "Who said anything about hanging him? We are only going to hang the other one." Thus the punishment the twins had evaded in their first trial for assault and battery is finally inflicted—intensified by the community's earlier, humiliating lack of power and by its continuing lack of knowledge, of which the twins' presence is a constant unwanted reminder.

The double lynching concludes *Those Extraordinary Twins* in a grotesque epitome of all the paradoxes about control that Twain plays with throughout the farce. Both twins die when the one "in control"—that is, the one designated as legally responsible for their actions—is hanged, just as all the acts of the controling twin also affect the subordinate one. Their intertwined fates make a mockery of the importance they place on their ostensibly divided control. Their lives revolve around which controls the legs and occupies the dominant position, yet their deaths show that the distinction is ultimately a meaningless one. Similarly, in the legal realm, "which of them was in possession of the legs" does not "indicate where the guilt of the assault belongs." This apparently logical determination of identity is exposed as inadequate, as inadequate as the analogous "proof" of identity, fingerprints, prove to be in fully determining Tom Driscoll's legal status in *Pudd'nhead Wilson*.

Twain's "comedy" intersects with his "tragedy," then, in their mutual suggestion that identity, as codified by the law and verified in its judgments of innocence or guilt, is both a set of comforting fictions fostering the illusion of social control *and* an imprisoning reality. The legal system depends on categorization, the creation of artificial boundaries between the individual and the group, master and slave, the free and the not-free, those who are pardoned and those who are punished. Such divisions provide the law with a means of measuring and controling what is essentially indivisible and unquantifiable, just as the "regular alternation" of the Siamese twins' "leg power" makes an even more specious attempt to deny and thereby control their total interdependence. Like masters and slaves, the twins are bound together equally in an attachment that only partially signifies superiority or inferiority, but fully demands that each twin, like each participant in the slavery system, must share the fate of the other. In their joint death by hanging—the fate that Tom Driscoll is ironically "spared" at the end of *Pudd'nhead Wilson*—the twins are thus a crudely literal analogue of the insight, more savagely realized by the end of that novel, that slavery is not simply an abhorrent social institution, but a metaphor for the individual's relationship to himself, to his intimates, and to his society.

IV

We have begun to answer the question of how and why *The Comedy "Those Extraordinary Twins"* remains connected to *The Tragedy of "Pudd'nhead Wilson"*, both in the form of a separate work and of separate twins, despite Mark Twain's protestations to the contrary. For Twain, Siamese twinhood embodied in simultaneously literal and farcical ways the difficult abstract issues of defining individuality and of assigning legal responsibility—issues that become all the more pressing when applied to a racial context. But if race did, indeed, function as an intensification of the same argument expressed comically in *Those Extraordinary Twins*, then why did Twain, in revising *Pudd'nhead Wilson*, alternately engage in and suppress the race issue?

This is no small problem for those readers who have valued the novel because they perceive it as grappling, however fitfully, with the problem of race slavery. Clemens himself appeared only partially to share that judgment. His enthusiastic appraisal of the newly separated and revised work *Pudd'nhead Wilson*, completed at the end of July 1893, does not grant race a privileged position. "*This* time 'Pudd'nhead Wilson' is a success!" he crowed to his publisher Fred J. Hall:

> I have pulled the twins apart and made two individuals of them; . . . *their* story has disappeared from the book . . . The whole story is centred on the murder and the trial; from the

first chapter the movement is straight ahead without diver-
gence or side-play to the murder and the trial; . . . Therefore,
3 people stand up high, from beginning to end, and only 3—
"Tom" Driscoll and his nigger mother Roxana; none of the
others are important, or get in the way of the story or require
the reader's attention. Consequently, the scenes and episodes
which were the strength of the book formerly are stronger
than ever, now.[18]

The strong scenes, in Clemens's estimation, involve primarily the
murder mystery and the trial, and only subordinately race. That is,
the "serious" racial concerns that draw critical praise were subor-
dinated by the author to what many may dismiss as the novel's
"melodramatic," even "sensational," aspects. So the problem remains: why does *Pudd'nhead Wilson* alternately acknowledge and
then deny the racial issues that constitute for most readers whatever power the novel may claim?

The novel's opening chapters prepare us for this disturbing alternation by offsetting an implicitly historical and contextualized
sensibility with a conventionalized, melodramatic mode. Precise
details of time and place frame the first chapter. It is 1830. "The
scene of this chronicle is the town of Dawson's Landing on the
Missouri side of the Mississippi, half a day's journey, per steam-
boat, below St. Louis." Such detail had framed the manuscript
from its inception, although it originally started with the arrival of
the Siamese twins and was dated "about 1850." After the addition
of the race plot, Twain rewrote the first chapters, incorporating the
history of the exchange of the babies in their cradles, and set the
date back twenty years so that the two children would be twenty-
two around 1850.[19]

The original date may have had no particular significance, but
recast in the setting of a "chronicle" of "a slave-holding town" (a
phrase added only during revision), 1850 becomes a memorable
year and the Mississippi River locale a special place. The census of
1850 counted mulattoes for the first time. In that year, in Ken-
tucky and Missouri, there was one mulatto slave for every six
black slaves. And in that year, Joel Williamson comments, "the
slave frontier was the trans-Mississippi South, and it was also
preeminently the area of mulatto slavery," and concludes, "Where
slavery was strongest and getting stronger, it was also becoming
whiter." One further paradoxical result of this racial mixing became apparent in the "new intensity of white racial exclusive-
ness" during the 1850s.[20]

These multiple historical contradictions are not exactly articulated in *Pudd'nhead Wilson* but rather registered, I would argue, as confusingly and as obliquely and inconsistently as Williamson's account of their historical manifestations indicates. That is, he shows how southern whites enabled themselves, ironically through increasingly stringent color consciousness and racial solidarity, to deny the apparently undeniable presence of increasing racial intermixture. With a similarly tortuous combination of denial based on acknowledgment, the two chapters of Twain's novel immediately following our chronological and geographic introduction to Dawson's Landing turn away from the historical context of the "chronicle," and instead plunge us into the narrative world of popular fiction (the Pudd'nhead Wilson/fingerprint plot and the Roxana/changeling plot). By thus submerging history in melodrama, or by uneasily combining these two modes, the novel participates in a strategy of presenting and yet denying its own historical and racial context. The ironic result: *Pudd'nhead Wilson* pushes us back to the cultural context that is missing.

We might also, however, take the lead from Clemens's own enthusiasm for the murder and trial as centerpiece of his book, and argue that those popular conventions play as critical a role in drawing out as in censoring the novel's vision of racial identity. From my point of view, *Pudd'nhead Wilson* is a transitional novel, posed midway in Twain's studies of identity. It encompasses his earlier tendency to comic role reversal (and resolution) and his later impulse to despair, as well as the whole range of conceptions of multiple identity in his writing, the external plot conventions (changelings, twinnings) and the internal psychological divisions.

The most notable example of the transitional status of this novel, Tom Driscoll is both conscious manipulator and victim of false identities. Not only does he disguise himself, in sequence, as a bearded white man, a young white woman and old white woman, a young black woman, and a tramp, but also under the cloak of respectability, he is a gambler, a thief, and finally a murderer—all versions of duality that are self-assumed and detectable, hence ultimately controllable by society. But as a mulatto with invisible "black blood," Tom also embodies a more threatening kind of duality: his second (slave) self is internal but also unwilled, an unwanted identity imposed by society's racial classification. Ironically, it goes almost undetected even by the very society that created it. Tom thus both harkens back to those pretenders, confidence men, and false claimants whose imposture is exposed, usually by the law, in Twain's fiction of the seventies and eighties and looks forward to the figure of the dream-self and other later formulations of internal psychic division that cannot be known by legal or any other standards. Finally, in its scepticism about the contemporary bodies of knowledge it draws upon—the "sciences" of race classification and the law—*Pudd'nhead Wilson* is linked proleptically with epistemological questions posed in the dream tales.

V

At the center of *Pudd'nhead Wilson's* problem of knowledge (social, scientific, legal) is the institution of race slavery. Committed to maintaining differences between racial groups as a means of distinguishing the slave from the free, American slavery spawned, and then tolerated, the anomaly Mark Twain calls the "pure-white slave": the mulatto who, appearing no different racially from his free white relatives, creates a pressing need for the many preposterous social and legal fictions of slave society. Partly a novel of detection and discovery, *Pudd'nhead Wilson* exposes a number of these fictions in the course of exposing a murderer. The murder plot culminates, as we shall see, by satirizing the legal fiction that a slave is both property (an extension of the master's will) and nonproperty (in that he can be tried for very willful, antisocial acts, such as murder).[21]

In addition, the novel's obsession with genealogy makes us aware of another social fiction, what George Fredrickson calls the "official dedication to maintaining a *fictive* 'race purity' for whites."[22] From the very beginning in which Roxana, trading literally on the babies' interchangeability, switches the two in their cradles, the novel detects a central ambiguity suppressed in law, if not custom, by slave society: if not by color or other unalterable physiological differences, how can we differentiate individuals and groups? How do we know who is master and who is slave, who is to be held accountable under the law and who is not? Finally, with the unsettling trial at the end, the novel asks, how sound is the basis of that knowledge? How do we know what we know is true? This line of questioning would have profound implications for the author of the novel, who we know represented his literary fiction as having taken control of its maker.

Within the novel itself, more than any other characters, Roxana and her son Tom trigger these questions through their multiple interchanges of race and sex. Not only does she engineer the switch of the babies, but also, like her son's numerous racial and sexual disguises, she puts on blackface and male clothing, ironically in her case, in order to escape from slavery. That they should be the novel's only explicit manipulators of identity is oddly appropriate, since as mulattoes their identity is, more radically than any white person's, tampered with by social fictionalizing. Both mother and son are products of racial intermixture in biological fact but not according to social fiction.

Yet precisely this societal denial of the products of interracial unions enables Roxana's switch of the babies' identities to go undetected. No one, not even the outsider Pudd'nhead Wilson, acknowledges what her successful switch implies: the logical extreme of a system that permits white men's illegitimate children to be enslaved is the enslavement of white men. When another outsider, the Count de Volney, visited the South in 1795, he traveled to Monticello and reported his shock at finding children there who looked as white as himself yet were called black and treated as slaves.[23] Precisely the same vision of racially indistinguishable children gives Roxana the initial idea of switching the babies ("Dog my cats if it ain't all *I* kin do to tell t'other fum which, let alone his pappy"), so that the exchange is enabled by the system and mode of thinking it violates. Her action may thus be classed with the kind of slave action that Eugene Genovese describes as proceeding within "narrow limits" but realizing "one vital objective": "it exposed the deception on which the slave society rested."[24]

Twain wants to show how ironically such deception, like any fictionalizing, can take on a life of its own, becoming an active force partially autonomous of, even turning on, its creator. And so he explains at some length how and why even Roxana, as a single individual, cannot fully control the consequences within herself of her own deception. As a result of exchanging her child for her master's son, she becomes more than merely "a doting fool of a mother":

> She was this toward her child—and she was also more than this: by the fiction created by herself, he was become her master; the necessity of recognizing this relation outwardly and of perfecting herself in the forms required to express the recognition, had moved her to such diligence . . . that this exercise soon concreted itself into habit; it became automatic and unconscious; then a natural result followed: decep-

tions intended solely for others gradually grew practically into self-deceptions as well; the mock reverence became real reverence, the mock obsequiousness real obsequiousness, the mock homage real homage; the little counterfeit rift of separation between imitation-slave and imitation-master widened and widened, and became an abyss, and a very real one—and on one side of it stood Roxy, the dupe of her own deceptions, and on the other stood her child, no longer a usurper to her, but her accepted and recognized master. (*PW*, 19)

Roxana's authoring of fictional identities is strikingly like the process of composition outlined in Twain's Preface to *Those Extraordinary Twins*. Like his story of the freak (or freaks), the "fiction created by herself" proliferates beyond her authorial control, creating unintended selves and scenarios and, finally, making the "fictional"—the "mock," the "imitation," the "counterfeit"—into the "real." For Roxana's author as well, we will see, fiction making eventuated in a similar overturning of distinctions between imagination and reality.

Moreover, in the moment when she becomes "the dupe of her own deceptions," Twain may well have been creating not only a premonitory image of his own career as author, but also an inadvertent (female) double of the King in *Huckleberry Finn*, who talks the Duke "blind" until, like Roxana, "he was actuly beginning to believe what he was saying, *himself*."[25] Becoming the dupe of one's own deceptions in this way is a fate popularly attributed to the confidence man. Horace W. Fuller's *Noted French Trials. Impostors and Adventurers* (1882), for example, a history of imposture that Clemens added to his library around the time of completing *Huckleberry Finn*, begins a chapter on the seven "false dauphins" with a qualified moral about imposture: "One does not know which most to admire, the persistency of the men who play a *role* in which they often end by being themselves their first dupes, or the imperturbable incredulity which is always ready to furnish them partisans."[26] The self-deceivers who become entangled in the world of their own invention always fascinated Mark Twain (one thinks of Colonel Sellers of *The Gilded Age*, the Yankee, and the inventor par excellence, James W. Paige of the disastrous typesetter); his own fiction after 1894 is obsessively preoccupied with narrators who trap themselves permanently in their own narratives by dreaming themselves into a nightmare from which they cannot awaken.

Clemens may well, then, have read as well as written about such figures. When he writes, for example, that Roxana's son is "no longer a usurper to her, but her recognized and accepted master," he may have been reminded of the paradoxical fate of several well-known frauds or impostors whose trials he followed: to be defined negatively by the identity that is *not* theirs. The "Tichborne claimant," for example, was almost never referred to by his legal name, even after prolonged legal efforts established his identity as the butcher Arthur Orton. At the end of *Pudd'nhead Wilson*, too, Roxana's son, the "usurping little slave," is still called "Tom" or Tom or "the false heir"—the fact of his imposture still our only reference point—and worse yet, the text never even refers to "the real heir" by any proper name whatsoever. The "real" "Thomas à Beckett Driscoll" ends essentially identity-less, his "true self" permanently usurped, an exile in the no-man's land between the races:

> The poor fellow could not endure the terrors of the white man's parlor, and felt at home and at peace nowhere but in the kitchen. The family pew was a misery to him, yet he could nevermore enter into the solacing refuge of the "nigger gallery"—that was closed to him for good. (*PW*, 114)

The identity ultimately usurped, Twain shows, may thus turn out in more ways than one to be the usurper's own. Roxana, we remember, does in fact become the "slave" of her son and "master"—to the extent that even after being freed by Percy Driscoll, she allows herself to be re-sold back into slavery to pay off her son's gambling debts.

"By the fiction created by herself," then, Roxana authors a reality: the "very real" "abyss" separating black slaves from white masters. Like her author, whose story, he said, grew, beyond his intentions, from ahistorical farce to social chronicle, Roxana's creation unwittingly places her right back in the world of slavery that she intended (her son) to escape. It is the real world, as well as the world she creates of imitation master and slave, Twain ironically shows, whose reality consists of social contructs. Virtually all of the identities in the novel advertise themselves as constituted culturally, primarily around names, titles, and clothing. In an early passage deleted from the final version, Twain specifically links the custom of naming in the South with racial distinctions. For an elderly person to be called "Uncle" or "Aunt" is the highest title of honor and affection, and the most gracious, that is known to the South. Negroes get it by mere age, and then it does not mean a great deal; but with the whites it is the assayer's stamp upon the golden ingot of character, and stands for a thousand carats fine.[27]

The published narrative elaborates ironically on the belief in these stamps of character. Dawson's Landing's white aristocracy, collectively titled within the narrative as the "F.F.V." (First Families of Virginia), bestow proudly upon themselves names and titles that do not actually mark any individual stamp upon them: to the reader, Judge York Leicester Driscoll sounds very much like Percy Northumberland Driscoll, which sounds like Thomas à Beckett Driscoll, which sounds like Colonel Cecil Burleigh Essex.

The absence of noble name or title defines other kinds of status recognized by the community. The marginal position of Mr. David "Pudd'nhead" Wilson is marked by the combination of his nickname and surname; he is most often called Pudd'nhead Wilson. And Roxana names her son Valet de Chambre: he had "no surname—slaves hadn't the privilege . . . It soon got shortened to 'Chambers,' of course." But as the "fine sound" of the name suggests, even those denied the "privilege" make the same assumptions as "white folks" about how names mark personal identity and enhance self-respect. Witness Roxana's pride in the old family names of her own genealogy and that of her son (his "Essex blood" combines with that of his "great-great-great-great-gran'father," "Cap'n. John Smith, de highes' blood dat Ole Virginny ever turned out," and that of his "great-great-gran'mother, or somers along back dah," Pocahontas "de Injun queen"), a pride which, so many critics have pointed out, both reflects and parodies the genealogical obsessions of white society (*PW*, 9, 70).

The novel's exuberant satire on naming reconfirms Twain's uncanny ear for linguistic nuance as a means of cultural critique. Eugene Genovese's magisterial study of slave life, *Roll, Jordan, Roll*, documents the importance of slave names, particularly surnames, to both masters and slaves. Not only does the "strongest evidence" of antebellum slave pressure to compel slaveholders to grant them the "privilege" of surnames come in part from the Mississippi Valley ("the scene of this chronicle," the novel's first sentence tells us), but after the war, slaves throughout the South either took surnames or openly went by those they already had. "Appropriately," Genovese remarks, "they called them 'entitles.'" Most important, he argues for a "formidable black initiative" in the creation of names; by going back in time to take names with origins in white families, as Twain has Roxana do, the slaves recaptured, as best they could, their own history. ("The name had to be 'real'; it had to embody a living history without which genuine identity could not have become possible.")[28] Such a genealogy as Roxana's everywhere acknowledges what the novel's white fathers do not, that the lives of the slaves and their masters had become so intertwined that to divorce them would to a great extent rob both groups, but the blacks especially, of the only history they had. Hence Roxana appropriates as her own those mythologized colonial ancestors Captain John Smith and Pocahontas.

Clothing, too, enforces race and class distinctions in the novel. Most clearly with the two identical infants, as Wilson points out to Roxana, clothing is necessary to offset their essential indistinguishability: "How do you tell them apart, Roxy, when they haven't any clothes on?" At the moment of making this casual remark to Roxy, planting in her mind, of course, the possibility of exchanging the babies, Wilson is engaged in taking their fingerprints (one of the hobbies he has cultivated in lieu of practicing law), the very marks that will eventually expose their switched identities. Because the two incidents occur side by side, the reader is led to anticipate that if one system of personal identification in the novel—names, titles, clothing—is patently unreliable, the other—fingerprinting—may prove to have more accurate differentiating power. But we also begin to wonder whether the issue is less one of accurately reflecting individual differences and more one of actually creating those differences. Twain introduces the little scene of the two babies, each with "blue eyes and flaxen curls" but dressed differently ("the white babe wore ruffled soft muslin and a coral necklace, while the other wore merely a coarse tow-linen shirt . . . and no jewelry"), by explaining "what *made* . . . a negro": "a fiction of law and custom" dictates that any amount of black "blood," supposedly measurable down to one-sixteenth in Roxana's case, one-thirty-second in her son's, "makes" "a negro" (my emphasis; *PW*, 9).

The visual deception created by this system of racial identification is embodied in Roxana, "as white as anybody" but "a slave, and salable as such." Assuming false roles, then, as both she and her son repeatedly do, is a learned response in this slave society, perhaps most of all for those who have historically been the victims, not the perpetrators, of the "fiction of law and custom" that defines racial identity. Particularly when mother and son assume both racial and sexual disguises, they enact the tangle of fact and fiction with which identity is constituted in this world. Each taking on aspects of the other's gender, they act out a mingling of boundaries which stands for the mingling of blood denied by the biracial society through its policies of racial classification.

The result of those overt policies is a covert crossing of the color line, or "passing," an implicit collapsing of boundaries that is brilliantly contained in Roxana's argument with "the ostensible 'Chambers'" over whether they are "imitation nigger" or "imitation white." Responding to his supposed mother's insulting him as a "misable imitation nigger," Chambers asserts that they are both "pow'full good imitation" whites, but "we don't 'mount to noth'n as imitation *niggers*." "Imitation nigger" makes a kind of physical sense in that Twain's "white negroes" are only a literally pale reflection of "coal-black" blacks like Jasper, the male slave with whom Roxana flirtatiously spars. "'You black mud-cat!'" she taunts, "'I got sump'n better to do den 'sociat'n wid niggers as black as you is'" (PW, 35, 8). In a broader, metaphysical sense as well, Dawson's Landing is populated by nothing but imitation whites whose very names, customs, and values ape those derived from an archaic feudal system with very little material relevance to their own reality. Moreover, as Chambers's amused rejoinder implies, it is not easy to decide what he and Roxana are imitations of. Although the word "imitate" and its synonyms assume the presence of some originating reality to be imitated, in this case there is no such certain reality to be the same as. This is a society radically confused about what people are, who is black and who is white, what is imitation and what is real, a society whose laws create and enforce strict boundaries to mask those confusions. Indeed, we remember Twain's comment on how Roxana becomes the "dupe of her own deceptions": "the little counterfeit rift of separation between imitation-slave and imitation-master" becomes "an abyss, and a very real one."

Thus in order to conceal a white appearance, Roxana and Tom assume the mask of precisely what Dawson's Landing has arbitrarily defined them to be—black. The fact that disguises identical to the social reality serve to hide both that reality and the self reveals how foundationless are these categories, which can be so readily reversed and righted, taken on and off like a suit of clothing. In fact, the existence of Tom's female persona—he disguises himself as a girl for his "theft-raids" on the village—is coextensive with his female attire; to shed the clothes is to shed the self. The "shameless young creature" in Tom's bedroom who puzzles Pudd'nhead Wilson will arouse no more dangerous curiosity, Tom knows, once "the clothes that gave her her sex [are] burnt up and the ashes thrown away" (*PW*, 102). If Tom paradoxically disguises himself as himself, he, like his mother, also disguises himself as what he is not. Each undertakes the role of transvestite in blackface, conflating categories of gender identification with racial categories. The implication, explicitly pursued by Twain after *Pudd'nhead Wilson* in his tales of sexual transformation, comes through partially even here: if "male" and "female" are as readily interchanged as "black" and "white," then gender difference may prove to be as culturally constituted, as much "a fiction of law and custom" as racial difference.

The fictive quality of these systems of identification emerges most graphically amid what might be called the novel's numerological fetish. Pudd'nhead Wilson's conspicuously numerical joke about halves of dogs enigmatically opens the novel. That joke, part of the earliest section of manuscript that Twain wrote in Bad-Nauheim during the summer of 1892,[29] remained part of the novel's opening throughout all subsequent revisions and is clearly both seed and fruit of Twain's developing conceptions of *Pudd'nhead Wilson*. The villagers' obtuse response to Wilson's deadpan line ("I wish I owned half of that dog . . . because, I would kill my half") takes the joke literally as a mathematical proposition to be solved like any problem. Counterparts of the village witnesses at the Siamese twins' trial for assault and battery, Wilson's audience is similarly faced with the problem of numerically classifying a human action. Of the different equations about fractions and whole numbers which they debate, the most difficult for these literalists is why Wilson would not want to own the whole dog, "knowing that if he killed his half and the other half dies, he would be responsible for that half, just the same as if he had killed that half instead of his own" (*PW*, 5–6).

Like fools who tell the truth in riddles, the villagers take to its logical extreme a process of mathematical reasoning we have already seen similarly perverted by one of the witnesses at the Siamese twins' trial. In their witless way, the villagers are making exactly the point Mark Twain himself makes farcically in that trial: precise definitions of human identity based on fractional division do not hold up under legal procedures of investigation and punishment. "If you kill one half of a general dog, there ain't any man that can tell whose half it was," just as no one can tell which "half" of the twins "belongs" to the crime of kicking Tom Driscoll, and just as Jim argues in *Huckleberry Finn* that King Solomon's decision to cut the disputed baby in half would not solve the case:

> De 'spute warn't 'bout half a chile, de 'spute was 'bout a whole chile; en de man dat think he kin settle a 'spute 'bout a whole chile wid a half a chile, doan' know enough to come in out'n de rain . . . *He* as soon chop a chile in two as a cat.[30]

The common denominator in all these cases is quantification, the numerical thinking so basic to the law's way of knowing that, however disastrously flawed in its logic, it is nevertheless applied to differentiate the innocent from the guilty and to determine punishment. The law, Twain shows, persists in arguing in precise terms of halves and wholes in spite of gruesome evidence that there does not seem to be anything capable of affecting one "half" of a whole and not the other. Both Siamese twins die when only one is hung, just as many social and legal efforts to exert control through punishment result in indiscriminate, rather than pre-cisely delineated, violence. The novel's opening "lesson in frac-tions," it has been argued, shows the destructive effects of defining identity through "any arbitrary division or artificial quantifica-tion."[31]

While I do not question the soundness of this conclusion, I do want to ask why Mark Twain was compelled only to half-express it, almost to make light of it, through the media of an absurd farce, a failed joke, and the voice of Jim. Although these examples do not betray anything dangerously attractive, I will argue that Twain was ambivalent about such systems of knowledge—epitomized by the law—that create fixed boundaries and thereby control human beings. He was as much attracted to their promise of order and control as he was suspicious of that promise and repelled by its violent results. The best evidence, however, for the sometime de-sirability of division and difference is not Twain's jokes about killing halves of babies or dogs or Siamese twins, but rather his complicated and contradictory attitudes toward fingerprinting. A system of identification roughly equivalent to the law's methods of detection, fingerprinting intrigues both author and reader all the way through *Pudd'nhead Wilson*, disappointing him (and us) only at the very end.

VI

Before we arrive at that final moment of discovery, however, this detective novel begins by displaying another important numerological scheme—racial classification based on fractional divisions of "blood." The infamous formula that makes Roxana—"to all intents and purposes as white as anybody"—a black slave is, we remember, only a fraction: "the one-sixteenth of her which was black out-voted the other fifteen parts and made her a negro" (*PW*, 8–9). And what enforces this illogical arithmetic other than the socially sanctioned contract summed up by the verb "out-voted"? The verb reminds us that these measurements measure ideologically rather than naturally produced differences between the races. Roxana's racial identity is socially created, "a fiction of law and custom," but a fiction shored up and made to look like fact through the pseudo-mathematics of blood lines. For Twain the apparent precision implied by minute fractional divisions (one-sixteenth, one-thirty-second) only underscores their disjunction from reality. All that counts racially in Dawson's Landing are two categories: black and white.

Mark Twain's representation of racial identity as a system of deceptive mathematics has historical precedent in the unique "descent rule" that has been the principal basis of racial classification in the United States. According to this ancestry rule, all descendants of mixed unions are classed with their black ancestors. The resulting two-category system (such as Twain depicts) originated in efforts, mandated by state legislation since the colonial era, to restrict interracial marriage and to determine the status of mixed offspring; by the time of the Civil War, in order to facilitate enforcement of anti-miscegenation laws, more precise definitions were formulated as to what proportion of black ancestry placed an individual on the other side of the color line. The usual antebellum rule for determining who was what was that anyone with one-fourth or one-eighth proportion of black "blood"—meaning anyone with a black or mulatto ancestor within the previous two or three generations—must be classified as black. This "statutory homogenization of all persons with Negro ancestry" was peculiar to slavery as it developed in the continental United States. Not even in South Africa, George Fredrickson notes, "despite the triumph of white supremacy and segregationism," has such a "rigorous ancestry principle been used to determine who is white and who is not."[32]

The rigor of the American two-category system can be judged by common linguistic usage. Other than the term mulatto (which was indistinguishable from "Negro" for legal purposes), no terminology existed in the U.S. with which to recognize varying degrees of intermixed "blood" or to define a hierarchy of status derived from those shades of distinction. Elsewhere, studies of comparative race relations show, racially mixed offspring ("half-caste" or "half-white") have usually been acknowledged as an intermediate group in systems of racial stratification with varying degrees of fluidity among white, "colored," and black. Such acknowledgment was reflected in the development of terminology to distinguish various racial mixtures. In Latin America and the British West Indies, for example, racially mixed offspring were labeled according to fractions of "blood": "mulatto" meant one-half white; "sambo," one-fourth white; "quadroon," three-fourths white; and "mestizo," seven-eighths white.[33]

Twain's minute fractions (one-sixteenth, one-thirty-second) mock the absurdity of this way of quantifying the genetic makeup. But however theoretically and genetically untenable, this complex linguistic machinery establishes a fact of social practice: miscegenation was a publicly accepted, almost institutionalized practice in some New World slave societies, whereas the absence of analogous terms in the U.S. suggests that racially mixed offspring simply were not officially acknowledged.[34] The reasons for such denial may be summed up in the language of a pioneering Virginia statute of 1691 that banned, for the first time in the colonies, all forms of interracial marriage. The legislation's stated purpose was "the prevention of that abominable mixture and spurious issue."[35] The essential word is "mixture." Mulattoes blurred the clear separation between the races essential to American race slavery, and miscegenation was thus perceived as a threat to a biracial society. Particularly threatening to this two-part order were the "free persons of color," most of whom were mulattoes. "We should have but two classes," declared one grand jury deliberating on the expulsion of the "free colored" from South Carolina in the late 1850s, "the Master and the slave, and no intermediate class can be other than immensely mischievous to our peculiar institution."[36] The grand jury testimony verges on acknowledging the contradiction that this "intermediate" group—an "abominable mixture," neither white nor black, slave nor free—violates the logic of the institution that produced it and therefore must be suppressed.

If, as a result, the mulatto was legally erased, deprived of any status under the law, the problem of race mixture itself was not altogether suppressed in contemporary political, scientific, and religious writing. A widespread proslavery argument of the 1850s drew on current knowledge of heredity to theorize that the off-spring of miscegenation would be an unnatural type, the mixture of races adapted to very different geographic regions, and hence unable to procreate beyond two or three generations. The eventual result of race mixture was inevitably sterility, according to another "scientific" argument offering "proof" in the sterility of an animal hybrid, the mule—an analogy linguistically enforced in the word "mulatto," borrowed from the Spanish and derived from the Latin *mulus*. Scientific justification was not the only authority appealed to in antimiscegenation writing. Immediately after the war, miscegenation became for some the essential sin against God that caused the South to lose. Defeat "is the judgment of the Almighty," wrote one low-country Carolina planter in 1868, "because the human and brute blood have mingled to the degree it has in the slave states. Was it not so in the French and British Islands and see what has become of them."[37]

The widespread revulsion against race mixture expressed in all of the above writings—the Virginia statute, the grand jury testimony, the scientific arguments on hybridism, and the planter's religious argument—helps to explain both why and how the fiction of race purity was maintained in the face of so much evidence to the contrary. As Winthrop Jordan puts this contradiction: "By classifying the mulatto as a Negro [the white slaveowner] was in effect denying that intermixture had occurred at all."[38] When Mark Twain, later in the 1890s, framed racial identity in *Pudd'nhead Wilson* as an issue of acknowledgment and denial, both for himself as an author and for Southern society, he was thus openly articulating the *sub rosa* judgment of many of his contemporaries.

Indeed, once slavery was abolished, the question of the color line and its impact on the representation of race relations became, if anything, all the more pressing. For many white southerners, George Washington Cable pointed out in 1885, looming in the passage of the Fourteenth and Fifteenth Amendments and the freedmen's participation in Reconstruction governments was the "huge bugbear of Social Equality": equality meant the "social intermingling of the two races," with its "monstrous" suggestion of "admixture of the two bloods" and "the utter confusion of race and corruption of society."[39] What Jordan calls the "peculiar bifurcation" of American racial categorization represented, then, for Twain and others, even more than purely a legal effort to control the results of interracial sex. The restrictive policy attempted broadly to control "black" encroachments on "white" identity, to fix racial identity as an absolute quantity with clear boundaries rather than on a continuum of fuzzy gradations, one shading into another. Fears expressed about "amalgamation," an antebellum term equivalent to miscegenation, corroborate what I will show to be Twain's association of race mixture with the destruction of basic assumptions about identity—not only racial, but also social, even sexual identity.

One traveler in the antebellum South singled out what he called the "bugbear of 'amalgamation.'" The traveler's journal noted that even the reform-minded Lyman Beecher was "so far jaundiced" that he supported African colonization, because "he considered it a salutary preventive of that amalgamation, which would confound the two races and obliterate the traces of their distinction." Similar arguments, bent on maintaining these "irresistible" "natural" differences, were advanced from colonial days through the Emancipation Proclamation by other, even more eminent advocates of black emancipation and colonization. In 1781 Thomas Jefferson asked in *Notes on the State on Virginia*, "Will not a lover of natural history, then, one who views the gradations in all the races of animals with the eye of philosophy, excuse an effort to keep those in the department of man as distinct as nature has formed them?" Jefferson's argument against race mixture was reiterated in 1862, when Abraham Lincoln addressed a small group of black leaders in the White House on the subject of returning all American blacks to Africa. "You and we are different races," he said. "We have between us a broader difference than exists between any other two races."[40]

Jefferson and Lincoln were articulating a general fear of amalgamation shared both by those who advocated some form of black emancipation and by the anti-abolitionist "gentlemen of property and standing" in antebellum America. For the latter, especially, Leonard L. Richards has asserted, amalgamation was personally and intimately threatening: it tapped the "fear of assimilation, of being 'mulattoized,' of losing one's sense of identity." For such men, tied to family, class, community, and position, race mixture went beyond a threat to race purity: it was a harbinger of "the breakdown of distinctions among white men, the blurring of social divisions, and the general levelling process that they saw enveloping ante-bellum America"; it was a first step to becoming "cogs in a mass society."[41] For southern women of the same class, such as Mary Boykin Chestnut, amalgamation also threatened a more private, familial order, as a well-known 1861 entry in Chestnut's diary suggests:

> Like the patriarchs of old, our men live all in one house with their wives and their concubines; and the mulattoes one sees in every family partly resemble the white children. Any lady is ready to tell you who is the father of all the mulatto children in everybody's household but her own. Those, she seems to think, drop from the clouds.[42]

For both men and women, proslavery apologists, abolitionists, and reform-minded anti-abolitionists alike, the issues of race mixture and interracial sexual relations struck at the heart of basic assumptions about the individual's place in his home and his society.

The "stock" changeling formula in *Pudd'nhead Wilson*, then, altered by Twain so that "twinned" black and white babies are exchanged in their cradles, acts out an interchangeability between the races that resonates with anxieties of the 1890s as well as of the antebellum years. For the 1830s saw a surge of enthusiasm for abolition, followed by a mounting resistance to that idea, culminating in the early 1850s in the Fugitive Slave legislation. Just so, the end of the Civil War and Reconstruction were characterized by optimism and even by radical thinking on race relations that gave way in the eighties and nineties to something old, something new. The law, once used to regulate the peculiar institution of slavery, now underwrote the far more broad-reaching ideology of white supremacy in state laws regulating relations between the races and establishing rigid lines of segregation. By the beginning of the twentieth century, for example, laws against intermarriage were passed in all but one of the seventeen states that had made up the slave South in 1861, and up to as recently as 1930, twenty-nine of the forty-eight states had made intermarriage illegal. At the same time, for the purposes of racial identification, the color line was more stringently and narrowly defined. As late as 1970, for example, in Louisiana the legal fraction defining blackness was still one-thirty-second "Negro blood." George Fredrickson argues that "most southern states were operating in accordance with what amounted to a 'one-drop rule,' meaning in effect that a person with any known degree of black ancestry was legally considered a Negro and subject to the full disabilities associated with segregation and disfranchisement."[43]

Such heightened awareness of what George Washington Cable called "the Negro Question" characterized the years during which Twain wrote *Pudd'nhead Wilson*. The new race laws and the accompanying cultural conversation about the South's "race problem" articulated for Twain, in concrete social and political terms, a longstanding problem: the connection between the maintenance of social control and the construction of identity. During this period (extending roughly from the late 1880s through the 1890s), the debate over race relations brought to the fore two bodies of contemporary knowledge—one legal and one scientific—that asserted the feasibility of drawing sharp racial, sexual, or social lines around groups of human beings, thereby ensuring the divisions many believed necessary to social stability. For Twain the possibility of such certainty as held out by the law and by the science of heredity was as deeply attractive as it was illusory and destructive. These contradictions finally collide in the conclusion of *Pudd'nhead Wilson*, when lawyer/detective/scientist David Wilson puts to the legal test his hobby of fingerprinting—a method of differentiating "each man from all the rest of the human species," according to the geneticist Francis Galton, "to an extent far beyond the capacity of human imagination."[44]

VII

Alone among Mark Twain's fictional detectives, most of whom, he once commented, "extravagantly burlesque the detective business—if it *is* possible to burlesque that business extravagantly," David Wilson is genuinely adept at the procedures of detection and proof.[45] His chosen profession, the law depends upon this skill, but since his fatal half-dog joke prevents him from practicing law in Dawson's Landing, his ratiocinative powers reveal themselves in more eccentric ways. Wilson's eccentricity as well as his outsider status remind us that he was created in the image of Sherlock Holmes, one of Twain's several forays in deliberately exploiting the contemporary market for detective fiction. Conan Doyle's Holmes had been a best-selling phenomenon in America ever since the first Sherlock Holmes story, *A Study in Scarlet*, appeared in *Beeton's Christmas Annual* (1887). An alienated intellectual, Holmes had popular appeal in part because he stood out from the institutionalized police detectives of the Pinkerton series or the Beadle dime novels. Holmes's "passion for definite and exact knowledge," for example, sometimes isolates him even from the devoted Watson, who criticizes the detective's intellect in *A Study in Scarlet* as "a little too scientific," approaching "cold-bloodedness."[46] In creating his own detective, Twain draws on the somewhat alienating ratiocinative powers of Conan Doyle's popular character: Tom Driscoll snidely sings Wilson's praises as the "great scientist running to seed here in this village" (*PW*, 49). In *Pudd'nhead Wilson*, as in popular detective fiction, one condition of intellectual power is isolation from the community, which, like Dawson's Landing, both fears and needs its scientists.

Mark Twain also appropriated from popular fiction the equation between seeing and deductive power, perhaps most memorably expressed in the insignia of the Pinkerton agency, which bore an open human eye with the motto "We Never Sleep" beneath it. Sherlock Holmes's power, too, is notably ocular; his special vision enables him to deduce biographical facts from ordinarily unnoticed details. Wilson's superior intellect also expresses itself through superior visual observation. Both his hobbies of reading palms and collecting fingerprints demonstrate a type of Holmesian second sight, for they emphasize the reading and interpreting of signs that are visible (to the interpreter) traces of the past in the present. In this fascination with ocular proof, Twain draws upon the popular caricature of the detective with magnifying glass, bending over what seems like invisible matter, collecting all possible facts because even trivial details may prove to signify.

When a whole elaborate plot may be thus untangled by discovering one essential fact, we have abandoned the problematic nature of causation in the real world of masters and slaves, where victim and victimizer are bound together by the institutional effects of slavery. No such entanglements can remain in the secure universe of the detective story, where fixed laws give meaning to particular events, and, through the detective's knowledge, random events are ultimately rearranged into one coherent line of causality from the murderer to the deed.

The characters in Twain's novel react to the deductive powers of the detective with much the same combination of awe and scepticism that Twain himself sometimes expressed toward the writer's omniscient eye. Indeed, we know, he went so far as putatively to reject his own authorial omniscience in the preface to *Those Extraordinary Twins*. And of David Wilson's own interpretive abilities, Tom Driscoll mocks, "Dave's just an all-around genius, . . . a prophet with the kind of honor that prophets generally get at home—for here they don't give shucks for his scientifics" (PW, 49). If Twain's detective, like the "jack-leg" novelist himself, is less a prophet than a disturber of the peace, and if his "electrifying revelations" at the end of the novel are more disruptive than restorative, then what judgment are we to make of his solution to the mystery of a murderer's identity? More particularly, what are we to make of how rather than what he knows: along with the murderer, what is on trial in the courtroom conclusion is Wilson's method of deducing identity, his "scientifics," the fingerprinting system.

In this case, the author shares his character's passion for scientifics, for while writing Pudd'nhead Wilson in 1892, Clemens "devoured," as he put it, Francis Galton's Finger·Prints, just published that year. In part his enthusiasm came from the novelty, and hence, he thought, saleability of this material. "The fingerprints in this one is virgin ground," he assured his publisher Fred Hall, "absolutely fresh, and mighty curious and interesting to everybody."[47] But in larger part Clemens was fascinated by both the scientific findings and the credentials of the eminent geneticist (and cousin of Charles Darwin) Galton. Recalling in 1897 how he had relied on Galton's book while composing Pudd'nhead Wilson in 1892, he wrote in a letter: "The finger-mark system of identification . . . has been quite thoroughly & scientifically examined by Mr. Galt [sic], & I kept myself within the bounds of his ascertained facts."[48] Chief among the facts on which the plot turns is Galton's demonstration that fingerprints can establish the identity of the same person at any stage of his life between babyhood and old age (and for some time after his death, Galton adds), as well as differentiate between twins ("It would be totally impossible to fail to distinguish between the fingerprints of twins, who in other respects appear exactly alike" [FP, 113, 167]).

Even more provocative for Clemens, I would argue, than these particular "ascertained facts" was Galton's broad and spirited endorsement of the wide-ranging potential of fingerprinting as a method of "personal identification." The prints would be of value not only in identifying criminals, Galton points out, but also in ferreting out the less willful kind of imposture that we know interested Clemens: the possibility "of a harmless person being arrested by mistake for another man," for example, "and being in sore straits to give satisfactory proof of the error" (FP, 149). "Let no one despise the ridges on account of their smallness," Galton urges a possibly sceptical readership:

> They have the unique merit of retaining all their peculiarities unchanged throughout life, and afford in consequence an incomparably surer criterion of identity than any other bodily feature . . . To fix the human personality, to give to each human being an identity, an individuality that can be depended upon with certainty, lasting, unchangeable, always recognisable and easily adduced, this appears to be in the largest sense the aim of the new method. (*FP*, 2, 169)

Apparently persuaded as much by Galton's impassioned tone as by his facts, Mark Twain puts all of these claims to the test in the dramatic courtroom conclusion of *Pudd'nhead Wilson*. When Wilson unveils his theory of who murdered Judge Driscoll and presents the evidence that proves its soundness, he also implicitly tries the case for what Twain learned from his research in Galton's *Finger Prints*. This "mysterious and marvelous natal autograph," Wilson argues, constitutes virtually perfect proof of identity:

> Every human being carries with him from his cradle to his grave certain physical marks which do not change their character, and by which he can always be identified . . . This autograph cannot be counterfeited, nor can he disguise it or hide it away, nor can it become illegible by the wear and the mutations of time. (*PW*, 108)

Like Galton's, Wilson's tone becomes more impassioned, his parallel clauses building in length and intensity, as he moves beyond the data to contemplate the potential of what he calls these "sure identifiers." Fingerprints, in Galton's terms, reliable means of "Personal Identification," render deception through impersonation or accident impossible by enabling each individual to be absolutely differentiated from the rest of the species. Wilson waxes eloquent about this method, building suspense in the courtroom audience by defining what the method is not. This signature is not a person's height, "for duplicates of that exist; it is not his form, for duplicates of that exist, also, whereas this signature is each man's very own—there is no duplicate of it among the swarming populations of the globe!" Even identical twins, Wilson pointedly concludes, "carry from birth to death a sure identifier in this mysterious and marvelous natal autograph. That once known to you, his fellow-twin could never personate him and deceive you" (*PW*, 108–9).

At this point in the argument, Wilson pauses and, as Mark Twain used to "play with the pause," theatrically lets his silence "perfect its spell upon the house," before putting on his final display, submitting himself to an actual, on-the-spot test of his claims. While his back is turned, he asks several members of the jury, whose fingerprints he has collected over the years and knows well, to make their prints on a glass window in the courtroom, where the two accused twins will also make their marks. This procedure, as he requests, is repeated twice on different panes, for, as he puts it, "a person might happen on the right marks by pure guesswork, *once*, therefore I wish to be tested twice." The reader is almost as gratified as the courtroom audience when Wilson correctly identifies the various prints ("This certainly approaches the miraculous!" says "the Bench"). But the source of our gratification is different from theirs. For us, the only real suspense in the novel has been waiting not for the identity of the murderer (which we've known all along) but for the moment when Wilson would discover that he has the means to prove it. And that moment finally arrives in the suitably theatrical trial, which opens in Chapter 20 with this rather ominous entry from "Pudd'nhead Wilson's Calendar": "Even the clearest and most perfect circumstantial evidence is likely to be at fault, after all, and therefore ought to be received with great caution" (*PW*, 99).

How, then, ought we to receive the evidence of the fingerprints? What do those "sure identifiers" actually reveal? Wilson, no longer the flamboyant rhetorician but the dispassionate man of science, now draws on the ostensibly neutral, value-free variables of science and the syllogistic structure of logical reasoning to complete his presentation of the evidence. The fingerprints tell us first, he argues, using the notation preferred by Galton, that "A was put into B's cradle in the nursery." "In the majority of cases," Galton remarks, "the mere question would be, Is the man A the same person as B, or is he not? And of that question the fingermarks would give unerring proof" (*FP*, 151). In the case Twain creates, things are not quite so clear. What happens next, Wilson explains, is that "B was transferred to the kitchen, and became a negro and a slave . . . but within a quarter of an hour he will stand before you white and free!" (*PW*, 112).

Neither the triumphant tone nor the burst of applause from the audience nor the aura of logical deduction and absolute clarity disguises the fact that Wilson's conclusion, though strictly "the truth," is also illogical and arbitrary, almost more confusing than clarifying. Fingerprints appear theoretically to be the one measure of unique, non-contingent, individual identity, but are in practice relational indices that must be read in and against the context of other sets of prints. Yet in spite of the methodologically essential social context, the fingerprints tell us nothing socially, as opposed to physiologically, significant about either A or B as individuals, much less about the lives of "Chambers" or "Tom." What they prove, in fact, is that one can be interchangeably "white and free" and "a negro and a slave." In this way Mark Twain thus out-Galtons Galton. Galton finally had to admit that fingerprints do not reveal racial grouping or characteristics; he acknowledged "great expectations, that have been falsified, namely their use in indicating Race and Temperament" (*FP*, 1–2, 26). Rather than stopping at this point, Twain goes even farther than Galton, showing that though fingerprints do, indeed, establish racial difference, those categories are not biologically fixed but rather culturally defined. Knowing, then, by evidence of the fingerprints, that Tom, considered white, was born black and enslaved and is once again so constituted does nothing to fulfill Galton's promise that fingerprinting will "fix the human personality" and "give to each human being an identity, an individuality." Instead, like any other "natural" index of the self—race or gender, for example—fingerprints point toward the culture that appropriates nature as the basis of socially constructed identities.

Rather than leading to any stable, independent determinant of identity, then, the fingerprints focus attention on the social context that authorizes their use in the science of "personal identification." That social context most explicitly enters the novel during the sentencing phase of the trial, the moment in the courtroom when the social voice speaks most directly to reaffirm its values and to reestablish the order disturbed by the crime. In Twain's case, though, the sentence accomplishes no such return to order. Although the murderer, now defined as "the false heir," makes "a full confession" and is "sentenced to imprisonment for life," the creditors of his ultimate victim, not Judge Driscoll but "the Percy Driscoll estate," argue that "a complication" has ensued. Building much the same structure of logical reasoning as Wilson does, they establish first that "the false heir" should have been "inventoried . . . with the rest of the property" at the time of its owner's death; that he was thus "lawfully their property"; and furthermore, "that if he had been delivered up to them in the first place, they would have sold him and he could not have murdered

Judge Driscoll." Hard on the heels of this stunning conjecture, in a triumphant burst of illogic, comes the conclusion to both the creditors' argument and the novel:

> Therefore it was not he that had really committed the murder, the guilt lay with the erroneous inventory. Everybody saw that there was reason in this. Everybody granted that if "Tom" were white and free it would be unquestionably right to punish him—it would be no loss to anybody; but to shut up a valuable slave for life—that was quite another matter.
>
> As soon as the Governor understood the case, he pardoned Tom at once and the creditors sold him down the river. (*PW*, 115)

The author and his reader see a different "reason" in this. If "Tom" or Tom or "the false heir" (the proliferation of names seeming to replace human substance with linguistic form) is pardoned only to be sold down the river, we reason, then words like "pardon" and "punish" (and "reason") have lost their meaning in Dawson's Landing, a society where an "erroneous inventory" can first assume the human burden of guilt and then, logically, escape human punishment. By the same agreed-upon fiction, a "valuable slave" is defined as chattel, not to be held accountable for human antisocial acts, and therefore even the law must obey the rules of logic and conclude of the murderer that "it was not he that had really committed the murder." Furthermore, only "if 'Tom' were white and free" would it "be unquestionably right to punish him, so it also follows that in this case a valuable slave—will-less chattel—must be "pardoned" for a crime he could not by definition have committed. Finally, if the guilty party is the "erroneous inventory," then all of southern society is implicated in the crime, since it participates in and oversees the slave system that requires such inventories. The trial thus bears witness to the anguished tangle of contradictions surrounding the slave system, and further, to the strange fact that while these contradictions expose themselves in the legal and linguistic fictions of slave society, they also keep that world from falling apart under their weight.

To thus discover that the criminal in a detective story is not one individual but an entire society is to disrupt the premise of narrative order and social justice upon which the story is based. Fomenting such disruption, Twain, as we know, in the later stages of composition, wanted everything in his novel to center on the

murder and the trial, invoking expectations of the ritual confrontation between law and criminality that concludes most detective
fiction with the restoration of order. Rather than coming to a schematic resolution, though, the conclusion of *Pudd'nhead Wilson*
initiates polarities between innocence and guilt, slave and free
man, loss and profit, punishment and pardon, only to expose them
finally as "fictions of law and custom." Similarly, the changeling
plot does not culminate in the conventional discovery of the
child's noble birth, a discovery which ordinarily vindicates the
noble behavior he has exhibited from the beginning as it restores
class lines and fulfills the audience's desire for order, both narrative and social.

Pudd'nhead Wilson deliberately denies such wish fulfillment.
Through the detective plot that its author so admired, the novel
arouses the reader's craving to discover, the desire to turn the act of
reading—palms, fingerprints, or texts—into a means of discovery
and resolution of apparently impenetrable mysteries. But if
Twain's detective acts out the author's desire that human knowledge could so accurately systematize the world, the character also
oversees the author's deconstruction of his own fantasy. Wilson's
classification system helps him to discover the false Tom (or
"Tom"), but in exposing a "white" man as a "black" slave, it also
exposes the whole society that created, but does not acknowledge,
its own nemesis. Whether one calls this a discovery of America's
"own secret self" (Leslie Fiedler) or of "the repressed guilt which
has gathered at the heart of slavery" (James Cox), such a discovery
makes knowledge more of a threat than a deliverance.[49] Tom's fate
threatens that the hidden taint of black blood could be disclosed in
any white person, tapping the dread that all "secret murderers are
said to feel when the accuser says 'Thou art the man!'" (*PW*, 45).
The craving to discover has reversed itself, as Barnum once noted it
could, into fear of exposure.

Thus Pudd'nhead Wilson's Calendar entry for the final chapter
reads ironically, "October 12, the Discovery. It was wonderful to
find America, but it would have been more wonderful to miss
it."[50] For a murder mystery, in which the murderer's identity has
been known from the very beginning, to close with a problematic
discovery is to confirm the earlier hint that *how* we know has
replaced *what* we know as the object of inquiry. When the novel
ends, its various scientific and legal bodies of knowledge—definitive means of identification and differentiation—result in no
certainty at all.

More disturbingly, the contortions that the law goes through at the last moment to reverse or undo itself in Mark Twain's courtroom—the guilty party, once white and free, identified as slave, defined as property, and pardoned—are analogous to the process of legal reversal enacted after Reconstruction. In a series of state laws and Supreme Court cases, the "freedmen" saw their legal rights reduced, eroded, and eventually nullified by the law. The process that once outlawed slavery in the late 1860s legalized segregation in the 1870s and 1880s, culminating most explicitly two years after the publication of *Pudd'nhead Wilson* in the "separate but equal" doctrine of the 1896 Supreme Court case Plessy v. Ferguson.[51] The novel confirms in an American context what Mark Twain's later anti-imperialist essays would conclude globally: that in spite of the Fourteenth and Fifteenth Amendments, the law had not only failed to solve the "Negro Question," but worse still had been positively enlisted in the service of reconstituting white supremacy, both in the United States and abroad. That many of the world's "civilized," "Christian" powers were, under the banner of imperialism, justifying the colonizing of Kipling's lesser breeds without the law meant for Twain a double defeat. Thereafter, neither the law, which permitted and enforced the farce of "separate but equal," nor science, which shored up racism with theories of "natural" degeneration, would hold out any promise of addressing America's most pressing social problem.

But as well as casting doubt on these hallowed bodies of knowledge, two great allies of late-nineteenth-century American civilization, the novel also implicates the author's own omniscience and control over his text. Mark Twain's preface, we remember, brings his own intentionality under suspicion, deriding himself as the author of a tale that "changed itself from a farce to a tragedy" while it was also "spreading itself into a book." Perhaps what he most rejected was how both stories resist the project of definitively separating the innocent from the guilty in social, racial, and sexual terms. Neither the farcical issue of the Siamese twins' singular/plural duality, nor the tragic issue of black/white division is ever resolved. The trials—a total of three in the two works—fail to ascertain individual responsibility in the face of necessity (either the twins' physical bond or the biological, social, and economic ties of slavery). And finally, the specific methods of identification through readings of the body (skin color, fingerprints) also fail, in Galton's terms, to "fix the human personality, to give to each human being an identity, an individuality." Neither the twins' legs nor Wilson's fingerprints prove to be a socially adequate means of differentiating individual responsibility.

Instead of a "true self" and clear standards of verification, what Twain discovered in his own fiction was the constructed and artificial character of essential social measures of identity—measures that, as the history of race relations demonstrates, we nevertheless totally depend upon. The novel, therefore, also exposes even as it exemplifies the mechanisms by which we persuade ourselves that the constructed is real. For without such constructs, or when they are momentarily inverted, the conclusion of *Pudd'nhead Wilson* suggests, the individual may find himself permanently displaced, nowhere socially recognizable. The "real heir," we remember, ends without a proper name or place or self, while the "false heir" disappears, pardoned and sold down the river. Mark Twain himself ends with his sense of authorial omniscience shaken, the writer still bound, the preface to the farce admits, by and to the unintentional disclosures of his own writing. Not even in the world of his own making could he imagine liberation under the law or discover a secure basis for knowledge of self and other. Like Aunt Patsy Cooper in *Those Extraordinary Twins*, Twain came increasingly to doubt whether he could "know—absolutely *know*, independently of anything [others] have told [him]" even that "reality" exists (*PW*, 152). Following *Pudd'nhead Wilson*, Twain's last major set of writings becomes obsessed with the question, "how do we know what we know is not a fiction or a dream?" The tendency in the thoroughly grounded, deeply historical *Pudd'nhead Wilson* to question conventional boundaries of racial identity expands in the dream tales into challenging the borders of reality itself.

CHAPTER FOUR

TALES OF SEXUAL IDENTITY: FEMALE FATHERS AND MALE IMPERSONATORS

Evelyn Thaw acquitted 1907
—graffiti, Princeton, New Jersey

During the year (1895–96) following the publication of *Pudd'n-head Wilson*, the Clemens family journeyed around the world on a lecture tour designed to pay their debts and recoup their bankrupt finances. Only Susy, the eldest daughter, remained at home in Hartford where she died suddenly of spinal meningitis in August 1896, just before the family was to be reunited. The trip, itself immensely successful, from packed lecture halls in the Pacific Northwest to sold-out performances in Australia, New Zealand, Ceylon, India, and South Africa, produced a profitable travel book, *Following the Equator* (1897). Oddly enough, this book that helped to accomplish Clemens's "rehabilitation in the business line" not only was written during the hellish period immediately following Susy's death but also addressed, under cover of the "travelogue," the potentially explosive issues of race and sexuality that had been kept on the margins of *Pudd'nhead Wilson*.[1] "I wrote my last travel-book in hell," Clemens told Howells in 1899. "But I let on, the best I could, that it was an excursion through heaven. Some day I will read it, & if its lying cheerfulness fools me, then I shall believe it fooled the reader."[2]

The excursion through heaven records with lying cheerfulness what James Cox calls Mark Twain's "trip around the equatorial black belt of the world," where what he saw of the politics of world imperialism reminded him of American race relations, past and present.[3] Foremost among the insights forged in lying cheerfulness is to join the lie behind imperialist pretensions to "civilize" the natives with American devotion to the color line, to guarding "race purity" by keeping the Negro "in his place." Signaling the link between Twain's 1894 novel on race and his 1897 travel book are the maxims from "Pudd'nhead Wilson's New Calendar," used as chapter headings in *Following the Equator*. These two works, along with Twain's later anti-lynching and anti-imperialism pieces, place themselves squarely in the global context of the

1890s, when racial violence and discrimination at home in America and colonialist ventures abroad (the U.S. in Cuba and the Philippines, the British in South Africa, and several Western and Eastern powers in China) brought to the fore "The Negro Question" on a worldwide, multiracial scale. At roughly the same time, late in the 1890s through 1907, Twain wrote a number of little-known but, what I will argue to be, related stories and articles in which stereotypes of sexual rather than racial difference are at issue. Because the affinities between the two types of difference were important to Twain's thinking and writing, my argument starts first with *Following the Equator* as an exemplary 1890s text, traversing race and sexuality.[4]

II

The second of the two volumes of *Following the Equator* covers Ceylon, India, and South Africa, places striking for "the massed dark complexion of the public," and opens with an outburst of praise for native as opposed to western clothing.[5] The contrast does not stay long on the material surface, though, but quickly takes the reader from outer coverings to skin to the bodies beneath—the contrast turning on the opposition between the fluid, undifferentiated, almost transparent relationships among black bodies, skin, and clothing, and the deceitful quality of white clothing that hides the body and of white skin that is so often artificially made up. Groups of natives walking in Ceylon appear strikingly individuated yet harmoniously joined in their "Oriental conflagrations of costume":

> Each individual was a flame . . . And such stunning colors, . . . such rich and exquisite minglings and fusings of rainbows and lightnings! And all harmonious, . . . never a discordant note, never a color on any person swearing at another color on him or failing to harmonize faultlessly with the colors of any group the wearer might join. The stuffs were silk—thin, soft, delicate, clinging . . . Sometimes a woman's whole dress was but a scarf wound about her person and her head, sometimes a man's was but a turban and a careless rag or two—in both cases generous areas of polished dark skin showing . . . I can see it to this day, . . . that incomparable dissolving-view of harmonious tints, and lithe half-covered forms, and beautiful brown faces . . . and movements, free, unstudied, barren of stiffness and restraint. (*DE*, 21: 9–10)

Sensuality consists here in the overwhelming sense of harmonies, minglings, fusings: boundaries in the process of dissolving, so that colors shade into one another, individuals meld into groups, female costume is one with male costume, and clothes and bodies become a single lithe form. Even the past mingles with the present, we note, in Twain's memory of this "dissolving-view" visible "to this day."[6]

Suddenly, in "grating dissonance" to "this dream of fairy land and paradise," come sixteen little Christian black girls, "Europeanly dressed," "marching two and two." Not only does the rigid line of their formation contrast to the formlessness of the first groups of natives, but also their clothes ("ugly," "barbarous," "repulsive") signal in Twain himself a sensation of boundedness. He is bound by his own intense self-consciousness, a sense of separation instead of identification, an awareness of the difference between native costume and that of himself, his family, and his culture. ("I looked at my women folk's clothes . . . and was ashamed to be seen in the street with them. Then I looked at my own clothes, and was ashamed to be seen in the street with myself" [DE, 21: 10].) Self-consciousness is followed by a long analysis of American clothing that emphasizes the boundary separating outer covering in "democratic America" from the tyrannical desires of the inner self. Needless to say, where there is fluidity between the bodies and clothing of the native other, there is tortured disjunction with ours:

> They are on us to expose us—to advertise what we wear them to conceal. They are a sign; a sign of insincerity; . . . a pretense that we despise gorgeous colors and the graces of harmony and form; and we put them on to propogate that lie and back it up . . . But . . . when we step into Ceylon we realize that we have not even deceived ourselves. We do love brilliant colors and graceful costumes . . . Yes, our clothes are a lie . . . They are insincere, they are the ugly and appropriate outward exposure of an inward sham and a moral decay. (DE, 21: 11)

Clothes as a lie: they distance us from ourselves; they mark the gap between private and public selves. The "frank honesty" of "a little brown boy's" costume—nothing but a string around his waist—stands out "in pleasant contrast" to the "masquerading" of "the little Sunday School dowdies" in western clothes. The contrast between honesty and masquerade pits the easy transparency, the fluid boundaries of Ceylonese clothes and bodies against more conflicted western signs—clothes as lies that inadvertently expose the self-deception they simultaneously propogate. Western clothing, that is, gives the lie to itself, whereas the native experiences no such divisions in Twain's view of the prelapsarian world on the equator.

What Twain finally admires in Ceylonese "harmony" is a fundamental absence of differentiation in all spheres, even and perhaps especially the sphere of sexuality. He associates the bright colors and silky fabrics of both native men's and women's clothing with the "ladies' toilette" on shipboard, and delights, as we shall later see, in stories of cross-dressing. The fascination with all in Ceylon that seems to unsettle sexual differentiation shows itself most immediately, if enigmatically, in the record of the very first day on shore, in a portrait of Clemens's Singhalese man-servant at the beginning of volume 2, chapter 1:

> January 14. Hotel Bristol. Servant Brompy. Alert, gentle, smiling, winning young brown creature as ever was. Beautiful shining black hair combed back like a woman's, and knotted at the back of his head—tortoise-shell comb in it . . . ; slender, shapely form; jacket; under it is a beltless and flowing white cotton gown—from neck straight to heel; he and his outfit quite unmasculine. It was an embarrassment to undress before him. (*DE*, 21: 7)

What is notable here, even more so than in the rest of the book's close readings of native dress, skin, and bodies, is the almost tangible connection Twain draws between the race and sex of this young brown creature, so clearly an other situated in a world *between:* between black and white, masculine and feminine. The liminality of the equatorial inhabitants extends even to the way these Africans and Indians seem to exist for Twain between their present and his past; they readily blend themselves into memories of the slaves of his Missouri boyhood. "A score of colored women," for example, dressed in a "showy mixture" and "mincing" with "divine delight in their finery" across a square in King William's Town, South Africa is "just as I had seen it so often at home":

> I seemed among old, old friends; friends of fifty years, and I stopped and cordially greeted them . . . All answered at once. I did not understand a word they said. I was astonished; I was not dreaming that they would answer in anything but American. (*DE*, 21: 362–63)

Despite the linguistic barrier, the essence of Mark Twain's equatorial experience remains one of identification with otherness; thus the voices, if not the words, of the African women "were familiar to me—sweet and musical, just like those of the slavewomen of my early days" (DE, 21: 363).

Less than a year after Clemens finished writing *Following the Equator* in May 1897, his notebook (dated January 1898) records another memory of another slave woman, his dream, we recall from my discussion in chapter two, of the "Negro wench" and her "hot mushy apple pie." Like her male counterpart, the "unmasculine" young native servant of the travel book, she represents Clemens's association of the images of blackness and sexuality—an interrelationship between images of difference by no means peculiar to him. Rather, as Sander L. Gilman reminds us in *Difference and Pathology*, the most powerful stereotypes in nineteenth-century Western Europe and the U.S. were those that associated images of race, sexuality, and pathology.[7] Gilman's account of the "protean nature of stereotypes" (the tendency of categories of difference, for example, anatomical differences such as skin color or the shape of the genitalia, to become linked without any recognition of inappropriateness, contradictoriness, or impossibility) suggests the broad social and psychological process underlying Twain's personal association of race and sexuality.[8] For a white male in particular, what blackness and femaleness have in common is that they afford a psychic means of staking out an identity and of individuating the self by dint of difference and separation. One could argue that culturally, too, for the late nineteenth century, both women and blacks, in their expanding political and economic demands and in their role as objects of state control (through segregation for blacks and medico-legal regulation of women's everyday lives), had been clearly differentiated, put "in their place."[9] Yet despite these psycho-social structures of difference, Mark Twain, we know, identified himself politically, culturally, and perhaps most important, authorially with the excluded. The rhetoric of vernacular humor through which Mark Twain created an authorial (and authoritative) identity celebrates itself, constitutes its values as the language of the outsider. Twain's writings on race and sexuality, therefore, reveal him to be in tension with himself as well as with the cultural stereotypes that he simultaneously assumes to be "natural" and challenges as "fictions of law and custom."

No better evidence for the conflicted, often only half-acknowledged, associations Twain drew between the exotica of blackness and sexuality can be found than in the opening and closing chapters of volume 2 of *Following the Equator*. Framing this volume of the travel book covering the equatorial black belt are two brief portraits of unresolved sexual ambiguity. The first, we recall, is that of the servant Brompy, that "young brown creature," "quite unmasculine," before whom it is "an embarrassment to undress." The second is an actual portrait—"a picture of a pale, intellectual young man in a pink coat with a high black collar"—that Twain says he saw in an old Dutch house in Cape Town. The "quaint old picture" is linked, à la Hawthorne, to "a curious romance," the tale of a Dr. James Barry, military surgeon, who came out to Cape Town from England, led a life of wild dissolution, never married ("evidently . . . not a marrying man"), and then died. "The story seems to be arriving nowhere," Twain apologizes, whetting his reader's appetite for the punchline: "only after Dr. Barry died was it discovered that he was *a woman*" (Twain's emphasis). The daughter of a great English house, goes the legend, she was spared punishment for her dissolute life on the Cape. Only two more sentences complete Twain's brief rendition of the legend: "Her name was an *alias*. She had disgraced herself with her people; so she chose to change her name and her sex and take a new start in the world" (*DE*, 21: 379–81). We hear no more from Twain on the subject of Dr. Barry; the next two paragraphs summarize the Clemenses' departing journey, and there the book ends. A trivial, if provocative, aside, it seems. Indeed, most readers would probably not even remember either anecdote of something like cross-dressing, that of the native servant outfitted "like a woman" or of the full-fledged transvestite Dr. Barry.

However difficult to take on their own, these two cases bring into focus the materials I want to explore in this chapter: a group of writings, largely unfamiliar, which I call the transvestite tales, most written after *Following the Equator* in 1897 but not published until well after Twain's death in 1910, and all dealing with cross-dressing or with otherwise reversing or inverting gender differences. Several of the tales enact variations on a common plot: a seduction occurs; a female transvestite is (of course, wrongfully) accused of fathering the illegitimate child; a (paternity) trial is held to determine the alleged (female) father's innocence or guilt; and the narrative comes to an abrupt and inconclusive end, the law unable to get its man, since in these cases the man is a woman. Because legal control over sexual identity is thus at issue (much as the law's definition of racial identity is the issue in *Pudd'nhead Wilson*), I will also look at two non-fiction pieces, written during the same period (1897–1907), which address the legal issue of age of consent. These argumentative pieces (one published and the other in manuscript) appear firmly to stand behind the very same sexual stereotypes turned upside down in the transvestite tales. Investigating this apparent opposition between factual and fictional modes will be one of the main tasks of this chapter.

Grouping the pieces as I have done itself constitutes the beginning of my argument. First, so much of this material is either unfinished, textually problematic, or "unliterary" that it would be difficult to read or make a case for any individual piece on its own. Second, the direction of my whole study of Mark Twain has moved toward the law as the cultural determinant he sees as fundamental to shaping the concept of individuality in all spheres, including the sexual one. (Hence the paternity trial is a common denominator of some of the transvestite tales I have chosen to focus on.) Finally, as we have already seen, Twain's interest in how a sense of indivuation is constituted focuses on moments when individuals are transformed almost beyond all recognition, moments of unraveling, disintegration, and, sometimes, reconstruction. The transvestite tales all entertain such moments. I have therefore chosen to examine the particular window they provide on the subject of "Mark Twain and sexuality," while excluding other possible approaches (Twain's characterization of women in fiction; Twain's stances, public and private, on contemporary feminist issues; Twain and the female adolescent).

I want to argue, then, that in the protean, associative mode of stereotypes, Twain's writings on race that come out of the 1890s discourse of "race purity" give rise to analogous writings on sexuality that address the stereotype of the "purity of womanhood." Even before the transvestite portraits in *Following the Equator*, racial and sexual categories were linked in *Pudd'nhead Wilson*, we remember, where Tom Driscoll disguises himself as a girl and his mother Roxana ironically becomes a black male, her sexual identity masked in male clothing but her racial identity exposed in her cork-blackened face. In establishing Twain's pattern of association between racial and sexual categories, we must ourselves be careful, however, not to blur distinctions. Whereas he unequivocally condemned racial stereotypes and discrimination, his writing circles more hesitantly around the whole problem of gender difference, sometimes affirming, sometimes denying that such a clear-cut system of difference does in fact exist, sometimes defending, sometimes attacking the right or entitlement of such a system (whether natural or created) to exist. In short, Twain shows himself to be more aware of the invidiousness of racial than sexual stereotypes. Preserving the bounds of sexual propriety, as we will see he sometimes asserts, can mean preserving the "natural" hierarchy of the sexes and the social order, whereas racial boundaries, he always asserts, unequivocally distort both genetics and social relationships. As a result, there is in Twain's view an inevitability, a justice even, to crossing the color line that contrasts to the moral disorder he associated with violating—not merely "crossing"—the lines of sexual propriety. For Twain, then, the particular association between racial and sexual difference comes down to problems of boundary drawing: whether there are "natural" distinctions among races and between sexes; if so, are they founded on physiological or anatomical signs of difference (skin color, the ability to conceive and bear children); if not, what does this lack of foundations mean to institutions of social control, such as the law, and to the identities of individuals? We will begin first with Twain's expression, in the age-of-consent pieces, of traditional stereotypes of sexual difference.

III

When human beings are equated with property or possession, the equation has disastrous consequences in Mark Twain's view for the integrity of blacks. But when the possession at stake is a woman, or, more precisely, female honor, then the consequences suffered are all on the side of the male possessor: the father, the husband. Twain propounded this conventional view both publicly and privately in two pieces arguing against the "age of consent," a legal boundary limiting the prosecution of potential defendants in rape cases. Age of consent may broadly be defined as the legal age of puberty, the moment at which the law recognizes the physiological capacity to consent to sexual intercourse (and to marriage). British common law fixed the boundary at fourteen for males and twelve for females, but by 1900 this early marriageable age had been altered in most of the U.S. to eighteen (males) and sixteen (females).[10] Outside of marriage, the law serves the even more stringent regulatory function of defining statutory or child rape. Then, as now, the law considers that below a certain age the victim is too immature to be capable of giving intelligent consent to the act of intercourse, and that any such act, regardless of the victim's personal feelings, constitutes statutory rape.[11] For Twain, age of consent thus raised the specific issue of legal protection granted or denied on the basis of age and sex, and the more general problem thereby implied of drawing sexual boundary lines.

"In the morning paper," Twain dictated on 20 April 1907, "I have once more come across that phrase which—considering its awful meaning—I think is the blackest one that exists in any language. It always unseats my self-possession." This unpublished autobiographical dictation rages against that blackest of phrases, age of consent, by drawing an analogy between the crime of murder, for which there is no such exculpatory condition as the victim's consent, and the "living death" of seduction, which may go legally unpunished if the victim consents to her own "murder." "It is my hope," the dictation concludes,

> that the ass who invented the "age of consent"—*any* age of consent between cradle & grave—is with his progenitors in hell, & that the legislatures that are keeping the resulting law in force will follow him soon. Women are denied the suffrage . . . If they had it, how long do you think this most infamous of all laws would continue to defile the statute books? (Twain's emphasis)[12]

Precisely why Twain directs such censure at the law itself and what exactly "unseats" his "self-possession" about age of consent emerge more clearly in an earlier, more extended piece published in *Harper's Weekly* for 2 May 1903 and entitled "Why Not Abolish It?"

The "it" was the age of consent, which, Twain argues, ought to be entirely abolished because it misconstrues the roles of seducer and seduced (the "criminal" and *his* "victim"). By limiting the chronological parameters of the "crime" of "seduction" only to the actual act of intercourse, the law not only minimizes the "perpetrator's responsibility" but also puts the onus on the victim. It does not take into account the role of non-physical but forceful means of "persuasion" that may have led to the act itself:

> "Consent" necessarily argues previous persuasion. It indicates who the instigator of the trespass was—that is to say, the offender-in-chief. Instead of magnifying his crime, this actually diminishes it, in the eyes of the law . . . Consent means previous persuasion—and there the crime *begins* . . . I would punish the beginner, the real criminal, and punish him well; society and civilization can be depended upon to punish

with a ten thousand times exaggerated and unjust severity his thoughtless victim.[13]

Lest we see Mark Twain in the light of today's few male crusaders for rape victims' rights, lest we mistake him, that is, for one who explicitly rejects the accused rapist's defense that the victim "enticed" or "provoked" him, we need to understand how utterly incapable of such aggressive sexuality Twain assumes the woman to be—and how much in need of male protection (from other men, from society) she is. We can always assume a division between male strength and female weakness, Twain argues, even in cases where we do not actually know which sex occupied which role:

> If a man and wife are drowned at sea, and there is no proof as to which died first, the law—in some European countries and in two of our States—decides that it was the wife. She is the weaker vessel. It is usually so in the matter of seduction. She is young, inexperienced, foolish, trustful, persuadable, affectionate; she would harm no one herself, and cannot see why anyone should wish to harm her; while as a rule the man is older and stronger than she is, and in every case without exception is a scoundrel. The law protects him now; it seems to me that it ought to protect her, instead. (*MTS*, 182–83)

The consent law itself, we note, as in the 1907 autobiographical dictation, comes in for its share of censure from the nineteenth-century man who assumes such sexual divisions. While the seducer violates the body of his victim, the law violates boundaries of another kind, those that equate femininity with passivity and female sexuality with (male) property. Age of consent assumes that females over a certain age limit—legal adults—are responsible for and in control over their own sexuality—what Twain calls being "privileged to help commit a tremendous and desolating crime against herself and her family" (*MTS*, 182). A woman's authority over her own body, the word "privilege" suggests, represents a sexual prerogative that violates Twain's concept of womanhood. Not only is woman "the weaker vessel" with whom he cannot associate the privilege of sexual choice or even the aggression of refusing unwanted sexual advances, but also her "good name" is not only her own but also the pride and joy—the possession—of her family:

> There is no age at which the good name of a member of a family ceases to be a part of the *property* of that family—an asset, and worth more than all its bonds and moneys. There is

no age at which a member of the family may by consent, and under authority of the law, help a criminal to destroy the family's money and bonds. Then why should there be an age at which a member, by consent, and under connivance of the law, may help a criminal to destroy that far more valuable asset, the family's honor? (Twain's emphasis; *MTS,* 182)

The age limit, then, permits the violation of both the female body and the family's fundamental right to protect its property. Therefore, Twain concludes, "I should say simply that commerce *with a spinster,* of whatever age or condition, should be punished by two years of solitary confinement or five years at hard labor; and let the man take his choice" (*MTS,* 183).

The harsh penalty, Twain frankly confesses, speaks to the personal anxieties he feels as a father of young daughters. Any jury would agree that was made up of men like himself, "fathers of families—families with young girls in them, the treasures of their lives, the light of their homes, the joy of their hearts" (*MTS,* 183). In "treasures" as well as "bonds," "moneys," and "valuable assets," we recall the same metaphoric accent on familial property that characterizes Twain's language when grieving over the deaths of both his wife and eldest daughter. But in addition to assuaging paternal anxieties over specific male threats to his female treasures, rejecting the legal concept of sexual responsibility based on age effectively reclassifies all females as legal children—as spinsters "of whatever age or condition." However, only the sexually innocent, that is, the spinster, the woman not yet sexually active, is recognized by Twain as woman. His penchant for images of child-women—his adoration of Susy, his admiration for Joan of Arc, even his late cultivation of the Angel Fish as adoring retinue—suggests how often his constructions of femininity were defined by powerlessness, vulnerability, virginity. On Susy's sudden death: "Susy died at the right time, the fortunate time of life, the happy age—twenty-four years."[14] Quite apart from the grieving father's need somehow to justify his daughter's untimely death, the time was right because, though well past adolescence, she was still a child in his eyes.

Twain's legal arguments against age of consent issue similarly from the common Victorian equation between femaleness and childlikeness. "Why Not Abolish It?" ends with a newspaper report (from which Twain quotes) of a case of infanticide in which public opinion is strongly in favor of clemency for the young mother convicted of drowning her illegitimate child. "The girl is a most pitiable creature," the article asserts. "She seems crazed by the happenings of the last few weeks, and is utterly unable to comprehend the enormity of her crime, or the hopelessness of the doom which is hanging over her. She is like a child" (*MTS*, 184). Popular sentiment for the "crazed" mother, perceived as herself more child than responsible adult, reflected legal practice in this and many and other cases of infanticide throughout the nineteenth century. The success of the insanity defense, in such cases often based only on a lay definition rather than medical evidence of insanity, is only one indication of the legally exculpatory attitude taken by the courts toward infanticidal women—and toward other "insane murderesses," as Twain refers in *The Gilded Age* to Laura Hawkins, his fictional version of Laura D. Fair, who successfully used the "emotional insanity" defense at her murder trial in 1871–72.[15] Few women actually faced a capital sentence for murdering their children. Roger Smith, a medico-legal historian of the nineteenth century, concludes of the Victorians' "remarkable willingness" to excuse these women: "lay and medical discourse coincided to render women—especially in activities connected with reproduction—lacking in responsibility."[16] Thus when Twain argued in his age-of-consent piece for the sexual innocence and essential passivity of female victims of seduction, he was voicing an assumption so widely and so deeply held that it extended even to those women who murdered their infants. Such an accommodation had to be made for women who were felt to be passive by nature and circumstance, even in the face of their active sexuality or violence.

Small wonder, then, that Twain's autobiographical dictation privately describes age of consent as a phrase that "always unseats my self-possession." In all of the ways that I have outlined above, the very concept of consent disrupts the cultural network of correspondences among woman, passivity, emotion, and irresponsibility, correspondences that existed in a socially contingent contrast to man, activity, intellect, and responsibility. For Twain, disrupting this network of correspondences meant in part the unseating of the foundations on which his sense of self—of self-possession—was predicated. At virtually the same time, though, that he therefore fought in the age-of-consent pieces for distinguishing the sexes in terms of traditional traits, Twain was also writing his transvestite tales, expressing in fiction, if not in fact, a fascination with all that seems to unsettle sexual differentiation. The writings of this period, then, appear initially to set up oppositions between restrictive social convention and the more open-ended creativity of fictive modes, one extreme of which is the rigid boundary drawing of the non-fiction age-of-consent pieces, the other the whirling boundlessness of the transvestite tales. If all the tales feature cross-dressing, though, not all of them criss-cross sexual boundaries and so threaten the stable distinction between the sexes. Instead some simply invert traditional gender stereotypes while preserving a conservative role structure. The opposition that seems to comprise the writings of this period and that we sense animates Twain's written representations of sexuality must, then, be more complicated than the model of repressive fact versus freeing fiction would suggest. To understand the precise dynamic of that crucial opposition, we must look to the transvestite tales, first and briefly to the more conservative group, and then to those that enact, via the conceit of female fatherhood on trial, an open-ended confounding of sexual categories.

IV

Personal Recollections of Joan of Arc (1896), considered by Twain "the best" of his books, a tribute to a "stainlessly pure child," presupposes an utterly conventional attitude toward female purity.[17] The same attitude, simply reversed, also informs the stories of sexual role reversal which remained unpublished until after Twain's death. Both "1,002d Arabian Night" (1883) and "Hellfire Hotchkiss" (1897)[18] create a hero-heroine pair whose behavior reverses stereotypical masculine and feminine characteristics—but always the sexes are distinguished in terms of traditional traits, and always those traits group themselves in traditional clusters (active goes with assertive, courageous, intellectual; passive goes with patient, pure, intuitive) even when they are assigned to the opposite sex.

In Twain's burlesque of the Arabian Nights tales, for example, a "wicked witch" switches the genders of the two babies born on the same day to two potentates, making the boy seem a girl and vice versa. Yet although each is reared as the opposite sex, "people came to observe that Selim-Mahomet-Abdullah, the ostensible *boy*, always interested herself in feminine matters; and that Fatima, the ostensible *girl*, always interested himself in masculine things" (*MTSB*, 106). Aside from the strategy, reminiscent of the Siamese twins' pronominal confusion, of playing on the dual grammatical gender appropriate to each character, the story's humor (such as it is) works by assuming the separation between "matters proper to the manly sex"—sports, palace finances, bed-time stories of massacres and harems—and those "proper to the womanly sex"—dolls, kittens, baby carriages (*MTSB*, 107–8). Of Fatima, the seeming girl who detests his feminine costume and takes a fierce tiger cub for a pet, it is said (in Twain's burlesque of Arabian Nights talk), "Of a truth she is defective, in that she hath no sufficient modesty"; whereas of Selim's dolls and kittens it is said, "How despicable is this, in a boy . . . Verily he is a milksop" (*MTSB*, pp. 106–8). The plot of the switched sexes comes to a farcical end when the two, still reversed in gender, marry and have children (twins, Ethelred and Ethelbald). "To think that the father, and not the mother," the astonished populace exclaims, "should be the mother of the babes!" (*MTSB*, 132).

A similar comedy of sexual errors is created in "Hellfire Hotchkiss," a more compelling tale, however, than the earlier "Arabian Night," in part because Twain moves the setting from the remote region of farcical fantasy (where characters speak in "haths" and "verilys") to the place (and language) he knows best, the fictional world of a village on the banks of the Mississippi. This village, Dawson's Landing, the scene of exchanged racial identities in *Pudd'nhead Wilson* three years earlier, becomes in the unfinished 1897 story the scene of switched sexual characteristics. Oscar "Thug" Carpenter and Rachel "Hellfire" Hotchkiss conform to sexual stereotypes that are no less rigid because totally inverted. Her (masculine) "presence of mind," her "business head and practical sense" contrast with his (feminine) "changeableness," his susceptibility to "praise" and "encouragement," his "burning enthusiasms" (*MTSB*, 187, 191, 183, 178, 171). "Where the male sex is concerned," Thug's father comments, the word "encouragement" is "detestable": "The boy that needs much of it is a girl in disguise. He ought to put on petticoats" (*MTSB*, 178).[19] Whereas Oscar (like his real-life counterpart, Clemens's brother Orion) constantly changes his politics and religion (in turn, three months a Methodist, a Campbellite, a Baptist, a Presbyterian, then back again to Methodist), Rachel resolutely rejects the dull life of a village girl and, by whipping one or two of the boys, forces them to accept her and make her "competent" in the "masculine arts" (*MTSB*, 177–78, 195). When Hellfire rescues Thug from drowning in the Mississippi, one of the villagers remarks on their topsy-turvy sexual divisions:

> There's considerable difference betwixt them two—Thug and her. Pudd'nhead Wilson says Hellfire Hotchkiss is the only genuwyne male man in this town and Thug Carpenter's

the only genuwyne female girl, if you leave out sex and just consider the business facts. (*MTSB*, 187)

But as if in answer to this conditional liberation of the business facts from sex, the story breaks off just after Twain has Hellfire assert that sex just cannot be left out:

> Oh, everything seems to be made wrong, nothing seems to [be] the way it ought to be. Thug Carpenter is out of his sphere, I am out of mine. Neither of us can arrive at any success in life, we shall always be hampered and fretted and kept back by our misplaced sexes, and in the end defeated by them, whereas if we could change we should stand as good a chance as any of the young people in the town. (*MTSB*, 199)

A few paragraphs after this lament, the story breaks off, un-finished, as Hellfire vows to right those misplaced sexes by refrain-ing from "ungirlish things": she will "withdraw from the boys" and return to her own sphere.

Twain's ideal historical embodiment of "the girlish" was, rather paradoxically, the soldierly Joan of Arc, burnt at the stake, we recall, finally, not because of witchcraft and not because she refused to renounce her "voices," but because she again donned men's clothes after agreeing to abjure them. *Joan of Arc*, Twain's literary idealization of a life of female purity and inviolate maid-enhood, asserts far more categorically than "Hellfire Hotchkiss" (written in the year following *Joan*'s publication) that the woman operating in a masculine sphere is socially victimized by her mis-placed sex and must inwardly long to return to "the industries proper to her sex."[20] Joan herself appeals to her "nature," her "disposition," to "being made like this" when she asks the king and his advisors why, since the war has been won and the king crowned, she "should . . . not go to my village and be as I was before? It is heaven! and ye wonder that I desire it. Ah, ye are men—just men!" (*DE*, 18: 57–58).

The essential "female nature" of the Maid of Orleans remains untouched, Twain thus insists, even though she may dress as a man and lead armies into battle. "Womanly tears" run down her face as she comforts a dying enemy; the army recognizes "the girlish face of its invincible little Chief" with names such as "Daughter of God" and "Victory's Sweetheart" (*DE*, 18: 40). Twain particularly believes that Joan's male attire never unsexes her, as her father initially fears and as she is ultimately charged in her final trial at Rouen. Whereas the ecclesiastical court accuses her of discarding "the decencies and proprieties of her sex, irreverently assuming the dress of a man and the vocation of a soldier," Twain comes to her defense, arguing that because of the constant presence of male guards in her cell, "the male dress was a better protection for her modesty than the other" (*DE*, 18: 201, 189).[21]

For Mark Twain, the woman, or rather the girl, bears the burden of a fixed identity. "Modest," "delicate," "angelic," "childlike," and above all, "pure": these are the terms in which Mark Twain constructs in Joan his own cult of womanhood, or girlhood, to be more precise. "And always," Twain asserts worshipfully, cataloguing Joan's heroics at the close of a 1904 essay "St. Joan of Arc," "she was a *girl*" (Twain's emphasis; *DE*, 22: 381). So much a (prepubescent) girl, we might add, that Twain commented, in his copy of Jules Michelet's history of *Jeanne d'Arc* (1853), on the testimony of some Domremy women that Joan had never menstruated: "The higher life absorbed her and suppressed her physical (sexual) development."[22] Like Joan and like Susy (who provided the physical model for Twain's Joan), the Angel Fish who toward the end of his life made up Twain's "Aquarium"—a club that admitted, according to its constitution, "none above school-girl age," with the exception, of course, of the founder and chief member[23]—demonstrate that for Twain one ideal of womanhood was the innocent child-woman whose essential girlish nature remains unawakened, untransformed, that is, unsexualized: the "purity from all alloy" of "that wonderful child," Joan of Arc (*DE*, 18: 287).

V

If the transvestism in these three works (the Arabian Nights burlesque, the Calamity Jane frontier tale, the historical novel) momentarily confounds sexual categories, only in the end to give way to the clarification of gender and hence to proper, communally sanctioned identity, Twain's other transvestite tales (those that put the transvestite in a paternity trial) are at once less conventional and more socially grounded in the legal process of verification and proof. In contrast to the stable distinction between the sexes in the works I just discussed, where misplaced sexes may be replaced into their proper spheres, thus allaying any epistemological anxieties their exchange may have engendered, the three remaining tales do not right or reinscribe those readily reversible social codes. Instead, sexual difference turns out to be at its origin unstable and unprovable.

Written over a long span between the late 1860s and early 1900s, these pieces—"A Medieval Romance" (1868), "Feud Story and the Girl Who Was Ostensibly a Man" (c.1902), "Wapping Alice" (1898, 1907)—together create a narrative pattern as bizarre as it is clearly of longstanding fascination to Mark Twain. The plot, as I earlier sketched out, starts with involuntary transvestism (in two cases women are forced, for various reasons, to dress as men); in a parallel subplot, a different ("genuwyne") female character is seduced and abandoned, and bears an illegitimate baby; the plots converge in Twain's version of a female revenge drama, as the unwed mother brings a paternity suit against the wrong man—or woman dressed as a man. Finally, all three tales culminate in some kind of official or informal trial which fails to identify the true father or to exonerate the wrongfully accused innocent or to discover the masquerade and replace the transvestite's misplaced sex. In short, these stories neither restore sexual boundaries nor resolve confusion over sexual identity.

In fact, the stories also notably fail to conclude themselves as texts. That is, each one ends ostentatiously incomplete, unbounded, unclosed, as though for their author, coming to a formal conclusion is out of the question when the issues are sexual indeterminacy and boundary breakdown. With the exception of the longest and latest work, "Wapping Alice," which I will argue should be considered inconclusive because of its several contradictory versions, the lack of closure is the most telling, if not the most titillating, aspect of these transvestite tales. A brief summary of the two earlier stories will help to set the stage for a more extended look at "Wapping Alice."

"A Medieval Romance" (the only one of the three stories to be published during Twain's lifetime—in the *Buffalo Express*, 1 January 1870)[24] breaks off after only five rather thinly contrived chapters in which the noble heroine, named Conrad and referred to as "he," masquerades as a man in order to fulfill complicated dynastic rules and thus inherit the family dukedom, now in the hands of his uncle. Conrad's cousin Constance (who might succeed to the throne if she "retained a blameless name") is seduced, made pregnant, and abandoned by the "scoundrel" Count Detzin (sent on his "devilish mission" by her scheming uncle, Conrad's father); when she falls in love with Conrad, who rejects with horror these advances of his cousin (herself unaware that Conrad is a woman), she takes revenge on his spurning her by naming him the father of her child. At the moment when she "points her finger" at

Conrad in the ducal palace's packed "Hall of Justice" and says, "Thou art the man!", the story breaks off with Conrad's realization that "to disprove the charge he must reveal that he was a woman, and for an uncrowned woman to sit in the ducal chair was death!" (a reference to still more complicated dynastic rules) (*DE*, 7: 208). Twain then steps in to confess his inability either to end his story or to sort out the sexual confusions he has created:

> The remainder of this thrilling and eventful story will NOT be found in this or any other publication, either now or at any future time.
> The truth is, I have got my hero (or heroine) into such a particularly close place that I do not see how I am ever going to get him (or her) out of it again, and therefore I will wash my hands of the whole business . . . I thought it was going to be easy enough to straighten out that little difficulty, but it looks different now. (*DE*, 7:208)

Many years later, in the early 1900s, still unable to straighten out that little difficulty, Twain tried to write another story with the same narrative outlines—female transvestite, seduction and illegitimate birth, female revenge, paternity accusation—but ended with another unfinished manuscript.[25] Even more schematic than "A Medieval Romance," "Feud Story and the Girl Who Was Ostensibly a Man" is only nominally set in a generalized southwestern setting—no particular time, no particular place—and equally perfunctorily constructs the characters: a bitter old bachelor, once deserted at the altar; the daughter of his former love, forced by the vengeful old man to disguise herself as a man; a "heartless flirt" who, like Constance of "A Medieval Romance," bears an illegitimate child, and by naming "the girl who was ostensibly a man" as the father, actually engineers their marriage. At this juncture, Twain, going even farther than in the 1868 story, has once again got his hero (or heroine) into such a particularly close place that he decides to wash his hands of the whole business. The two marry, we are told, but "do not live together"; the final sentence of the manuscript reads bluntly, "At last the child was born—a boy."

The narrative pattern that Twain creates but cannot control in these two unfinished stories repeats itself not once but in several different versions in "Wapping Alice," the work to which I will devote the rest of this chapter. In contrast to these skeletal stories, in which the seduced woman is also the vengeful aggressor, the retellings of the "Alice" tale attempt to rewrite and clarify this gender confusion. Textually the most fully realized of all the transvestite tales I have discussed, "Wapping Alice" is also the most culturally compelling. Unlike the remote historical romances or non-specific southern settings we have seen, "Alice" is a semi-fictional transformation of events that occurred in Clemens's own life, and hence has the autobiographical framework—and the biographical urgency—of much of his best writing. Moreover, as I will show, Twain's story intertwines itself with a major courtroom event of the early twentieth century, the sensational Stanford White murder case. Of all the transvestite tales, therefore, "Alice" deserves our sustained attention in spite of the fact that it is a "minor" work, of little "literary" value, virtually unknown and still almost unavailable (it has only recently been privately printed). Not only, I will argue, does this story supply a fresh perspective on the central dualities in Mark Twain's character, but also it shows how fiction and a major courtroom event can and do intertwine in the American republic of laws, and finally, more tentatively, it allows us to reach beyond its immediate subjects toward a larger portrait of American culture at the turn of the century.

VI

The story of "Wapping Alice" (1898, 1907) is best told by beginning where, as we shall see, it actually ends, with the Stanford White murder case. Early in 1907 one of the twentieth century's most notorious murder cases was making headlines in America and abroad with revelations of bizarre sex, violent jealousy, and hereditary insanity in the demimonde of New York's high society. On the evening of 25 June 1906, following the opening performance of *Mamzelle Champagne*, the Pittsburgh millionaire Harry K. Thaw shot the well-known architect Stanford White in full view of diners at the Madison Square Roof Garden—the building itself one of White's most acclaimed designs. Thaw, charged with first-degree murder and on trial for his life, pleaded not guilty by reason of temporary insanity. The defense argued that Thaw's long history of mental instability was aggravated by his wife Evelyn Nesbit Thaw's story of how, as a sixteen-year-old virgin, she had been drugged and seduced by the much-older Stanford White. Even though the alleged ruin of Thaw's wife took place some (unspecified) time before her marriage and years before the murder, still the defense claimed that after Thaw proposed to Evelyn Nesbit in June 1903 in Paris (the first of two premarital and, it was noted, unchaperoned trips the couple took to Europe) and heard her story of seduction, his mental condition gradually deteriorated until three years later when his delusions culminated in what he believed was an act of divine providence, the murder of his wife's alleged seducer, to him a symbol of all depraved men who ravish innocent women.

In summing up, chief defense attorney Delphin M. Delmas went so far as to generalize Thaw's condition, inventing a label and a national profile of symptoms for this newly discovered "species of insanity which has been recognized in every Court, in every State in this Union, from the Canadian border to the Gulf of Texas":

> Dementia Americana. It is that species of insanity which makes every home sacred. It is that species of insanity which makes a man believe that the honour of his wife is sacred; it is that species of insanity which makes him believe that whoever invades the sanctity of that home, whoever brings pollution upon that daughter, whoever stains the virtue of that wife, has forfeited the protection of human laws and must look to the eternal justice and mercy of God.[26]

But the claim of seduction—the "staining" of the "virtue" of the wife—was itself as hotly debated as the plea of insanity, opinion both inside the courtroom and out being divided over whether Evelyn Nesbit, an artist's model and chorus girl in the Broadway hit Floradora, had been a passive, deflowered victim (as she alleged) or a willing and even aggressive participant. Indeed, the only uncontested sensation in this sensational murder trial was the murder itself. Even the verdict was indeterminate: the trial closed on 12 April 1907 with a hung jury.

Such a brief narrative account of the Thaw trial only begins to suggest the complex issues it raised. First, for most of the public, the issue was not the murderer's innocence or guilt, but that of his wife, as evidenced in a most colloquial and popular form, the graffiti of my epigraph. The question "Who was Evelyn Nesbit Thaw?" posed itself in several different but overlapping ways. As a participant in the sexual act with White, was she the seducer or the seduced? (In Mark Twain's terms, was she the weaker vessel?) As a witness in the courtroom drama, was she an actress consciously playing the role of the wronged woman, or an actress who was not acting but being the victim? Second, these questions about individual character, sexuality, and theatricality led to the even more disturbing issue of how do or can we know the answers to such questions. Competing stories were being told on the witness stand and in the newspapers about things that couldn't be known. When exactly did the alleged night of seduction take place? How long was Evelyn Nesbit unconscious? How many times and on what occasions afterward did the two have "intimate relations"? In short, the point of the murder trial—not only for us now, but for the mainstream press at the time—is that even though the jury had only to be convinced about Thaw's state of mind, not the truth of Evelyn Nesbit Thaw's character, being convinced depended on how good an actress she was (that is, on her convincing them, too). The distinction between a woman's acting ability and her character thus proved to be not at all clear-cut, undermining public confidence in the law's ability to make other essential distinctions—between fact and fiction, innocence and guilt.

The issues in the Thaw trial did not need to wait for E. L. Doctorow's *Ragtime* to realize their potential as a historical intermingling of the factual with the fictional. In 1898 Mark Twain had already written "Wapping Alice," his own story of seduction with a judicial cast that eerily anticipated, if not the Thaw case itself, many of its sexual, psychological, and legal confusions. Moreover, the story was itself based on a case of seduction which had occurred in the Clemens household in 1877 and was first recorded in three letters, all written by Clemens (and signed "Saml.") to his wife Livy on the day when the case was actually breaking. Briefly summarized, the events of 17 July 1877, as Clemens reports them in his letters, are as follows: a Clemens family maid claimed that a household workman had made her pregnant during a long affair conducted in the basement of the family's Hartford home; the denouement was arranged by Clemens, who convened an informal court of inquiry (with himself as "judge, jury, & lawyer for both sides," he writes to Livy), convicted the supposed seducer, and sentenced him to a shotgun marriage.[27] Following this first epistolary version, and only after learning some years later that the supposed victim had never been pregnant at all, Mark Twain wrote up a semi-fictional account of the "Wapping Alice" incident in 1897 or 1898; in 1898 he tried but failed to find a publisher for this slightly risqué tale, and then shelved the story for nine years, until suddenly, apparently inexplicably, he began to rewrite it in autobiographical form during the final days of the Thaw trial. By this late date in his life, we recall, Mark Twain was dictating rather than writing his autobiography; the dictations for 9 and 10 April 1907—just before the trial ended in an inconclusive verdict—contain Twain's revised version of his own 1898 story of "Wapping Alice." So there are three different levels in the lineage of the "Wapping Alice" case: the three letters of 17 July 1877, the 1898 manuscript, and the 1907 Autobiographical Dictations.[28]

In that last version, at the end of the story itself, Twain notes that "the tremendous Thaw trial is approaching its end" and then appends, without further commentary or explanation, an "extract," as he calls it, from the New York Sun (dated in his handwriting "April 9, '07") containing a transcript of the section from Delmas's summary for the defense that re-tells Evelyn Nesbit's story. Clearly the two tales of seduced women were associated in Mark Twain's mind. The questions I want to answer are what connected the long-standing, long-pondered, much-revised "Alice" stories with one of the most celebrated murder cases of the twentieth century: how does Twain's "Alice" influence our understanding of the Thaw trial; and what do Twain's personal responses tell us about his culture?

Even such a brief sketch as I have just given of the outlines of the two cases shows that what is at stake in both is female power, that is, the use by a woman defined as sexually powerless of her own vulnerable sexuality. Both Twain's Alice and Evelyn Thaw tell stories of seduction, portraying themselves as victimized females and, more broadly, appealing to their audience's cultural definition of sexual identity based on fundamental differentiation between the sexes: male as dominant, female as submissive. Yet the circumstances and the outcome of the telling of the two tales, rather than enforcing those differences, blur them. In the end, both self-proclaimed "seduced-and-abandoned" women get their man where they want him to be: institutionalized, through either marriage or insanity.

My argument is that, faced with such reversal of stereotypical female roles, the culture (whether in the discourse of the Thaw trial itself, or of the journalistic accounts of the trial, or of Twain's autobiographical tale) relies on both the institution of the law and the custom of storytelling to reassure itself about boundary confusions—between guilt and innocence, man and woman, seductress and seducer, fact and fiction. The Thaw trial, however, shows that the law itself could not resolve any of those ambiguities, a predicament which, I will argue, Mark Twain entertains and creates in his own fictional courtroom but flees from in his response to the actual trial.

My argument thus depends upon establishing a particular dialogue between these two cases of seduction, for neither Twain's nor the journalistic accounts alone tell the story that the two together do. Both cases speak in common to two aspects of fictionality. One is a mode of social differentiation, the sexual and legal categories (passive/aggressive, victim/victimizer, innocence/guilt) essential to both cases, but whose actual application was, for different reasons in each, momentarily suspended. It was impossible to decide, for example, whether Evelyn Thaw or Alice or Twain himself, for that matter, should be classified as victim or victimizer, as playing the active or passive role in their respective narratives. The temporary suspension of these categories, I will argue, does not invalidate them or brand them as "fictive," but rather reveals them as culturally constructed and culturally applied, in Twain's words in *Pudd'nhead Wilson*, "a fiction of law and custom" (*PW*, 9). In both cases the response to this moment when cultural categories cannot be definitively applied is a process of storytelling—a second aspect of fictionality—that attempts to construct coherent narratives about those suspended "fictions of law and custom." Although Twain's "Alice" case opens in 1877, not until it connects with the Thaw trial in 1907 does the full story, as I have just briefly outlined it, emerge. It is precisely that double story that the rest of this chapter will tell: the story of how Mark Twain's personal compulsions met up with his culture's in the act of reporting, representing, interpreting, and finally making its own events mean.

VII

Mark Twain's autobiographical tale raises problems of interpretation similar to those in the Thaw case: the tangled chronology—events of 1877, recorded in letters as they are happening, written in 1898 into a piece that then reappears, slightly revised, in Twain's Autobiographical Dictations in 1907—creates even thornier anomalies within the tale itself. Because Twain wrote two slightly different versions, we have to contend with several layers of fiction that are themselves sometimes incompatible, sometimes contradictory, sometimes hard to tell apart. The story constitutes itself as narrative through a number of genres and forms: letters, fiction, autobiography, journalism. When "Wapping Alice" was printed for the first time in 1981, the editor Hamlin Hill included not only the tale itself but various supporting documents—the three letters from Clemens to Livy written in 1877 about the original incident, another story based on that incident, "The McWilliamses and the Burglar Alarm," and portions of the Autobiographical Dictation of 10 April 1907—as though this particular story could not be told without entangling many different versions.[29] But even Hill's fully documented and inclusive edition excludes the Thaw material (Twain's comments on the trial and the *Sun* excerpt) attached to the 10 April 1907 dictation; thus the only available text of "Wapping Alice" is still incomplete. No one has yet put together the two stories of seduction as Twain himself evidently did.

In "Wapping Alice" Twain represents the action for the most part straightforwardly, although he nominally tells the events as a mystery in the three 1877 letters as well as in the 1898 manuscript. But as observer, participant, and, finally, recorder of these events, Twain represents himself, even in the letters, as both a fictional character in them and creator of them. His roles run the gamut from actively engaged character detecting the mystery, to semi-detached "judge, jury & lawyer," to omniscient dramatist staging and directing the denouement of the shotgun wedding. One letter brags to Livy, "I have been detective Simon Wheeler for 24 hours now," and another describes in detail the "dramatic grandeur" of the "performance" that he, as showman, orchestrated, with each participant introduced by "Enter____," as though each were a player in a drama.[30]

Twenty years later, in the summer of 1897 or 1898, when Clemens put these events into narrative form, he dealt with the problem of his status in the story by at first using his own name and those of his servants, but later (in November 1898) he changed his name to "Mr. Jackson" (a southerner rather than a Connecticut resident) and his English housemaid Lizzie Wills's to "Wapping Alice" (because she was from that part of London), and he transformed the nondescript accused seducer into a Swede—and otherwise turned autobiography into more distanced fiction.[31] One change, however, was more substantial. Twain embellished the story with a surprise ending: the English housemaid turns out to be a *male* transvestite (the only one in all of the stories we have seen). The masquerade is a "secret" so unnecessary to the plot of the actual incident that Twain reveals it abruptly on the second page, claiming, "Some of the ridiculous features of the incident . . . will be better understood if I expose Wapping Alice's secret here and now, in the beginning—for she had a secret. It was this: she was not a woman at all, but a *man*" (*WA*, 42). Twain does not even bother to give any justification for this fiction, dismissing the sex change with "Why he unsexed himself was his own affair" (*WA*, 42). Nine years later, however, Twain did venture an explanation for this apparently inexplicable embellishment, an autobiographical explanation that actually forms part of the telling of the tale. In the Autobiographical Dictation of 9 April 1907, he dictated "Wapping Alice" almost exactly as he had first written it in 1898, instructing only that the fictional names should be changed back to the original ones (Jackson to Clemens, and so forth). On 10 April he revealed the other, far more bizarre fiction in the story—Alice's gender—and gave his "true" reason for making her male:

> I am aware that yesterday's dictation reads like a farcical fairy-tale and looks like an invention; . . . There is one considerable detail which is fictitious, but it is a non-essential. In that instance I diverged from fact to fiction merely because I wanted to publish the thing in a magazine presently, and for delicacy's sake I was obliged to make the change. But this Autobiography of mine can stand plainnesses of statement which might make a magazine shiver; . . . For my own pleasure, I wish to remove that fictive detail now, and replace it with the fact. . . . Wapping Alice was a *woman*, not a man. This truth does not relieve or modify by even a shade the splendid ridiculousness of the situation, but the temporary transformation of Alice into a man does soften the little drama sufficiently to enable me to exploit it in a magazine without risk of overshocking the magazine's readers. (*WA*, 71)

It is impossible to ignore the humor of this passage but next to impossible to tell what Twain is up to in his "plain statement" of "fact" that coyly raises more questions than it resolves. Can he be serious when he implies that readers will be less shocked by homosexuality than illicit heterosexuality? Or is it that he would never imagine such an implication—would in fact run from the slightest suggestion of it—so that if it is there, he is totally unaware? Twain's claim of making a true confession must seem blatantly deceptive, for while his bizarre fictional strategy may have avoided one sexual peccadillo (an illicit affair and illegitimate pregnancy occurring belowstairs in his own home), it created another (an apparent homosexual affair) which he neither acknowledges nor comments upon. If we suspect that Twain's autobiography is just a telling of another story, his tone of confidential candor just creating another persona, that suspicion is confirmed when he ends the day's dictation by revealing (creating?) yet another "fictive detail": how he discovered that the real Alice had never been pregnant at all. This autobiographical recollection characteristically verges on fiction. Three years after the marriage, Clemens recalled, he returned from Europe and on a visit to Hartford met a well-dressed couple who turned out to be his former housemaid and her husband. Their prosperity, the husband explained, was due to his wife's shrewdness, so he was grateful to Clemens for forcing them to marry, "but as to that child, it hasn't ever arrived, and there wasn't the damndest least prospect of it the time that she told you that fairy-tale—and never *had* been!" (*WA*, 74).

The revelation of the fictitious pregnancy furnishes the surprise ending not only of the 10 April dictation but also of the oral versions of the tale that Twain is known to have told. It must have been one of his favorite after-dinner entertainments, acceptably off-color for an all-male audience, since at least two different sources record its telling at two different men's clubs. During his stay at the Villa di Quarto in 1904, the *Italian Gazette* (a paper for the Anglo-American colony in Florence) reported that at a dinner at the Ponte Vecchio Club, Mark Twain told "an excellent story of how he drove an unwilling man into matrimony"—needlessly, as it turned out.[32] Two years later at another dinner at the Players Club in New York, Walter Oettel, majordomo at the club, recalled in his memoirs that Mark Twain told "the amusing story of English Mary." This version, according to Oettel, ended with exactly the same punch line as the 10 April dictation: there was no child because there had never been a pregnancy.[33]

The "surprise" ending of the "Wapping Alice" manuscript is even more scandalous than the outcome of the actual incident, and Twain permitted himself to include it only in those versions not intended for a public audience. The cryptic last line of the story, "The couple never lived together, nor had any family," flirts, however obliquely, with the possibility of sexual activity between two men (much as the end of "Feud Story" does with two women), surely equally "indelicate" and "shocking" as the drama of an unmarried woman pretending to be pregnant.[34] Furthermore, that final sentence somehow reverses the effect of the Mark Twain character's action—as if to make his attempts to "force" a marriage fruitless and, by alluding to the fact that only those directly involved in a sexual act can really know the true story, to refute the assumptions he'd made about their sex lives. The "surprise" ending that unmasks both the fictitious pregnancy and the fictitious gender thus makes a rather unsettling conclusion to the whole "mystery" of "Wapping Alice."

Why would Twain have changed the serving girl to a male transvestite? If not "for delicacy's sake," as the Autobiographical Dictation ingenuously claims, then for what fictional and psychological reasons? This strategy accomplishes several things at once: it overtly preserves the morality of "delicacy" by not making the woman guilty of sexual transgression, yet it covertly violates those mores even by imagining two men, one a transvestite, "living together" and having a family. But by thus affirming that sexual aggression is exclusively male rather than female, this violation simultaneously reasserts the cultural assumptions about gender distinction and sexuality that Mark Twain's story questions, even tends to subvert. If aggressive female sexuality is problematic for a culture that recognizes only the passive woman as woman, then Twain, one of its representative men, avoids that problem by disguising female sexual aggression, projecting it onto a male character. The "he" that Twain creates, a "comely young creature in blossomy hat and fluttering ribbons and flowing gown" whom "it is awkward and unhandy to call . . . anything but 'she' " (WA, 42) is the image of a "phallic woman": he claims to have a baby but really has a penis.[35] In this guise Twain's Alice acknowledges the New Woman emerging at the turn of the century but simultaneously reasserts the gender differences threatened by the breakdown of sexual boundaries.[36] So the change of sex that appears only to violate the bounds of morality also restores other boundaries that have been threatened. For by the end of Mark Twain's tale, not only has Alice been unsexed and unmasked, but also the problems of knowledge raised by her tale of seduction have been masked. We are left with the apparent assurance that male experience is accessible (he cannot be pregnant), even if woman's is not (she could pretend to be pregnant). But this somewhat equivocal conclusion masks the more threatening unknowability, dramatized by Alice's tale, of whether this woman is sexually active or passive, that is, the seductress or the victim.

There are also other, somewhat different reasons for the sex change that are only partially related to the belief in female sexual passivity. From the very beginning, Twain stresses theatricality not only as his own but also as Alice's modus operandi, characterizing their relationship as a rivalry between equally accomplished role players. "It is very creditable to his ingenuity that he was able to masquerade as a girl seven months and a half under all our eyes and never awake in us doubt or suspicion," Twain grudgingly admits. Yet Twain the tall-tale-teller extraordinaire, proud of his own "native appetite for doing things in a theatrical way," cannot stand the prospect of having been beaten by a rival liar, and so, early in the story itself, hastens to assure us that the neighbors, too, were completely deceived: "They knew Alice almost as well as we knew him, yet no suspicion of the fraud he was playing ever crossed their minds. He must have had years of apprenticeship in his part, or he could not have been so competent in it" (WA, 60, 42). This passage, in the story, explains Mark Twain's fictionalization of sexual identity from fact to story. Part of the logic of the sex change may be to explain away the problem of how a female could lie as well as Mark Twain does. He (the author) has been fooled by this person who conned him with her tale of a fictitious pregnancy. But men are better liars (hence better storytellers, better authors)—he himself being a champion liar/storyteller. Therefore the person who beat him at this game must really be a man.

It is thus both as rival liar/storyteller and as aggressively sexual female that Alice represents for Twain the boundary-transgressing woman. And it is in part this boundary breakdown that pushes Twain toward the repressive resolution of legalistic language and reasoning. Resolving to "hold a court in the morning and fan out the evidence and get at the bottom facts of this dark episode," Mark Twain plays the interrogator with Alice as prime "witness" and acts out his fantasy of aggression against her. He delights first in "disordering her story" and then in trapping his victim with a particularly competitive and hostile relish:

> I wove the stories of the servants into a clear and compact narrative, and reeled it off like a person who had been behind the door and seen it all . . . It was as if I was plucking the secretest privacies out of her heart, one by one, and displaying them before her amazed eyes. (WA, 57)

The gleeful tone here betrays how entangled storytelling is with voyeurism, seduction, and sexuality. It is as though since Alice, a serving girl, victimized Twain, her employer, with her story of seduction, the only way for him to try to regain his sense of masculinity is to exert his authorial power to penetrate her story and thereby restore the hierarchical relationship that she had reversed. And yet the last laugh is still on Mark Twain himself, as character in the story.

As the perhaps unwitting link between these two sharp-eyed competitors—he who has "seen it all" and she of the "amazed eyes"—suggests, Twain identifies with Alice. The details of this male transvestite's clothing ("a white summer gown with a pink ribbon at the throat and another one around her waist" [WA, 56]) remind us of the various kinds of cases of cross-dressing in Twain's writing. Not all represent a structural identity between man and woman. Huck Finn poses unsuccessfully as a girl, revealing his male self when he catches a lump of lead with his knees (betrayed by the phallus?); both Roxana and her son become trapped by either their true race or their true gender when they try to escape those selves by combining sexual with racial disguise; and Joan of Arc's male attire leaves her female self unaltered. More significant than this textual evidence in establishing Twain's fascination with the theatricality of cross-dressing is his own attitude toward the white costume he wore so self-consciously in his later years. In the fall of 1906, according to Albert Bigelow Paine's biography, Mark Twain ordered only white suits from his tailor and made the following confession:

> I can't bear to put on black clothes again. I wish I could wear white all winter. I should prefer, of course, to wear colors, beautiful rainbow hues, such as the women have monopolized . . . I should like to dress in a loose and flowing costume made all of silks and velvets resplendent with stunning dyes, and so would every man I have ever known; but none of us dares to venture it. (MTB, 3: 1341–42)

Female clothing in this fantasy expresses the powerful attraction of an exotic other, and wearing it acknowledges the presence of that other within the self. But as we recall from Following the Equator, such clothing is not monopolized by women. For Twain, we know, native costume shares all of the allure of women's dress, from the rainbow hues and stunning dyes ("such stunning colors" in Ceylonese dress, such "fusings of rainbows"), to the loose and flowing lines (the "unmasculine" brown servant wears a "beltless and flowing" gown), to the silky fabrics (the Ceylonese "stuffs were silk—thin, soft, delicate, clinging"). Associated with both blackness and femaleness (in the protean mode Sander Gilman identifies in stereotypes), this "loose" and "flowing" and "fusing" costume is a means of liberation, of imagining the dissolving of rigid dress codes and of racial and sexual distinctions.

Such an associative identification may even promise a means of regeneration. For Twain also comments in the same passage that women's clothing makes an opera audience into "a garden of Eden for charm and color," whereas the men, "clothed in odious black, are scattered here and there over the garden like so many charred stumps." Anxieties about sexual differences and racial differences are tortuously, almost impenetrably, entangled here. In a kind of male inversion of penis envy, Twain asserts that every man, each of those phallic, black, charred stumps, feels and desires to feel the latent power of—not white but all-color—female fluidity. Yet Mark Twain's very identification of himself and "every man" with the opposite sex is a source of anxiety, just as his detailed pleasure in the hair, dress, and "shapely form" of the "unmasculine" young brown servant at the Hotel Bristol ends in his confessing, "It was an embarrassment to undress before him." Such lack of differentiation, blurring both gender and racial distinctions, seems a harbinger of loss of identity as self and other mingle. Even the admiring William Dean Howells sensed something dangerously unsettling in his friend's white clothing, praising it as "an inspiration which few men would have had the courage to act upon."[37] Hence the jocular certainty about gender of the ending of "Wapping Alice" ("blame her skin—she's a *man!*") actually casts doubt on all the epistemological assumptions of the story: "I keep calling her *she*—I can't help it; I mean *he*" (WA, 66–67).

The dramatic "showy effects" that Mark Twain loved in white costuming and cross-dressing speak to a similar theatricality in the law, ironically the cultural institution to which he looked to resolve the very sexual and epistemological disorder generated by his tale of transvestism. He delighted in the variety of legal roles he played in the actual "Wapping Alice" drama, as he confessed in the letter to Livy I quoted from earlier: "I haven't had so much chin-chin for some years. I have enjoyed it very much; I am judge, jury & lawyer for both sides. Moreover, the Court of Appeals being in Elmira, I have a pretty swinging jurisdiction here & it sets me up & makes me feel my oats."[38] The "Wapping Alice" manuscript, too, makes much of the Mark Twain character's "detective skill," his "examination" of the "witnesses" culminating in the theatrical denouement of the wedding arranged by Mark Twain the show-man. "Each actor was in his place at his appointed time . . . I was in the schoolroom; at 8 the bridegroom was with me, and the bride had taken post in the nursery. The curtain was up, the performance ready to begin" (*WA*, 60). All of these theatrical hijinks, however, deliberately disguise "Wapping Alice's" problem ending that comically casts doubt on the efficacy of both detection and the law.

The institutions of the law thus seem to Mark Twain to operate as though in a theater where fiction and fact can never be wholly disentangled. Twain's theatrical performance written into the trial in his story underscores the theatricality of the legal process itself, as we shall see, even as it obscures the threatening collapse of distinctions that occurs as he simultaneously acts in and observes the drama he also creates. Hence his apparently untroubled enjoyment of the triple roles of "judge, jury & lawyer"—"for both sides." Like some of his most flamboyant characters who so often end up in a courtroom, where both the individual's capacity for self-deception and the culture's capacity for fictionalizing can be put on trial, Twain revels in the law's problematic theatricality. As an author-character in a semi-fictional story, he suggests that we who authorize legal power also become its enactors, its audience, and its victims. Yet fiction did not alone provide the grounds for such investigation; the highly publicized Thaw murder trial in 1907 linked sexuality and theatricality with law even more problematically than Twain's fictional trials did.

VIII

The Harry K. Thaw murder trial sounds like the kind of case that Mark Twain should have seized upon as an updated version of "Wapping Alice." The Thaw case as a whole involved a series of sexual, psychological, and legal uncertainties that correspond with striking affinities, as I will show, to those of the "Alice" tale. In particular, we know that Evelyn Nesbit Thaw's seduction story was the subject of Mark Twain's dictations on 28 February and again on 10 April, the very same day he concluded dictating his account of "Wapping Alice." What is especially significant is that, following his plan in his autobiography to drift from subject to subject, in a kind of free association, the "methodless method of the human mind," he proceeds with no break from the "Wapping Alice" incident to the "tremendous Thaw trial."

It is really not surprising that such a sensational case should have in some way caught Mark Twain's eye. From the opening day the press covered the trial as a theatrical event performed before a mass audience. On 23 January 1907 the *New York Times* announced:

The Thaw trial is being reported to the ends of the civilized globe. The eminence of the victim, the wealth of the prisoner, the dramatic circumstances of the crime, and the light it sheds not only on Broadway life, but on the doings of the fast set in every capital have caused special arrangements to be made for the press.

The facts of the case—other than the murder itself—were as dubious as they were sensational—indeed, maybe even sensational because of their dubiety. Not only, we recall, were the sanity of the murderer and the moral/sexual character of his victim and his wife hotly debated by various kinds of "expert witnesses" in court, but the seduction of Evelyn Nesbit by Stanford White was itself open to question.

To compound the problem, although the story of seduction was very much on trial in the newspapers, in court the legal rules of evidence forbade any questioning of a narrative of a sexual act that, it was alleged, had taken place years before. The chronological sequence is as anomalous as that of the "Alice" tales; moreover, one of the participants (the alleged seducer) was no longer even alive to tell his own story. In spite of these uncertainties, Evelyn Thaw's version of the seduction story was admissible as evidence regardless of its veracity, but only insofar as it had been told to Thaw as she claimed and insofar as it affected his sanity or insanity. And so the rules of evidence forced the court to allow one cultural narrative—that of the woman seduced and abandoned— to be reenacted in its forum, and forced it to exclude other roles— the Camille, the seduced maid, the whore, the scheming woman, the showgirl/courtesan.

If Twain entertained all of these ambiguities in his own courtroom, he refused to look beyond the stereotypes when faced with a similar situation in the Thaw trial—just as he stood resolutely behind the same stereotypes in his two age-of-consent pieces. Fiction might have freed him at the very least to question Evelyn Thaw's story (not to mention his role and those of the various legal and journalistic audiences in shaping her story), as we know he cross-examined not only his housemaid's story of seduction but also his own theatrical response implicating him in the story of her story. He must have known that it was possible for an elaborate charade to be staged, with Evelyn Thaw at its center, since that was exactly how he had represented the "Alice" incident. But when that possibility emerges in the Thaw trial, he denies it, just as he ultimately asserted that only a male Alice could be actively deceiving him in order to get her man.

In his autobiographical dictation on the Thaw trial, echoing the age-of-consent pieces, Mark Twain spoke as Victorian patriarch, raging at "the middle-aged architect" who had "eagerly and diligently and ravenously and remorselessly" hunted the "slender and illustriously beautiful girl-wife" to her destruction.[39] Using these words in the dictation, just after Evelyn Thaw had completed her testimony, Mark Twain went even further and attacked not only White's character but also that of the public, those whom we know Twain despised because of their cruelty to seduction victims, and in this case who "have fed at this horrible Thaw banquet" with a ravenousness equal to White's sexual appetite. Yet in his own story of seduction, the Twain character brags about how his "native appetite for doing things in a theatrical way feasted itself with a relish on this spectacular program" (WA, 60). There seems to be no dialogue at all between Mark Twain's overt, sexually and socially conservative response to the Thaw case, expressed in the most outworn of clichés (the same clichés invoked in the consent arguments), and his covert, humorously farcical questioning of those very clichés in "Wapping Alice."

In contrast to Twain's certainty about assigning sexual innocence and guilt in the Thaw case, contemporary newspaper accounts show how polarized public opinion was over the characters of the major players in the drama. In his outrage at White and sympathy for the "victim," Mark Twain represents those who focused on the seduction rather than the murder and interpreted that former event by upholding prevailing sexual stereotypes. Most striking, what he refused to or could not see in the Thaw trial—the theatricality of the law—was exactly what he had flaunted in "Wapping Alice" and exactly what both fascinated and repelled his contemporaries about the case.

It was not simply because Evelyn Thaw had been an actress that her testimony was repeatedly characterized as an accomplished performance, although that made explicit an otherwise implicit suspicion. District Attorney William T. Jerome offered this kind of critical analysis of both her role and her melodramatic story in his summing-up on 9 April. Exhibiting some early photographs of Evelyn Nesbit, he addressed the jury:

> Do those look like the girl in the little sailor suit who came here to testify? Or do they show a wise young actress who knew her business? Gentlemen, this is no case of a Saint George rescuing a maiden. This is a mere, common, sordid, vulgar, everyday Tenderloin homicide.[40]

A frequent focal point, her appearance was interpreted by some as having been deliberately shaped to evoke what became the most often-used adjective in the newspapers: childlike. Her courtroom costume—a navy blue tailored dress with a shirtwaist and Buster Brown collar—was invariably compared, sometimes admiringly, sometimes critically, to that of a schoolgirl. The *New York Times* was openly sceptical of her "schoolgirl garb" and the "childish lisp in her voice." During her testimony (which revealed to the sympathetic shock of some, the cynical outrage of others, the most intimate details of her sexual life), in contrast to Thaw's visible agony, which had "no hint of theatrical effect about it," her self-possession was marked: "The lisp in her voice . . . was not missing when she sat and coldly told of the attentions of Barrymore, of White, and of Thaw . . . Dressed as a child, she comported herself as a woman of many years in the ways of the world."[41]

Suspiciously theatrical to some, Evelyn Thaw's role as ravished child-woman largely captured public sympathy. Even those who spoke as though hers could have been a self-fashioned act raised that possibility only to deny it. "She was not acting a part," insisted Irvin S. Cobb, covering Evelyn Thaw's testimony for the *Evening World*. "She could never have counterfeited it—the tortured twitch of the red, vibrant lips literally shrinking away . . . from the words they must frame . . . The best emotional actress in America couldn't have done it as well."[42] More typical, though, than Cobb's oddly double-edged defense was the sheer sentimental outcry over Evelyn Thaw's cross-examination by District Attorney Jerome, such as the columnist Nixola Greeley-Smith's description of "the vivisection of a woman's soul": "To me she remains what she seemed from the beginning—the child that was not given a chance; the frail reed bent to hideous purposes because it grew in a quagmire of vice and knew nothing else."[43]

This narrative of seduction reached its apogee when it was recapitulated by Delmas in his summing-up for the defense on 8 April. It was on the following day that Mark Twain picked up the 1898 story, reworked it, and dictated the revised version into his autobiography. Attached to the 10 April dictation is the clipping from the *New York Sun* with quotations from Delmas's impassioned argument about Evelyn Thaw's "ravishment" by the "tempter," as he called Stanford White. The excerpt makes clear that in part what drew Mark Twain to the Thaw case was the lawyer's highly theatricalized narrative of seduction—at its center the child-woman as tragic heroine:

> To a gilded den fitted with luxuries and adornments this
> man, old enough to be her father, enticed this child and there
> he ruined her . . . He had committed the most hideous crime
> that man can commit—to gratify his passion. He had crushed
> the poor little thing—the sweet little flower that was strug-
> gling toward the light and toward God.[44]

Alice's story of seduction, as Mark Twain reconstructs it, has similar melodramatic tones: "She told me that by persuasion of the
[seducer's] damnable fascinations she had 'fallen'; that her time
was approaching, and that she should presently become a mother"
(WA, 71).

But the point of Mark Twain's story of her story is that he had
himself passively "fallen" victim to Alice's aggressive "persuasion," reversing the sexual roles enacted in her melodrama of
seduction. Both cases, then, Twain's and Thaw's, involve the paradox that for each "fallen" woman, convincing the audience—
either Mark Twain or the jury—of the moral sincerity of her story
and of the sexual innocence of her character depends in part on
how knowing an actress and how dramatic a storyteller she is.
Especially when successful, her tale telling emplots her equally,
and ambiguously, as seduced victim and as victimizing storyteller.

The Thaw trial illuminated these interpretive difficulties
through the rules of evidence that framed Evelyn Thaw's seduction as story rather than event. The District Attorney attempted,
more than once, to remind the jury that hearing her testimony was
like listening to a story:

> The purpose . . . is purely to show that the mind of this de-
> fendant was affected by the narration of these facts by the
> witness, and . . . the rules of evidence do not permit the Dis-
> trict Attorney to controvert the facts as ever having
> occurred, . . . only . . . to controvert the question whether it
> was or was not told to this defendant.[45]

Legally speaking, the state's case was hamstrung by the evidential
technicality which permitted—indeed required—the jury to
weigh Evelyn Thaw's crucial evidence without regard to its truth
or falsity. When the trial ended in an inconclusive verdict, the lack
of formal closure only recapitulated a general sense of irresolution
that many were aware had plagued the entire case. Yet confronted
with such undecidability—no one could be found guilty—many
newspaper editorials found a more generalized place to lay the
blame: the guilty party was the legal system itself, which was

forced by its own ideology of factuality to authorize a kind of fictionality—Evelyn Nesbit Thaw's story of seduction admissible in evidence only *as* story.

Most papers, though, focused not on the general issue of the law's ability to know but rather located blame in specific procedural terms: it was the rule of evidence which, by prohibiting any distinction between fact and fiction, encouraged "much defiant perjury," in the words of the *New York Times*. On the morning after the trial closed without ending, the rest of the *Times* editorial indicted the evidentiary rules in the Thaw trial:

> We trust that no such extraordinary theory of justice as that which permitted the wife of the defendant to tell her preposterous story at great length while at the same time forbidding the prosecution to prove it untrue will ever be accepted and acted upon in another murder trial.[46]

This critique of our "theory of justice" manages both to question and to uphold the law's most basic premises of truth and proof—that is, the very terms challenging the law's authority also reinforce it by assuming that a "preposterous story" can be proven "untrue." The *New York Tribune*, too, argued that our system of justice had itself been put on trial, and yet it also managed in the teeth of the accusation somehow to reaffirm the validity of that system:

> We are entering into no apology for the private life of Stanford White, but . . . the slaying of the character after the slaying of the man, for the defense of the slayer, with the aid and sanction of the law, whose rules of evidence afforded no protection to the dead man's memory, offends the public sense of justice.[47]

That last ringing phrase asserts that a "sense of justice" exists apart from legal justice, a "public" justice that can still be offended even when the very system that creates, defines, and gives life to the concept of justice denies its existence.

Responding more explicitly to these contradictions than Mark Twain does, the newspapers rail against the law; they do so, however, in the language of the law, speaking from within the legal system, granting its premises, assuming its modes of inference. Even the jury's inability to reach a verdict was itself ironically seen as an appropriate kind of decision, reflecting, according to one British paper, "the verdict of the world, upon which the human tragedy beneath has produced like utterly contradictory impressions."[48] Although the only agreement is that there is no agreement among "like contradictory impressions," still, if legal language is the currency, that constitutes the only possible verdict. In addition to such legal terminology, the papers, like Mark Twain, use theatrical metaphors, as the *Evening Mail* did when it called the Thaw trial "a terrible example of the scandal and fatuity of our system of jurisprudence" and lamented the necessity of a retrial: "Well, we shall have it all over again, with the theatrical properties a little frayed, some of the tinsel missing."[49] By thus replacing with their own narrative and moral authority the legal authority that had been threatened, and even temporarily lost, during the trial, the newspapers restored a kind of informal judicial authority as journalists drew their own conclusions from a trial that officially ended inconclusively and was followed by Thaw's second trial.[50]

What we ultimately hear in these journalistic voices condemning the Thaw trial is a shrill cry of frustration, expressed in both legal and theatrical language, at the contradictions and uncertainties of the case. Not only did the public understand the rules of evidence as the court's open admission that, under certain circumstances, it would hear a witness's version of the story as *the* story rather than one of many competing narratives, but also the whole trial was perceived as theater, simultaneously enacting mutually exclusive dramas. In the journalists' discourse, Evelyn Thaw had to be characterized as either the innocently seduced or the guilty seductress; legal discourse, however, reflecting the adversarial nature of the legal system, constructed equally convincing cases for both roles. The Thaw trial, then, like Twain's "Wapping Alice," created rather than resolved confusions between factuality and fictionality and between stereotypical male and female roles. Finally, though, both journalistic and novelistic narratives of the trials contained these multiple uncertainties by representing them in terms of categorical certainties and dramatic oppositions. The newspapers created sexual melodrama and turned Evelyn Thaw into either virgin or whore; Mark Twain turned Wapping Alice from a woman into a man and created transvestite farce.

IX

When Mark Twain literally set "Wapping Alice" and the Harry Thaw trial side by side in his 10 April 1907 Autobiographical Dictation, he situated story and courtroom event at the intersection of the novelistic and the journalistic, where his personal obsessions meet up with those of his culture. Like many of his contemporaries (including, but not especially, Harry Thaw), Twain suffered from "Dementia Americana," a "species of insanity" so widespread, so common, indeed so much the "norm"—among American men—that Thaw's defense attorney coined the phrase to exonerate his client, assuming he was appealing to a shared cultural condition. The defense, we remember, defined Thaw's "insanity" to include every American who believes that "whoever invades the sanctity" of his home or "stains the virtue" of his wife or daughter "has forfeited the protection of human laws." By this definition Mark Twain was certainly among those insane Americans. Husband and father of a celebrated American family, Twain, we know, voiced the cultural concern with purity and violation—the assumption that males either protect or violate female purity and domestic sanctity—that Thaw's lawyer traded upon. Indeed, he goes so far as to characterize the male seducer, we recall from the *Harper's* consent article, as "the murderer of all that can make life worth the living—honor, self-respect, . . . the adoring worship of the sacred home circle" (*MTS*, 181).

But at the same time Twain diagnosed astutely his own and his culture's condition. While his "Alice" tales violate convention by creating and entertaining deliberate gender confusion and boundary crossing—boundaries of factuality and fictionality as well as of gender—his closing word on the case appears to suppress its sexual violations within the borders of a pure fact/fiction distinction. "I have now told all the facts and removed all the fictions," Mark Twain concludes the 10 April dictation, "and to my mind the facts make a plenty good enough tale without any help from fiction."

We should not conclude, however, that Twain was trapped by the distinction between repressive fact and freeing fiction. Instead, even in this late period he operated as he always had, by cultivating a self-image realized not despite but through oppositions between the constraint of social convention and the liberation of fictive creation. Both the literary voice and the living persona of Mark Twain required such resistance in order to achieve expression. In life he created himself through the self-conscious image of the domesticated humorist who accepts the genteel censorship of Olivia Clemens or William Dean Howells. The self-dramatizing, white-suited old man who would rather dress in even more dramatic women's colors is a version of the flamboyant young writer with flaming red hair and moustache and sealskin coat; he had a "keen feeling for costume" and "relish for personal effect," we recall Howells wrote, and "enjoyed the shock, the offence, the pang which it gave the sensibilities of others."[51] In his writing, as well, the most powerful images of freedom come into being only through opposition to real suppression and cultural conformity. The West of *Roughing It* is realized not as a place in itself but in the gap between conventional literary imaginings of that place and a more potent vernacular "reality," just as Huck and Jim's idyll on the raft enacts a fictitious freedom that the reader desires precisely because it is never actualized but made real in language.[52]

And so, too, with Twain's late encounters, both factual and fictional, with women who seem to speak as freely as men. Rather than despairing at the gulf created by sexual and legal paradoxes entertained in fiction but repressed in fact, Twain makes up his mind that "the facts make a plenty good enough tale"—a tale, we note, like his stories of his own boyhood, that refused its author's repeated efforts to conclude it, a tale whose telling generated new questions, new answers, new tellings—much as the Thaw trial itself did. Twain's last words on the "Alice" case thus come to an appropriately cryptic conclusion. They locate his own tale of transvestism in the same border place as the Thaw trial, somewhere in the oppositions among fact, tale, and fiction.

Delmas's invention of Dementia Americana unmakes the boundary between sanity and insanity, or at least for those convinced by the label and its point, discloses that boundary as vague and permeable. Twain had already been moving toward his own deliberate project of boundary dissolution in terms, we recall, of past and present in *Following the Equator*. The dark-skinned natives of India and Africa in the 1890s dissolve, under the pressure of the act of writing, into the slaves of the antebellum South of Twain's childhood. It is an experience of memory that Twain actively courts. The sight of an Indian servant meekly receiving punishment takes Twain back to the equally cruel customs of his boyhood—and then to an awareness of the power of his own imagining mind:

> It is curious—the space-annihilating power of thought. For just one second, all that goes to make the *me* in me was in a Missourian village, on the other side of the globe, vividly seeing again these forgotten pictures of fifty years ago, and wholly unconscious of all things but just those; and in the next second I was back in Bombay, and that kneeling native's smitten cheek was not done tingling yet! Back to boyhood—

fifty years; back to age again, another fifty; and a flight equal
to the circumference of the globe—all in two seconds by the
watch! (*DE*, 21: 19)

From here it is not very far, either narratively or chronologically, to
Twain's dream tales, the first of which he probably began in May
1897, a few days after finishing *Following the Equator*. Through
these stories of voyages to alternate worlds in decentered time and
space, Twain hoped to liberate his writing entirely from the con-
straints of history and reality and into a world of pure fictive
creation. As I will show in the next chapter, the so-called science
fiction writings give vent to the "space-annihilating power of
thought," the creative power of the mind to unmake stable distinctions—those of time, space, sanity/insanity, dream/reality—and
thereby to make new realities effectively come into being. Such
narrative experimentation was to reflect back in unforseen ways
on the writer himself, especially on the "all that goes to make the
me in me." Just as he discovered that what is deceptive about
sexual divisions is finally not their cultural constructedness but
rather the conclusion that we can do without such fictions of law
and custom, so, too, the dream tales would disclose that the creative self preserves its own reality only through the fictions it
constructs.

CHAPTER FIVE

THE DREAM WRITINGS
AND THE
COSMIC CONSCIOUSNESS

In 1898 when Mark Twain attributed his understanding of dreams and the unconscious to "the French experiments in hypnotism ten or twelve years ago, and the investigations made by our Professor William James," he was referring to a radical new field of investigation.[1] The First International Congress of Experimental Psychology held in Paris in 1889 was notable, as William James later commented, for bringing science and the occult together. In attendance were leading French psychotherapists Jean Charcot and Pierre Janet, joined by a delegation from the British Society for Psychical Research (SPR), including two of its founders, Henry Sidgwick, a Cambridge professor of moral philosophy, and F. W. H. Myers (later known for his theory of the subliminal self), as well as by William James, later the SPR's first American president (whose *Principles of Psychology*, a book Mark Twain read, was published the following year), and Francis Galton, main discussant in a session on psychological heredity. Not only were the participants themselves drawn from often inimical fields, but also their methods of research and treatment—hypnosis, inducement of trance states, dream analysis, automatic writing and talking—and their subjects—hysterics, mediums, and others with alleged "abnormal" or "supernormal" experiences—represented a heterogeneous mixture of the orthodox with the marginal and the outright outré.[2]

No better paradigm of this moment of crossover among disciplines, or of the type of scientific exotica that most energized Mark Twain, can be found than the "Census of Hallucinations," authorized by the congress as a whole and to be carried out by the SPR. The very title suggests how the methodologies of science were crossed with matters spiritual. The sample consisted of over 25,000 people of different nationalities, chosen at random and asked to fill out a long questionnaire beginning with a question phrased so as to define mental impressions by rigorous criteria:

"Have you ever, when believing yourself to be completely awake, had a vivid impression of seeing or being touched by a living or inanimate object, or of hearing a voice; which impression, so far as you could discover, was not due to any external physical cause?" Mark Twain himself cites this particular SPR requirement in an article entitled "Mental Telegraphy" to which we will return later. The results of the census were tabulated, analyzed, and then published, in the classic model of the scientific report, in the *Proceedings of the Society for Psychical Research* (1894).[3] William James comments in his article "What Psychical Research Has Accomplished" that the question still remaining from the results, themselves calculated, he notes, through the most sophisticated statistical theory available, was whether we must suppose "an occult connection behind these apparitions."[4]

Both the nature of the experimentation in the unconscious reported at the 1889 congress and the participation of ordinarily separate constituencies marked a new decade in experimental psychology, one that saw three more international congresses by 1900. At all of them, psychic researchers (whose province was the "supernormal") cooperated with psychotherapists (who treated the "abnormal") in investigating phenomena that James describes as "unclassified residuum," "usually treated with contemptuous scientific disregard": "Physiology will have nothing to do with them. Orthodox psychology turns its back on them. Medicine sweeps them out" (*WJ on PR*, 26). Revolting in common against the reigning physiological definitions of mental illness and unconscious mental states, the new research (whether it is called psychical or psychological) engendered its own self-conscious momentum through debates, conducted in newspapers and on the lecture circuit as well as in professional journals, over the methodology and status of the new theories and the emerging fields they signaled. Still more controversial were the wide-ranging applications of new psychological theories in the area of the law, especially criminal laws defining individual responsibility, diminished capacity, and the use of the insanity defense. Thus the new psychology of the unconscious, using suspect methods on disreputable subjects, was tinged throughout the 1890s, in the popular mind as well as the scientific, with an aura of the charlatan, the criminal, and the freakish.

It was this climate of opinion that ushered in Mark Twain's own "scientific" phase of literary experimentation during the final two decades of his life. The formative cultural context of this period has long been recognized, especially by biographers and by those who have edited Mark Twain's late writings.[5] So, too, has Mark Twain's primarily sceptical and humorous interest in phrenology, mental telepathy, séances—and other vaguely disreputable phenomena associated with spiritualism or the occult.[6] But during the 1890s, in writings on dreams and creativity, Mark Twain himself pointed the way to a perhaps even more deeply engaged interaction with contemporary psychological theories—the particular engagement of a writer long troubled by problems of authorial intentionality and control, for whom the experimental crossing of science with pseudoscience during the 1890s produced results speaking powerfully to his literary concerns.

The direct consequence of this constellation of interests, personal and cultural, was the outpouring of writings, almost all notoriously incomplete, that constitute what editors have called Mark Twain's "dream tales" or "symbolic writings" or "fables of man." To Justin Kaplan, this "nocturnal and irrational" material—"story after story about men whose dreams turned into reality"—exposed the writer to madness, "but by turning his dream life into a literary problem—into *work*—he saved himself from madness."[7] William James might have alternatively described Twain's dream stories as tales of "the cosmic consciousness": literary fantasies playing upon assumptions related to James's own "panpsychic view" (expressed in "The Last Report: The Final Impressions of a Psychical Researcher") that "there is a continuum of cosmic consciousness, against which our individuality builds but accidental fences, and into which our several minds plunge as into a mother-sea or reservoir."[8] The mental sea voyages depicted in several of Twain's dream tales, however, envision a self-devouring plunge not into James's nurturing and liberating mother-sea, but rather into "The Great Dark" or "The Devil's Race-Track" or "The Enchanted Sea-Wilderness." These are nightmarishly ambiguous regions in that they are not distinctly either dream or reality; their effect on the individual's sense of self is similarly unbounded. For Twain's narrators, whether a dreamer at the eye of a microscope whose dream-vision turns out to be overseen by the Superintendent of Dreams ("The Great Dark"), or a scientist transformed into a microbe and marooned in a vast microbic planet (actually the body of a tramp) where human existence is unknown ("Three Thousand Years Among the Microbes"), contact with the panpsychic undermines their sense of individuality. Whereas James sees in the continuum of cosmic consciousness an expanded self-awareness, Twain finds a progressively shrunken individual sense of self, until finally he arrives at the farthest point expressed in the Socratic dialogue *What Is Man?*: "Young Man. You really think a man originates nothing, creates nothing. Old Man. I do."[9]

As Mark Twain saw it, then, the climate of psychological experimentation spoke in new therapeutic and theoretical terms to his old problems with literary creativity and authorial responsibility. The whole issue of originality in particular was directly addressed by the SPR's experimental work in thought transference. Writing to the society in 1884 to accept the offer of a membership, Clemens links the work in what they call mental telepathy and what he calls mental telegraphy to his own long-standing views of authorship: "I have grown so accustomed to considering that all my powerful impulses come to me from somebody else, that I often feel like a mere amanuensis when I sit down to write . . . I consider that that other person is supplying the thoughts to me, and that I am merely writing from dictation."[10] The term "amanuensis," one we know he sometimes used to characterize himself as a writer, comes directly from the vocabulary of psychical research, used to refer to the so-called "spirit controls" through whom the medium's message was communicated. As we will see, the figure of the artist-as-amanuensis also animates Mark Twain's late writings, but only in conjunction with his opposite: the artist as creator/destroyer, as Twain's Satan/No. 44 of *The Mysterious Stranger*, whose multiple guises represent both the fecundity and the duplicity of genuine imaginative creation.

The narrators of the dream tales are all creators of one kind or another: dreamers dream themselves into nightmarish worlds in "Which Was the Dream?" and "The Great Dark"; the double-dealing George Harrison of "Which Was It?" commits a murder, frames an innocent man, and then himself acts the part of the innocent; the scientist-turned-microbe narrator of "Three Thousand Years Among the Microbes" tells stories of his memories of the human world unknown to his microbe audience; and finally, a figure not usually included in this group, the mysterious stranger whose "mind creates . . . out of the airy nothing which is called Thought" (*MS*, 114). Though sometimes separated off as a semi-canonical work of Twain's late years, *The Mysterious Stranger* belongs, in my view, to the series of bizarre visions of the creative, often near-insane, imagination that we get in the dream tales. These contradictory conceptions of the creative unconscious may be traced to contemporary debates within the new psychology over the nature of the artist and artistic creation. Some argued for the "degeneracy," the maladaptation of genius, others for "cryptomnesia" behind much apparent original creation, and a very few for the clearly "mythopoetic" functioning of the unconscious.[11]

It is not only in these various refractions of the unconscious that the dream tales assimilated some of the best-known findings in psychological research. The tales are structured to be explicitly self-questioning in ways that engage with the popular awareness of the problematics of scientific methodology and standards of experimentation. That is, public debate during the 1890s over legal applications of psychological theories highlighted the issue of what constitutes evidence and proof in both the laboratory and the courtroom. Some of Mark Twain's writings, we will see, incorporate this atmosphere by internally testing the narrative grounds on which they rest. The nightmarish narratives of disaster and freakish reversal (of fortune, scale, time, and space) are all set within an outer frame, purported to be the "real," creating an ostentatious structural division that gradually becomes blurred, calling into doubt the foundation and authority of both the inset tale and the frame, the "dream" within and the "reality" without. The question these writings leave open, then, is not simply whether we know "Which Was the Dream?" or "Which Was It?", but rather how can we know, what is the basis of our knowledge. The interrogative tales take off at the point of a narrative imagining of the absence of a state of mind capable of knowing. "It isn't safe to sit in judgment upon another person's illusion," the microbe-narrator concludes. "While you are thinking it is a dream, he may be knowing it is a planet" (WWD, 492).

II

Such epistemological speculation in Mark Twain's writing took shape during a period when controversial developments in psychology and criminal law led to a public accustomed to the vocabulary of evidentiary analysis. Since the well-publicized Rochester "spirit-rappings" of the Fox sisters in upstate New York in 1848 and their subsequent investigation and exposure, the widespread perception of fraud among mediums and the need to control it were instrumental in creating the professional psychical researcher. Founded in 1882, the Society for Psychical Research expressed its intent, in a statement printed at the front of every issue of the society's *Journal*, to examine "without prejudice or prepossession and in a scientific spirit, those faculties of man, real or supposed, which appear to be inexplicable on any generally recognized hypothesis."[12] As the Census of Hallucinations demonstrated, to the SPR the scientific spirit represented in part a procedural method of data collecting and testing for psychical researchers experimenting primarily with the mental phenomena of hypnotic subjects (mediums, clairvoyants, and others) but also with grosser physical manifestations (motor automatisms, apparitions, haunted houses).

More important, though, than actual experimental practices or results (both often disputed and ridiculed), the SPR's claim to a scientific spirit translated for supporters and critics alike into a self-conscious appraisal of science and its organization of knowledge. Constant attention was paid in the society's reports, as well as in reviews of its work, not only to what James criticizes as "quiddling discussions" of the "precise coefficient of evidential value," but also to a broader discussion of the boundaries of contemporary science (*WJ on PR*, 30, 39, 59). The American philosopher C. S. Peirce, for example, wrote a scathing review of *Phantasms of the Living* (1886), a two-volume study of cases of telepathy collected and classified by three SPR leaders, in which he criticized the study on the grounds that every single one of its visual-crisis cases violated one or more of the eighteen conditions which they should have fulfilled to be acceptable as evidence.[13] G. Stanley Hall, well-known American psychologist and an original sponsor and vice-president of the SPR, dismissed out of hand the reports of cases collected in *Phantasms*, arguing that sceptical scientists demanded at the very least "a single fact that can be demonstrated regularly in a laboratory." Although Hall later confessed "an attraction to all the works and ways of believers," still the best that could be said of psychical researchers is that they are "believers," but never men of science. The worst that could be said relegates psychical research to the outer margins of the regressive and primitive realm of the nonscientific: Hall deplores "the recrudescence in this cult of a savage superstition which belongs more to the troglodyte age than to our own."[14]

More than anyone else, sceptic or believer, William James explicitly addressed what were most often veiled assumptions, held by both camps in the debate, about the proper boundaries of scientific research. His 1890 article "What Psychical Research Has Accomplished" first reassures his scientific audience that the efforts of psychical research to normalize itself and to classify heretofore unclassifiable phenomena aspire to "the ideal of every science . . . , that of a closed and completed system of truth." Such a neat system, however, James points out, ignores—"not accidentally but systematically"—those "wild facts" that cannot be pigeonholed within the existing theoretical structure of nature. Indeed, James argues, turning back on itself the language of the "rigorously scientific mind,"

> Although in its essence science only stands for a method and for no fixed belief, yet as habitually taken, both by its votaries and outsiders, it is identified with a certain fixed belief—the belief that the hidden order of nature is mechanical exclusively, and that non-mechanical categories are irrational ways of conceiving and explaining even such things as human life.

If the suggestion implicit in such terms as "votaries" and "belief" is at all muted, James brings the accusation into the open when he asserts of science, "To suppose that it means a certain set of results that one should pin one's faith upon and hug forever . . . degrades the scientific body to the status of a sect" (WJ on PR, 26–27, 44–45, 41). Thus he expresses a critical and anti-foundationalist view of positivist science.

The argument *for* psychical research, as opposed to the argument against "the irreversibly negative bias of the 'rigorously scientific' mind," draws James into the rhetoric of yet another camp, that of "the professional logic-shop." As he had done with orthodox science, he turns the language of the logicians against itself. "If you wish to upset the law that all crows are black," James, the logician-turned-psychic-researcher argues, "you must not seek to show that no crows are; it is enough if you prove one single crow to be white. My own white crow is Mrs. Piper," James concludes, forcing the abstract formulas of logic to incorporate the human phenomenon of a Boston trance-medium well known through the Northeast for séances that could not be proved fraudulent. Finally, though, James abandons the rhetorical effort to use precise logic as a means of falsification ("It is a miserable thing for a question of truth to be confined to mere presumption and counter-presumption") in favor of a looser, more colloquial evidentiary rhetoric derived from the law. The SPR's *Proceedings* have "conclusively proved one thing to the candid reader; and that is that the verdict of pure insanity . . . which the scientists of our day are led by their intellectual training to pronounce upon the entire [spiritual] thought of the past, is a most shallow verdict" (*WJ on PR*, 41, 45).

As to why it is shallow, we are best told twenty years later in James's 1909 "Last Report, The Final Impressions of a Psychical Researcher." Public opinion in his view has not changed significantly in the twenty years since "What Psychical Research Has Accomplished" was first published. In judging psychic phenomena, both spiritists and sceptics still make the same faulty division of either genuine or fraudulent, "revelation or imposture," "spirits or bosh." These "naive alternatives" have resulted in an "inconceivably shallow state of public opinion on the subject," shallow because "man's character is too sophistically mixed for the alternative of 'honest or dishonest' to be a sharp one." Instead, James concludes, "there is a hazy penumbra in us all where lying and delusion meet, where passion rules beliefs as well as conduct, and where the term 'scoundrel' does not clear up everything to the depths as it did for our forefathers" (*WJ on PR*, 314–18, 312, 321).

Precisely the same problems that James perceives in 1909 in public opinion on the field of psychical research were raised with even greater social force by the extension of clinical psychology into the courtroom, particularly when the insanity defense was invoked. The central problem is the difficulty of defining absolute "proof," either of spiritualist phenomena or medico-legal sanity. Like the sharp division between spirits and bosh, the alternatives of sanity or insanity were rigidly conceived and applied. Since the landmark M'Naghten case in England in 1843, the legal test of criminal insanity (the M'Naghten Rules) adopted in England and in most American jurisdictions was in effect a "right-wrong" test: the accused is not responsible for his crime if, at the time of committing it, he was unable to know that the deed was wrong.[15] Critics of the M'Naghten Rules noted that this legal test for responsibility (rather than a medical test for sanity) assumed a narrow identification of insanity with disordered reason, a view incompatible with emerging psychotherapeutic descriptions of insanity as disease affecting not only the cognitive or intellectual faculties, but the whole personality, including will and emotions. "The fundamental defect in the legal test of responsibility," noted Henry Maudsley, a mainstream leader of British physiological psychology, in 1864, "is that it is founded upon the consciousness of the individual. And while this is so, it is admitted in every book on mind published at the present day . . . that the most important part of our mental operations takes place unconsciously."[16] Toward the end of the century, experimental hypnosis underscored this view of unconscious or "automatic" or "involuntary" mental operations and even demonstrated the widely discussed possibility (if not actuality) of crime committed under hypnosis and of post-hypnotic criminal suggestion.[17]

Fueling the medical establishment's criticism was the problem that in theory the law allows insanity as an exculpatory condition, yet it proved difficult, if not impossible, to demarcate such conditions. The courts relied increasingly throughout the nineteenth century on expert witnesses from the medical science community, whose evidence must often be mustered to support opposing sides of cases, even though neither judge nor jury is considered competent to adjudicate between opposing expert testimonies. In the Laura Hawkins murder trial (based, we recall, on the successful insanity defense in the Laura D. Fair case in 1871–72) that culminates *The Gilded Age* (1874), for example, Mark Twain directs his most scathing satire at the jury system rather than at the plea of emotional insanity that results in her acquittal (after "four weary days" the jury selection process was completed satisfactorily; only two jurymen could read; "some had a look of animal cunning, while the most were only stupid").[18] Whether the jury or the expert witnesses were specifically censured, as a whole the M'Naghten Rules were widely criticized by doctors, lawyers, and laymen alike for failing to regularize the law and even leading to contradictory verdicts. As early as 1854, one English legal authority on insanity located the problem particularly in the law's lack of recognition of degrees of responsibility; one was either sane (knowing and responsible) or insane (not knowing and not responsible). Yet, John C. Bucknill argued,

> in nature we find no such sharply defined classification . . . and in the kingdom of mind, mind itself is scarcely able to conceive the gradations of power and knowledge. But nature herself must bend to the laws of man! and a dozen farmers and shopkeepers are compelled to divide the world of mind into two parts; and . . . to discern what the most scientific often fail to do.[19]

The problem with the "sharply defined classification," whether in medico-legal discourse or psychical research, is, as James would say, the absence of a *tertium quid:* "In law courts no *tertium quid* is recognized between insanity and sanity . . . And it is seldom hard to find two experts who will take opposite views of his case. All the while nature is more subtle than our doctors." This passage comes near the beginning of the seventh of James's 1896 Lowell Lectures on Exceptional Mental States, in a lecture on "Degeneration" that immediately precedes the eighth and final lecture on "Genius." "Our transition to genius," James notes, is provided by a group of (noncriminal) individuals that exemplifies the wide reach of the problem of the absence of a *tertium quid:* the "one-idea'd" persons (for example, the abolitionist, John Brown, the crusader for the mentally ill, Dorothy Dix) who "are *not* insane, not maniacs, not melancholics, not deluded; yet they are not sane." Still, James concludes, when we examine them in detail, "they show under a microscope the play of human nature."[20]

Ranging from such concerns with a *tertium quid* between sanity and insanity and the delicate balance between degeneracy and genius to the subjects of dreams and hypnotism, multiple personality, demoniacal possession, and witchcraft, James's lectures assume a diverse complex of familiarities—and interests—in his educated Back Bay audience of Wednesday and Saturday evenings. The same kinds of shared knowledge shaped the contours of Mark Twain's last two decades, as did the same ease of movement among an international variety of sources and references.[21] James's lectures touch not only on Pierre Janet and F. W. H. Myers but also on the criminologists Cesare Lombroso and Max Nordau, on the Irish historian W. E. H. Lecky, as well as on Bonaparte, Paganini, Shelley, Jay Gould—and Mark Twain. The brief mention of Mark Twain himself in the middle of one of James's long lists would not count for much, except for its context: Twain's name appears with those of several other writers in James's final lecture on genius, part of his attempt to refute "the prevailing opinion of our time" which "supposes that a psychopathic constitution is the foundation for genius" (*WJ on EMS,* 159–60, 149). That final lecture demonstrates how explicitly the well-publicized psychological and legal controversies over the unconscious engaged themselves with issues of creative genius, whether, James notes, that of the philosopher, scientist, or literary man. The fields of both psychology and psychic research addressed the question of what constitutes genius, with examples frequently drawn from literary ranks, most often cited to support the medical view that genius was allied with degenerative insanity. For Mark Twain, all of these interlocking interests in creativity, criminality, and the unconscious signaled the emergence of a volatile cultural context in which to place both his long-standing exploration of the divided self and his longstanding engagement with the problems of authorship in nineteenth-century America.

III

Many of the psychic phenomena investigated at the turn of the century would not immediately strike us now as particularly pertinent to the situation of the American artist. But both Hawthorne and James recognized in the mesmerist's hold over his usually female subject a potent metaphor for the moral perils they associated with the act of writing. Mark Twain's version of the metaphor, however, reverses that relationship and turns the artist from mesmerizer into mesmerized subject, controlled or possessed by his own literary creations, his own performance, his own audience. Twain's self-described experiences with writing reiterate many of the central motifs associated in the public mind with the hypnotic or mediumistic trance. Like the professional medium who, investigators reported, often communicated through "controls" in messages formed vocally or by automatic writing, Twain's artist-as-amanuensis writes "automatically," producing words dictated by some "other person." Indeed, man's mind, he says in the formulaic phrase of these years, is "a mere automatic machine," "a machine of which we are not a part, and over whose performances we have nothing that even resembles control or authority."[22]

A similar phenomenon known as "self-suggested automatism" was often observed in experiments on writing obtained in different stages of the hypnotic trance. In *Human Personality and Its Survival of Bodily Death*, for example, Myers interprets Janet's results with automatic writing in language that defines the hypnotized subject as the kind of reluctant author that Mark Twain so often represented himself to be. Automatic writing demonstrates that

> fresh personalities can be artificially and temporarily created, which will write down matter quite alien from the first personality's character, and even matter which the first personality never knew . . . If these writings are shown to the primary personality, he will absolutely repudiate their authorship . . . It is noticeable, moreover, that these manufac-

tured personalities sometimes cling obstinately to their fictitious names, and refuse to admit that they are in reality only
aspects or portions of the automatist himself.[23]

Such celebrated nineteenth-century cases of multiple personality
as Mlle. Hélène Smith (a medium studied by the Swiss psychiatrist
Théodore Flournoy) communicated in several flamboyantly alien
personalities and languages; among her controls, or "manufactured personalities," were a fifteenth-century Indian princess, a
Martian, and Marie Antoinette.[24]

Psychic researchers like Myers, then, perceived the mediumistic trance in terms that replicate Mark Twain's own experience of authorship: the manufactured personalities with fictitious names, created through writing by the primary personality,
who repudiates them as alien and even unknown to him. When
Mark Twain himself recognized the overlap between his craft and
the findings of psychical research, though, the link in his mind was
not mediumistic performance but rather, as we have already briefly seen, the phenomenon he called "mental telegraphy." In
Harper's Magazine for December 1891, he published a long article
entitled "Mental Telegraphy" that begins with a telling introductory note explaining why this piece, originally written in 1878 for
A Tramp Abroad (1880), should not have appeared in print until so
many years later. It was the old predicament, which so often drove
Mark Twain to repudiate his own art, of the humorist doubting
whether his writing will be taken seriously. That predicament was
only intensified at a time when the subject of psychic phenomena
aroused either ridicule or scepticism. While revising the travel
book, Mark Twain says he "removed" the "Mental Telegraphy"
piece, "for I feared that the public would treat the thing as a joke
and throw it aside, whereas I was in earnest." In 1881 he submitted
the essay to the North American Review, hoping, the humorist
derides himself, to publish it anonymously and "creep in under the
shelter of an authority grave enough to protect the article from
ridicule." The "wary" editor of that authoritative journal insisted,
however, that the article must be signed, but the author refused to
use either his name or nom de plume ("It would be the surest
possible way to defeat my desire that the public should receive the
thing seriously"). What, then, has so changed the climate in 1891
that even this checkered publication history may be divulged?
"The flood of light recently cast upon mental telegraphy by the
intelligent labors of the Psychical Society":

Within the last two or three years they have penetrated toward the heart of the matter . . . and have found out that
mind can act upon mind in a quite detailed and elaborate way
over vast stretches of land and water. And they have succeeded in doing, by their great credit and influence, what I
could never have done—they have convinced the world that
mental telegraphy is not a jest but a fact, and that it is a thing
not rare, but exceedingly common. They have done our age a
service—and a very great service, I think.[25]

They have also rendered a personal service to Mark Twain. The
SPR's work in telepathy has not only enabled him to speak out, but
has also provided him with "the solution of this hoary mystery,"
the apparent duplication of thoughts and actions between individuals, "exactly as if you two were harnessed together like the
Siamese twins" (*DE*, 22:114). Only "mind-telegraphing" could explain, perhaps even vindicate, the writer's long-standing sense of
illegitimacy, of not fully controlling his own thought process, but
of being rather an unwilling father or midwife to some alien creature, or the proprietor of a tank that often runs dry, or even an
unconscious plagiarist. He recalls an unnerving experience of such
thought duplication during the 1870s when "a red-hot new idea"
struck, telling him the time was right for a book about the Nevada
silver mines and further that an old journalist friend from his
Nevada days, William H. Wright ("Dan De Quille"), was the one to
write such a book. Learning within days that the far-off Wright had
independently come up with exactly the same idea, down to the
most minute detail, Mark Twain concluded not only that their
minds had been in "close and crystal-clear communication with
each other across three thousand miles of mountain and desert"
but also that Wright's later explanation showed that "his mind had
done the originating and telegraphing and mine the receiving."
The ultimate significance: "Consider for a moment how many a
splendid 'original' idea has been unconsciously stolen from a man
three thousand miles away!" (*DE*, 22: 116–19).

If the effect of this "unintentional and unwitting mental telegraphy" is to make permanently uncertain one's "right and title"
to ideas, at least, Mark Twain says, it accounts for "newspaper
wars over poems whose authorship was claimed by two or three
different people at the same time," as well as for discoveries made
simultaneously by different scientists. And at the very least, we
might add, the spectacle that Mark Twain conjures of "in-
ventors . . . constantly and unwittingly stealing each other's

ideas" redeems the writer, too, from any personal criminal complicity in producing his "own" writing. As he confesses at the end of the long 1898 letter to Sir John Adams, "I have one consolation . . . [my mind] is getting its scheme *from the outside* and therefore not personally blameable for its crazy work."[26]

Clemens's "plea for pardon," as Bernard De Voto called this theme, repeated in many forms in the group of unfinished manuscripts De Voto named the "Symbols of Despair," certainly issues, as De Voto says, and as Kaplan, among others, has reiterated, from "the terrible force of an inner cry: Do not blame me, for it was not my fault."[27] But all the publicity surrounding the new psychology of the unconscious meant even more: a broad-ranging debate, carried out at various sites of cultural discourse, reassessed the epistemology of individual responsibility and personal guilt. For Mark Twain this represented public corroboration and elaboration of the personal terms in which he had repeatedly conceived of his dilemma as a popular American writer driven partially against his will by his own brand of literary success. Such a writer may well never know, as the SPR's inconclusive experiments with the highly regarded medium Mrs. Piper demonstrated, whether he is plagiarist, charlatan, criminal, or savior—or all of these, as is Satan/44 in *The Mysterious Stranger*.

Before Mark Twain began writing the series of manuscripts with the mysterious artist-stranger at its center, he pursued what he called "the comedy-side of hypnotism" through the theme of the deluded inventor in *The American Claimant* (1892).[28] Based on the unsuccessful play "Colonel Sellers as a Scientist," written with Howells in 1883, *The American Claimant* creates a double variant on those scientist/poets in "Mental Telegraphy" who naively claim "right and title" to their own creations. The multifaceted claimant of the novel's title, Colonel Mulberry Sellers ("Attorney at Law and Claim Agent" reads one sign at his door) first appeared as the prototypical American land speculator/promoter in *The Gilded Age* (1873) and is here the same "visionary" staking his claim in a get-rich-quick scheme suitable to the 1890s: "a Materializer, a Hypnotizer, a Mind-Cure dabbler, and so on," the Colonel plans to make a fortune by materializing the dead and selling them as a cheap labor supply ("spirits won't eat, they won't drink—don't need those things"). Defending his brand of spirit-materialization as "scientific," Sellers derides the thing as practiced by ignorant charlatans . . . where there's a dim light and a dark cabinet, and a parcel of sentimental gulls gathered together, . . . and one and the same fatty degeneration of protoplasm and humbug comes out and materializes himself into anybody you want, . . . Witch of Endor, John Milton, Siamese Twins. . . . But when a man that is competent brings the vast powers of *science* to bear, it's a different matter.[29]

The self-proclaimed scientist with an eye to commercial value also lays claim to a title of an aristocratic kind: rightful heir to the earldom of Rossmore, an inheritance that Sellers, like Clemens's distant cousin James Lampton, believes has been usurped by the English branch of the family. Clemens's fascination with "the Claimant market," as the present old Earl of Rossmore derides it, goes back not only to the Tichborne claimant's trial of 1873, but also to family stories of the "great tribe of American Lambtons" (English spelling) and their prolonged legal efforts to reclaim their rights to the title and estates of the earldom of Durham. It was a family dream that Clemens gently mocked in his mother but which he himself drew on, at least for literary capital, to the extent of reporting in "Mental Telegraphy" how Livy once anticipated, without his telling her, the outcome of one of his own private fantasies—that on his deathbed someone should rush in with a document and announce that all the heirs are dead and he is the Earl of Durham.[30]

Although such dreams of the aristocratic heritage, wrongfully withheld but finally restored, are again and again satirized in Mark Twain's fiction, he identified himself with Sellers's inexhaustible capacity for dreaming, his comic refusal to allow "mere" reality in any way to impinge upon his imagination. So convinced is Sellers of his right to the earldom, for instance, that he names his "rickety old house" "Rossmore Towers" and takes the parlor portraits of famous dead Americans for various Rossmore ancestors (Andrew Jackson "does duty" as "Simon Lathers, Lord Rossmore, Present Earl"). The comically incongruous world of Sellers's imagining, depicted in indulgent detail by Mark Twain, extends even, temporarily, to the "double personality" of his daughter:

> All day long in the privacy of her work-room Sally Sellers earned bread for the Sellers family, and all the evening Lady Gwendolyn Sellers supported the Rossmore dignity. All day she was American, practically, and proud of the work of her head and hands and its commercial result; all the evening she

took holiday and dwelt in a rich shadowland peopled with titled and coroneted fictions. (*DE*, 15:49–50)

Before long the double lives of the entire Sellers-Rossmore family are disrupted by a double mistaken-identity plot turning on the kind of absurd complications that Twain, like Sellers, loved to create. Intending to materialize the departed spirit of a dead bank robber and turn him in for a reward, Sellers mistakenly identifies as his "materializee" the Viscount Berkeley, son and heir to the earl of Rossmore, come to America disguised as a "struggling artist" in order to investigate the rights of the American claimants to his father's earldom as well as to see in action the democratic institutions he admires. Sellers remains unfazed by this surprising "spirit" ("this materialization is a grander and nobler science than we have dreamed of") until his daughter falls in love with "it": "Happy with a spectre . . . Oh, poor deluded child! . . . Come away from it! It isn't a man!" In the midst of so much comic delusion and pretension, Sally Sellers resolves to accept her role as American democrat, vowing to banish her father's aristocratic "dreams, visions, imaginings" and be herself—"my genuine self," "clear and clean of sham and folly and fraud." In Mark Twain's eyes, we might add, such a self is both dream and delusion. Even as the novel ends with a wedding at the Towers and the two families about to embark on a trip to England, the Colonel is absent, absorbed in the process of rebounding from the failure of his materialization scheme. He has invented "a grand new idea," "like all of my most notable discoveries and inventions, . . . based upon hard, practical scientific laws": regulating the earth's climates and furnishing them to order through control of sunspots. Like the boastful teller of an astronomical tall tale, reminding us of another "scientific" showman, the Yankee, who predicts an eclipse, the Colonel instructs the others to watch for a message from him: "I will waft a vast sun-spot across the disk, and you will say 'Mulberry Sellers throws us a kiss across the universe'" (*DE*, 15: 172, 208, 247–49).

The American Claimant unites several of Mark Twain's most persistent versions of double or duplicitous identity—dreamers, claimants, confidence men, unprovable rights to titles, lovers mistaken for someone they are not—with the theme of the inventor-artist deluded by his own imagining of mastery over modern technology. In Sellers, Mark Twain created a comic image of a figure that had long both attracted and betrayed him: the poet "whose

sublime creations are written in steel," "the Shakespeare of mechanical invention."[31] Although these phrases, written in 1890,
refer specifically to James W. Paige, whose typesetting machine
was by then well on its way to bankrupting Clemens (himself a
fatally irrepressible Sellersian "visionary" in matters of patents
and investments), other Shakespeares of mechanical invention
work their technologized magic—black and white, fraudulent and
genuine—throughout Twain's writing. Horace Bixby, master pilot
of "Old Times on the Mississippi" (1875), initiates his cub into the
science of piloting, enabling him to read the authentic language of
the river but lose its dreamy poetry; Simon Wheeler, amateur detective, badly bungles the science of deduction in an 1877 play, but
still upstages three professional detectives in the end; the Duke
and the King "work" a number of "lines" in *Huckleberry Finn*
(1885), among them jour printing, mesmerism and phrenology,
and "layin on o'hands—for cancer, and paralysis, and sich things";
the Yankee, of course, for whom the inventor is, "after God," the
creator of this world and, all unawares, by the end of the 1889
novel, its destroyer as well; Pudd'nhead Wilson, whose "scientifics" of fingerprinting can expose but not alter the illogic of
slavery; and finally, as we will see, the composite of all these
figures, the character at the center of the three versions of *The
Mysterious Stranger* (1897–1908), variously named Philip Traum,
(Young) Satan, and No. 44.

Behind all of these artist-inventors lies the shadow cast by the
irreverent impostor, with the *nom de plume* Mark Twain, whom
Clemens represented himself to be in "The Whittier Birthday Dinner Speech" (1877). His ambiguous portraits of the artist as nineteenth-century con man take their place in the "hazy penumbra"
that William James recognized, "where lying and delusion meet"
and "where the term 'scoundrel' does not clear up everything to
the depths as it did for our forefathers" (*WJ on PR*, 321).

IV

James's hazy penumbra also refers, of course, to the grey territory
occupied by the various "mental sciences" of Clemens's day.
Plagued by numerous ailments throughout their lives, the whole
Clemens family experimented with a representative sample of
contemporary health fads and faddists, from the mind-healer who
cured the adolescent Olivia Langdon of a mysterious paralysis, to
Clemens's brief flings in the 1890s with Plasmon (a patented high-

protein powder which, he assured William James among others, would cure all ills, physiological and financial) and with osteopathy (a Swedish body-manipulation therapy which the family particularly hoped would help their youngest daughter Jean's epilepsy).[32] As enthusiastic an endorser of these cures as he was a scoffer ("Damn all the other cures, including the baths and Christian Science," he wrote in a letter from Kellgren's clinic at Sanna, Sweden, "*this* is the satisfactory one!"),[33] Clemens accepted the general principle of mind cure, so long as it could be associated with a new experimental science rather than a charismatic (female) founder of a popular religious movement like Mary Baker Eddy's Christian Science. "Hypnotism & mind-cure are the same thing; no difference between them," Clemens wrote to Livy in January 1894 while he was in New York, she in Paris. After hearing how Elinor Howells's recent experience with a mind-healer had even "converted" her husband, "the scoffer," Clemens admitted:

> She convinced *me*, before she got through, that she and William James are right—hypnotism and mind-cure are the same thing . . . Very well; the very source, the very *centre* of hypnotism is *Paris*. Dr. Charcot's pupils & disciples are right there & ready to your hand without fetching poor dear old Susy across the stormy sea . . . *Do*, do it, honey . . . dang'd if I don't think I'll cable you to try hypnotism for Susy.[34]

But the equation of hypnotism with mind cure begs the question of the source of authority for these treatments, one representing itself as a cure to be taken on faith, the other an experimental method empirically tested in controlled conditions. Two years later, during the 1895–96 lecture tour, the anxious father was appealing to both belief and science, congratulating his daughter on being "a convert to that rational and noble philosophy," "your mental science." ("I always believed, in Paris, that if you could only get back to America and examine that system with your clear intellect you would see its truth and be saved.")[35] Susy's death in August 1896, six months after that letter was written, initiated a period of most intense bereavement in London the following winter, during which Clemens himself, in hopes of seeing some "truth," "examined" a number of psychic and psychological "systems." He and Livy consulted a pair of mediums recommended by F. W. H. Myers and one of his associates in the SPR, but later in a 1901 letter he recalled one medium as a "transparent fraud," the other as an "innocent, well-meaning, driveling vacancy," and said of the séances that he had never had an experience which moved him to believe the living could communicate with the dead. Still, he concluded, he and Livy would continue to "experiment in the matter when opportunity offered."[36]

If, as the letter continues, further experimentation with mediums—one Missouri hypnotist and her "best subject," for example, were to sustain "strictly scientific tests before professors at Columbia University"—proved unpromising, and if even Mr. Myers ("President of the London Psychical Research Society," "a spiritualist" and "I am afraid . . . a very easily convinced man") admitted that Mrs. Piper had been discredited, still the evidence of Clemens's reading that fall and winter demonstrates his continued "intellectual examination" of psychological theories. Among particular works he mentions are "Prof. Wm. James's psychological book" (Principles of Psychology) and Phantasms of the Living (an 1886 study of cases of telepathy written jointly by Myers, Edmund Gurney, and Frank Podmore, all active in the SPR).[37] Of the latter Clemens comments in his notebook around Christmas 1896: "Been reading Apparitions [sic] of the Living—Gladstone suddenly appears—is solid—talks and disappears. Emperor William, Barnum, P. of Wales, & c."[38] Such apparitions, we know, are invariably satirized in Mark Twain's fiction; even Colonel Sellers mocks them, and of the villagers at Oliver Hotchkiss's séance in the "Schoolhouse Hill" version of The Mysterious Stranger, only an enthusiastic spiritualist like Hotchkiss can welcome the "poor things" and "remarkable English" of the spirits of Lord Byron, Napoleon, Shakespeare, and a throng of Roman statesmen and generals" (MS, 206–7).

But Phantasms attempts more than a simple compendium of cases of materializations and dematerializations; Myers's introduction sets forth what would become for Mark Twain a potent theory of the paradoxical value of the mesmeric or hypnotic trance: "We have found a mode of shifting the threshold of consciousness which is a dislocation as violent as madness, a submergence as pervasive as sleep, and yet is waking sanity."[39] In Twain's experimental tales of the 1890s and after, Myers's oft-repeated central concepts of threshold of consciousness, madness, sleep, and waking sanity found, if not complete acceptance, an extended literary testing ground.

Spiritualism and related psychic experimentation drew in Mark Twain (and many others), as most critics have recognized, on the one hand as a satiric sceptic, on the other as a would-be believer

vulnerable in illness and bereavement. But more significant for
Twain than these two irreconcilable poles (much like those James
excoriated as naive alternatives between "spirits" and "bosh") is
the attraction exerted by the questionable status itself of psychical
and psychological research. Perceived at the time as a genuine
border area of knowledge, displaying all the chaos of a developing
discipline, the study of the unconscious proceeded, as we have
seen, by generating open discussion of experimental and evidentiary standards, as well as debate over its own claim to the status of a
science. Moreover, the central experimental technique of hypnosis demonstrated that it was often impossible to decide whether
trance phenomena were fraudulent or genuine, or if genuine,
whether evidence of pathology, normalcy, or genius. For Mark
Twain, such a developing field, self-conscious about its still-open
borders, represented a new frontier of knowledge and the liberating
possibility of lighting out for the unfamiliar territory of the
unconscious.

Throughout the 1890s dream writings, Twain cultivated this new
terrain, experimenting with his own literary versions of what were
termed "psychic excursions." The "comedy-side" of the possibility of "out-of-body" experiences is entertained not only as we
have seen in *The American Claimant*, but also in *The Mysterious
Stranger* as well as in detailed plans for a play to be called
"Shackleford's Ghost," all late works that associate disembodied
spirits with Twain's favorite comic, legal, and sexual conundrums.
Though never written, "Shackleford's Ghost" (dated by Paine in
the 1890s) contains *in ovo* the essential obsessions with fraudulence, mistaken criminality, sexual duplicity, and the problem of
legal proof that we have seen informing Twain's interests in psychical and psychological research.

A rich man invents a formula to make people invisible, successfully tries it on a young stranger, and then himself disappears. No
will is found, and an innocent man is accused of his supposed
murder. A séance is held during which the invisible young man
("I.M.") impersonates the spirits of "Webster, Byron, Shakespeare
&c," writes "foolish things on the slate," then writes a will ("a
complex and contradictory one"), and "makes love [on another
slate] privately to the prettiest girl—the principal legatee—
daughter of the disappeared man." The notes end, as so many
Twain fantasies do, with the "lynch-court trial" and conviction of
the accused murderer, the sensational disembodied voice of the

I.M. coming to the rescue, and finally his becoming visible again through the office of the rich inventor, who gives his daughter to the I.M.[40]

Variants on this sexual/legal spiritualist comedy of errors reappear, we remember, in *The American Claimant*, where Colonel Sellers mistakenly believes his daughter is to marry a "materializee" who is, of course, the rightful legal heir to the title mistakenly claimed by the Colonel. Even more explicitly than *The American Claimant*, *The Mysterious Stranger* speaks to the contemporary climate of psychical research, specifically to the sexual and legal complications—the possibility of immoral acts and crimes—popularly supposed to be a danger of the hypnotic or mediumistic trance.[41] The (usually) female subject's possession trance was understood to be a state of somnambulism so deep that the words delivered were supposedly not her own, but those of her spirit control or amanuensis. According to Laurence Moore's study of spiritualism in American culture, one American medium even tried (unsuccessfully) to plead irresponsibility as a legal defense against charges of fraud. There were also famous cases of nineteenth-century spirits reportedly ordering American wives to divorce their husbands, as well as rumors of promiscuity linked to mediumistic practices. In 1859, for example, Benjamin F. Hatch, the first husband of the well-known medium V. Cora Hatch, published an exposé, *Spiritualists' Iniquities, Unmasked, and the Hatch Divorce Case*, charging that one male spiritualist left his wife to travel with his lover, who "bore him what they call a spiritualist baby," and another harbored a wife "in every Spiritualist port."[42]

In two of the versions of *The Mysterious Stranger*, Mark Twain imported the aura of sexualized manipulation between male hypnotist and female subject. Both Young Satan in the "Eseldorf" manuscript and what are called the "Duplicates" or "Dream Selves" in "No.44, The Mysterious Stranger" exert a strange, hypnotic hold over the female characters in the two stories. Satan's creative powers (displayed in his mesmerizing music and gorgeous embroidered pictures) so infatuate the village maidens of Eseldorf that their human lovers become jealous of this apparently nonfleshly rival. In "No.44" the narrator, August Feldner, falls in love with a girl (alternately named, in her different states of being, Marget and Lisbet) who, we are told, cares nothing for him in his "flesh-and-blood personality" (his "Waking-Self"), but his "presence as a spirit acted upon her hypnotically—as 44 termed it—and plunged her into the somnambulic sleep . . . Steeped in the hypnotic sleep, I was the idol of her heart" (*MS*, 342). The result is that August becomes jealous of himself, or rather of his Dream-Self's embodiment ("this odious Dream-stuff") and a comic rivalry ensues. It is a spiritualized and sexualized version of the Siamese twins' predicament: "I could have only half of her; the other half, no less dear to me, must remain the possession of another. She was mine, she was his, turn-about" (*MS*, 344). The solution to "this fiendish complication": to attempt a marriage "by suggestion," carrying overtones of the contemporary rumors of "spirit-marriages" performed during séances:

> By "suggestion," as 44 had told me, you make the hypnotised subject see and do and feel whatever you please: see people and things that are not there, . . . carry out all suggested acts—and forget the whole of it when he wakes, and remember the whole of it again whenever the hypnotic sleep returns!
>
> In obedience to suggestion, Lisbet clothed herself as a bride; by suggestion she made obeisance to imaginary altar and priest. (*MS*, 349)

Such absolute obedience to another's will, it was perceived, could as readily promote crime as seduction, both committed without any clear legal indication of individual responsibility. A set of working notes for "No.44" indicates Mark Twain's (unused) plans to involve the Duplicates in just such a spectral murder case that ends as unsatisfactorily as most of his trials:

> GHOST-NIGHT—castle full of spectres & wandering lights. Distant groans & cries—flight & pursuit, noiseless.
>
> The murderer is I *or* my Duplicate, they can't tell which; I confess I did it but I won't *tell* which. The indulgence names the Duplicate & 44 claims to be he & that a duplicate is not human & not amenable to law. Court is uncertain. (*MS*, Appendix B, 460)

Pursuing the "comedy-side of hypnotism," as Mark Twain called it during these later years, thus clearly spoke to his longstanding involvement with the rhetoric of legal and sexual responsibility. More broadly, as well, the whole study of the unconscious, whether associated with the techniques of hypnosis or dream analysis or the "talking cure," provided Mark Twain with a new focus for questions of authorial creativity and new ways to formulate the protean figure of the artist/inventor/scientist/poet. We have already seen how his writing during the nineties became increasingly self-absorbed, focusing on the twin issues of his own creativity and its seeming control over him. His letters after Susy's death, we remember, reflected the bereaved father's guilt over the artist in him, whose creative powers continued to function, virtually in spite of himself. And the fiction written during this difficult period, we know, also spills over with ambiguous representations of the artist, most of which present him as ultimately compromised by his art and barely in control of his own creative powers.

These figures represent Twain's anxieties, the hostility and guilt associated with his literary craft, but they do not acknowledge the desire whose repression originated the guilt: a deep attraction to authorial power. Not until the writing of *The Mysterious Stranger* did an avowedly all-powerful creator—that is, a figure totally opposite to the amanuensis or plagiarist or proprietor or midwife Twain represented himself to be as an author—finally emerge in the composite "mysterious stranger" figure of all three versions who bodies forth the artistic imagination.

The three versions are not, however, equally central to the issues I have been discussing. The most explicit embodiment of the creative unconscious occurs in the last version of the tale (the "Print Shop" manuscript), the only one for which the title "Mysterious Stranger" is used and the only one in which the identity of the strange protagonist remains a genuine mystery. In all three a youthful figure arrives in an isolated village (the Austrian Eseldorf of 1702 in the earliest version, "Chronicle of Young Satan;" nineteenth-century Petersburg in the "Schoolhouse Hill" fragment; and in the latest version, "No.44," another Austrian setting, this one a printshop in 1490) and spends his time entertaining and instructing a group of boys who become his comrades. Of the three young strangers only the last (full name No.44, Series 864,962) gives no indication of his origins, whether human or superhuman. In contrast, Satan in the "Eseldorf" version announces himself as the nephew of the fallen angel and consistently occupies the perspective of a divinely omniscient commentator on human nature. And although the magical boy of "Schoolhouse Hill" calls himself 44, he too reveals his angelic identity as Satan's son, born before Adam's fall.

"No.44, The Mysterious Stranger" also singles itself out as the only one of the three manuscripts with a conclusion written expressly for it, the celebrated dream ending, in which 44 reveals

himself as the dream-self of the boy narrator, August. It is important to acknowledge, though, that this ending also clearly works
successfully to conclude the "Eseldorf" manuscript, as demonstrated by the bowdlerized Paine-Duneka edition, published in
1916 and still preferred by some readers. It *is* true, as James Cox
maintains, that the dream ending, written in 1904 for "No.44,"
"turned out to be an Eseldorf ending after all," or as 44 tells August, "the dream-marks are all present," including Eseldorf's
dreamy beginning (*MS*, 405).[43] But despite this overlap, most readers would agree that the whole dream structure—not just the
"dream-marks"—is most fully realized in the last version. So, too,
does the whole contemporary psychical/psychological context
burst forth most dramatically in "No.44," although it is also visible in the other two manuscripts. For all of these reasons, the last
version deserves our special attention, most particularly as the
culmination of a long process of composition (1897–1908) that
coincided with a period of unusual cultural awareness of the concept of the unconscious. It is to that context, and *The Mysterious
Stranger*'s dialogue with it, that we now turn.

V

The bizarre tricks performed in all three manuscripts by Satan/44,
also known as Philip Traum ("traum" the German word for
dream)—mind reading, materialization of people and things from
other places and times, musical and dramatic impersonations—
may appear simply to be variants on Tom Sawyer's entertainments for the village boys. But in terms of the broader, nonliterary
context, these particular mental feats are drawn from a general set
of theories concerning the potential of human creativity, theories
tested by psychic researchers in their experiments in the unconscious. More than anyone else in the field, F. W. H. Myers was
credited with attempting to inventory, classify, and synthesize
these findings in a series of articles on the "subliminal self," originally written during the 1890s for the SPR's *Proceedings*, and then
collected and published posthumously in *Human Personality and
Its Survival of Bodily Death* (1903), a book in Mark Twain's library.[44] What William James and others recognized as Myers's
genius for collecting and classifying disparate data from wide-ranging sources makes his work into a virtual bibliography of contemporary research into such topics as hypnosis and hysteria.[45]

Drawing on both clinical cases (Charcot's, Janet's, Binet's,

Breuer and Freud's, among many others less well known today)
and experiments in psychic phenomena (most conducted or collected by the SPR), Myers's interpretation of the human personality rejected traditional criteria for defining an independent,
distinct, and unified personality. Hypnosis revealed instead,
Myers theorized, the "multiplex personality," consisting of what
he termed the "subliminal" and the "supraliminal," those parts of
the mind that lie below the "threshold" of normal waking consciousness and those which remain above it.[46] This vocabulary
was developed specifically to reject what Myers saw as the dis-
missive or misleading connotations of the more widely used terms
"unconscious" or "subconscious" or "secondary self," all of
which, he felt, accord implicit superiority to consciousness.[47]

Myers's theory of the subliminal self, then, took essential shape
by defining itself against the judgments of mainstream psychologists, while simultaneously depending on their results. An
inverted hierarchy reversing the orthodox primacy of consciousness over unconscious becomes a central image for Myers, as we
will see it also does for Mark Twain. A well-known passage outlin-
ing his basic theory reveals how much Myers owed to his defensive
relationship to orthodox psychology. It begins in the negative,
suggesting that "the stream of consciousness in which we habitu-
ally live is not the only consciousness which exists in connection
with our organism":

> Our habitual or empirical consciousness may consist of a
> mere selection from a multitude of thoughts and sensations,
> of which some at least are equally conscious with those that
> we empirically know. I accord no primacy to my ordinary
> waking self, except that among my potential selves this one
> has shown itself the fittest to meet the needs of common life.
> I hold that it has established no further claim, and that it is
> perfectly possible that other thoughts, feelings, and memo-
> ries, either isolated or in continuous connection, may now be
> actively conscious, as we say, "within me,"—in some kind of
> coordination with my organism, and forming some part of
> my total individuality.[48]

These other thoughts, feelings, and memories constitute the subliminal self, for Myers a region of the mind associated with the
frequent incoherence of dreams and the bizarre phenomena seen in
hysteria, hypnosis, and somnambulism. But, Myers insists, the
subliminal is simultaneously the province of heightened "supernormal" faculties, both imaginative and ratiocinative, superior to

those of the empirical consciousness and even responsible for the inspirations of genius ("subliminal uprushes," as Myers calls them).

The triumph of Myers's theory of the subliminal self is thus to view the "spectrum of consciousness" as "infinitely extended at both ends," that is, to incorporate the so-called abnormal and pathological as fundamental parts of the "normal" mental constitution.[49] In this central tenet Myers departed from most contemporary psychologists (Pierre Janet his most frequently cited example), who viewed unconscious phenomena either as degenerative and aberrant splinters of the primary personality, or as freakish, rare, idiosyncratic. Even William James, who regarded Myers's *Human Personality* as one of the great radical texts of modern psychology, and who praised the theory of the subliminal self as a "momentous event in the history of our science," likewise lauded Myers for breaking with the "dogmatically negative treatment" generally accorded "multiple modifications of personality," and yet feared that Myers had gone too far in his "belief in the ubiquity and great extent of the subliminal."[50] James's reluctant criticism implicitly reiterates the special suspicion displayed by the psychological community toward claims for unconscious "supernormal" or "transcendent" abilities.

Even theories linking the creativity of genius to the unconscious went against the temper of the times. Thus when Myers defines an "inspiration of Genius" as a subliminal "uprush," underscoring, as Mark Twain does, the lack of willful control ("an emergence into the current of ideas which the man is consciously manipulating of other ideas which he has not consciously originated, but which have shaped themselves beyond his will"), he immediately follows with an address to his scientific audience's potential objections: "I shall urge that there is here no real departure from normality; no abnormality, at least in the sense of degeneration." Having thus at least acknowledged the orthodox view, Myers finally asserts, still, however, using a scientific metaphor, the transcendence of the subliminal: it is "a fulfillment of the true norm of man, with suggestions, it may be, of something *supernormal*—of something which transcends existing normality as an advanced stage of evolutionary progress transcends an earlier stage."[51]

Mark Twain's understanding of the unconscious—what he conceptualized as a dream-self—took shape in the same environment as Myers's and was in fact conceived as defensively as the subliminal self. Just as Myers insists that he accords no "primacy" to the ordinary waking-self, and indeed that sleep is "an independent phase of personality, existing with as good a right as the waking phase," so does Twain formulate his "multiplex personality" in "No.44, The Mysterious Stranger" by inverting the ordinary hierarchy of consciousness.[52] Like that of Myers, Twain's theory of double personality accords no primacy to the waking-self. As 44 explains to August: "One is your Workaday-Self and 'tends to business, the other is your Dream Self . . . It has far more imagination than has the Workaday-Self, therefore its pains and pleasures are far more real and intense than are those of the other self" (MS, 315). Before long August learns that this two-part self actually expands into a triadic theory of personality, the Waking-Self, the Dream-Self (or Duplicate, August also calls it), and the Soul. This last is the "immortal spirit," as powerfully endowed as Myers's subliminal self: "Freed from the encumbering flesh, it was able to exhibit forces, passions and emotions of a quite tremendously effective character." The Duplicate, too, though farcically incarnated in the story as August's love-rival Emil Schwarz, dominates over August, his "inferior self." "I was always courteous to my Duplicate," August tells us, "but I avoided him . . . , for he was my superior."

> My imagination compared with his splendid dream-equipment was as a lightning-bug to the lightning; . . . in the arts and graces of beguilement and persuasion I was a pauper and he a Croesus; in passion, feeling, emotion, sensation—whether of pain or pleasure—I was phosphorus, he was fire. In a word he had all the intensities one suffers or enjoys in a dream! (MS, 343–44)

More telling even, in terms of the contemporary psychological climate, than this inverted conception of the supernormal powers of the unconscious is the fact that of all the *Mysterious Stranger* manuscripts, only "No.44" does not project those powers onto a superhuman, transcendent figure, but instead, like Myers, incorporates them into the human personality. Not until the 1904 dream ending is 44, himself in command of tremendous creative powers, finally revealed as part of the narrator's psyche, his dream-self. It took Mark Twain four versions, which survive in three manuscript drafts, written over ten years, before he could do so. In the first two versions, most of 44's mental powers are attributed to the angelic youth, member of Satan's family (in "Chronicle" his nephew, in "Schoolhouse" his son), whose "supernormal" abilities are indeed just that. "Man's mind clumsily and tediously and laboriously patches little trivialities together," mocks Satan. "My mind *creates!* . . . Creates anything it desires—and in a moment . . . I *think* the whole thing,—and in a moment it is before you—created. I *think* a poem,—music—the record of a game of chess—anything—and it is there" (*MS*, 114). Such divine creation *ex nihilo* ("out of the airy nothing which is called Thought") can readily turn to destruction (the miniature castle that Satan creates and destroys, for example), thus appearing as pathological and freakish to Twain's human characters, burdened with the Moral Sense, as the sometimes self-destructive phenomenon of hysteria seemed to contemporary psychologists. What sets "No.44" apart from the two earlier, related versions, then, is that it celebrates the creative unconscious, as Myers does, by incorporating it into the ordinary human psyche.

Nearly all of the disparate psychic phenomena collected and classified by Myers in *Human Personality*—unconscious cerebration, thought transference, clairvoyance, dreams, hallucinations, apparitions of the dying, medium-trances, demoniacal possession, inspirations of genius, even ghosts—are replicated in some form in the *Mysterious Stranger* manuscripts. Satan of "Chronicle" reads minds, carries four games of chess in his memory a week, plays an old spinet so that it produces "marvelous pictures painted in music," and makes the whole history of the world "live before you when he told about them" (*MS*, 53, 93, 105, 50). The even younger 44 (or Quarante-Quatre, as he calls himself) of "Schoolhouse Hill" astounds the schoolchildren of Petersburg by learning English in an instant and shocks their elders by materializing himself at a séance and then hypnotizing most of those present (who wander "somnambulistically away") so that the next morning they will think it was all a dream.

No.44 of the latest manuscript is even more exuberantly playful and childlike than either of his surrogates, reminding us first of Twain's penchant throughout his writing career for boyish play.[53] But in addition, through his numerous masquerades and impersonations and the multiple languages he speaks, 44 reflects the tendency, identified by psychic researchers, for mediumistic performances to exhibit a rather childish, dramatic flair. In "Final Impressions of a Psychic Researcher," for example, William James asserts that the medium's "will to personate" raises "questions about our subconscious constitution and its curious tendency to humbug," tentatively concluding that far from being uncommon, "every sort of person is liable to it, or to something equivalent to it":

> And whoever encourages it in himself finds himself personating someone else, either signing what he writes by fictitious name, or spelling out . . . messages from the departed. Our subconscious region seems, as a rule, to be dominated either by a crazy "will to make-believe," or by some curious external force impelling us to personation. (WJ on PR, 317, 322)

Once Mark Twain lambasted the "curious tendency to humbug," which he, like James, found to be a common trait in the damned human race. "No.44," however, takes a more affirmative view of the "will to personate" by celebrating the fictive impulse of 44's imagination—an imagination, we remember, that first appears "supernormal," but is ultimately revealed to be coextensive with the human mind. With something akin to what Myers calls "subliminal inventiveness," 44 entertains narrator and reader with dramatic performances ranging from impersonations (as an aged peasant and a magician doing a disappearing act just as he is about to be burnt at the stake as a heretic), to musical and dance performances with instruments (a jew's harp) and songs ("Buffalo Gals" and "Swanee River") that come from the American South of the future, to the "best effect" ("it beat Barnum and Bailey hands down"), a kind of ultimate séance, the Assembly of the Dead, a procession of skeletons that turns time backwards. And in a different kind of comically literalized version of the medium's communication with other worlds, 44 even imports delicacies from the future: corn pone, fried chicken, and milk-and-flour gravy. Unlike Satan's bloody and essentially joyless visions of human frailty in "Chronicle," we are clearly meant to enjoy this "frivolous" and "feather-headed" boy, apparently compulsively given to the "most extravagant and stirring and heathen performances" (MS, 326, 299).

In accordance with what Twain calls the "innate frivolities of his nature," 44 exhibits the "crazy 'will to make-believe'" that James associates with the subconscious. Not only does he do a wild dance to the jew's harp and put on an incredible minstrel show with himself (as Bones) in traditional blackface singing a sort of "bastard English" (black slave dialect), but also he dresses in splendor more fit for a queen than a king, as August points out, and carries himself "like a princeling 'doing a cake-walk'" (MS, 299,

354–56, 303). In addition to this ostentatious theatricality, which we know also marks Twain's own creative impulses, 44 exhibits a facility for languages, real and invented, that matches the celebrated linguistic range (French, Italian, Martian) of Flournoy's medium Hélène Smith. He speaks to all animals, as well as to humans of the future, in their own tongues. A maidservant turned into a cat by 44's potent transforming magic, for example, is taught to do poetry recitations in "catapult, or cataplasm, or whatever one might call that tongue" (MS, 362). Whether all this comic absurdity—what the narrator calls "coarse and vulgar horseplay"— explicitly parodies spiritualist exploits, Twain's portrait of 44, a feather-headed boy with transcendent powers, reiterates the paradox that made James and others uncomfortable with Myers's conception of the subliminal: it is "so impartially the home both of evolutive and dissolutive phenomena." By this James means that "the fictitious personages of mediumship" reside in the subliminal—as in 44, Twain's "dream-sprite"—"side by side with the inspirations of genius, with the faculties of telepathy and telesthesia."[54]

A similar paradox had always tormented Mark Twain's relationship to his own creativity, whose expressions, epitomized by "The Whittier Birthday Dinner Speech," seemed inextricably bound to both evolutive and dissolutive impulses and consequences. With 44 and other late embodiments of the dream-self, Twain brought himself ever closer to the sources of that paradox, and closer, too, to embracing it as a necessary, empowering condition of his art. In "No.44" he expands speculative distinctions between dream and waking consciousness, first sketched out in 1898, into an elaborately farcical plot involving invisible Duplicates, or Dream Selves, created by 44 to break a strike at the printshop. The ensuing comedy, in which the Duplicates become visible and wreak sexual havoc by making love to the female Originals, seems disjoint and, as some have argued, appears to take place in a dramatic vacuum.[55] But we know from Pudd'nhead Wilson and other works that such disjuncture is often critical to releasing, and also to masking, Mark Twain's complex writing process. The Duplicates harken back not only to Colonel Sellers's materializees, but more tellingly to the Siamese twins: "Duplicates" is the term Twain coined, we recall, for the uncanny pair in Those Extraordinary Twins. Like them, these "Duplicates did not need to eat or drink or sleep, so long as the Originals did those things," but the trouble comes when an Original drinks and his Duplicate gets "the other half of the dividend," and is just "as insufficently drunk" as he is (*MS*, 316, 307).[56] Like the Siamese twins, the Duplicates comically undercut individuality. They are such "exact reproductions" of their Originals that "there's never any telling, in this bewitched place, whether you are talking to a person himself, or only to his heathen image." Indeed, "a mirror couldn't have told them apart" (*MS*, 373, 305).

Extending this characteristic expression of uncertainty, Twain has 44 explain the ambiguous ontological status of these apparently solid creatures made of "only fictitious flesh and bone." In language reminiscent of the literary Caesarean section performed by the author in producing *Pudd'nhead Wilson*, 44 says he "pulled them out of the Originals and gave them this independent life" (*MS*, 315). And again like Twain's perception of the alien, uncontrollable quality of his own fictional creations, the Duplicates and Originals are strangers to one another. "Whenever one of us was awake," August says of his fleshed Duplicate, "and in command of our common brain and nerves the other was of necessity asleep and unconscious, . . . never encountering each other save for a dim and hazy and sleepy half-moment on the threshold." He then proceeds equivocally to acknowledge his relationship to this strange self, much as Twain's genealogical preface literally joins, in one volume, *Those Extraordinary Twins* to *Pudd'nhead Wilson*, while ostensibly rejecting their kinship:

> Although we had been born together, at the same moment and of the same womb, there was no spiritual kinship between us; spiritually we were a couple of distinctly independent and unrelated individuals, with equal rights in a common fleshly property . . . My fleshed Duplicate did not even bear my name, but called himself Emil Schwarz. (*MS*, 343)

If this odd couple reminds us not only of the Siamese twins and of Twain's twin novels but also of his dream-self named Watson, the difference is in "No.44" 's far more extended meditation on doubling and identity than in any of these related writings. Here the relationship between the two identical selves rises above the farcical fraternal squabbling of the earlier figures toward a moving reconciliation, a sense of self-acceptance. As the "odious Dreamstuff" becomes "my brother," the stranger within is embraced.

In one of the last-written sections of the manuscript,[57] following a scene of jealous competition between August and Emil

Schwarz, the former attempts to give a psychological and philosophical account of the decentering he experiences in the en-
counter with his own mirror image. Seeing himself in a doorway
("that is to say, I saw Emil Schwarz, my Duplicate") moves August
to extended self-analysis:

> I had been used to supposing that the person I saw in the
> mirror was the person others saw when they looked at me—
> whereas that was not the case . . . In the figure standing by
> the door I was now seeing myself as others saw me, but the
> resemblance to the self which I was familiar with in the glass
> was *merely* a resemblance, nothing more; not approaching
> the common resemblance of brother to brother, but reaching
> only as far as the resemblance which a person usually bears to
> his brother-in-law. Often one does not notice that, at all,
> until it is pointed out; and sometimes, even then, the re-
> semblance owes as much to imagination as to fact . . . Well,
> there he stood, . . . and he hardly even reached the brother-in-
> law standard. I realized that I had never really seen this youth
> before . . . Well, there he was; that is to say, there *I* was. And I
> was interested; interested at last. (MS, 364–65)

This interior monologue apparently prefigures the dream ending,
where the "self" is revealed to be a fiction, a mere semblance
owing as much to imagination as to fact. At the same time, though,
August's speech departs from the conclusion in that his sensation
of self-doubt does not annihilate the self, but rather leads momentarily to a reconstruction of individualism—or at least a
resurgence of "interest" in the "I."

These are analogues of the two extreme perspectives between
which *The Mysterious Stranger* continually oscillates: to live trapped in a reality constituted by terrible contradictions (foremost
among them, a self that contains an alien other within, and a God
"who created man without invitation, then tries to shuffle the
responsibility for man's acts upon man"), or to escape by ex-
tinguishing that reality, transforming it into a fiction, "a grotesque
and foolish dream," as the conclusion states. But despite the dream
ending, and what so many have assumed of its solipsistic certainties, *The Mysterious Stranger* structurally resists coming to any
such resting place or any such stay against confusion. Instead the
narrative aims to decenter the reader, as the narrator is decentered,
by courting the confusion, which William James sees as inherent
to the exploration of all psychic phenomena, over whether fraud is
simulating reality or whether reality ("if any reality there be") has

the bad luck of being fated everywhere to simulate fraud (*WJ on PR*, 314).

At the point of August's reconciliation with his Duplicate, the moment when he hears him(self), as though in a dream, plea eloquently to be freed from the "bonds of flesh," from "this earthly life," the reader's own suspicions are clinched. Just as we've suspected, virtually from the beginning, the whole story of the mysterious stranger—his travels back and forth in time, his dramatic impersonations—turns out to be August's dream. The narrative is thus structured as an elaborate practical joke on the reader, who is meant to be partially in on the hoax, since, as 44 informs the necessarily dim August at the conclusion, "The dream-marks are all present—you should have recognized them earlier." "Strange!" he continues, "that you should not have suspected . . . that your universe and its contents were only dreams, visions, fictions! Strange, because they are so frankly and hysterically insane—like all dreams" (*MS*, 404).[58]

It is not in fact difficult to recognize the "dream-marks," various kinds of hints planted throughout the text that the characters and events apparently constituting this story are actually part of the narrator's dream, fictions within a fiction. Indeed, perhaps the most striking of these hints is the whole farcical plot involving the Duplicates, which is, as so many readers have noted, nothing if not "frankly and hysterically insane." From the very first chapter (the same one used in both "Chronicle" and "No.44"), set in an Austria "far from the world and asleep, . . . where news from the world hardly ever came to disturb its dream," the possibility of interpreting the story as a dream begins to take shape. Such an interpretation takes into account not only most of our boggled expectations, but also the illogical shifts in plot development, the displacements of individual characters and predicaments onto others, the repetitions and condensations, the skewed sense of place and time. The drowsy stillness of the opening, for example, returns eerily in the middle, when the invisible Duplicates of the printing crew do their work in the printshop amidst "the saddest, uncanniest silence, a sepulchral stillness" (*MS*, 282–83). This sense of solitude is, of course, not only a look back to the beginning but also an overdetermined prefiguring of the conclusion. Canceling out most of the frantic plot activity of the main body of the tale, the "soundless emptiness" of the printshop, filled with invisibles setting type and running the press, merges into the "empty eternities," the "shoreless space" of the conclusion in whose "limitless solitudes" August, "but a *Thought*," is left spectrally to wander (*MS*, 404–5).

The "dream-marks" are also present in the clues that a special relationship exists between the narrator and 44, anticipating the end when the latter reveals himself as the former's "dream, creature of your imagination." Between the two, as August frequently notes, there is almost never any need to say a word, so completely are their minds able, telepathically it seems, to communicate. And it is usually, but not always, August's mind that does the "receiving" and 44's that does the "originating and telegraphing," as, we remember, Twain says in "Mental Telegraphy." August's knowledge of printing, for example, communicated instantaneously and silently, enables 44 to pass a test put to him when he first arrives at the print shop, a stranger suspected of being an impostor or a jailbird, as his strange numerical name seems to the sceptical printers to suggest. Reversing the direction of this thought transference, 44 endows August with his ability to become invisible, so that long before the end, when August learns he is a "wandering and forlorn Thought," his occasional invisibility points toward that moment. At one point, for example, when 44 seems to have deserted him, August makes himself invisible and "floats upon the unrevealing air," "wandering here and there," "disconsolate," "aimless, comfortless, and forlorn," prefiguring the conclusion in which he is revealed to be "but a *Thought*—a vagrant Thought, a useless Thought, a homeless Thought, wandering forlorn among the empty eternities" (*MS*, 311, 405).

All of the "dream-marks" planted throughout the text have the intended effect of unsettling the reader, plunging us in a kind of narrative limbo where fictional conventions and categories jostle uneasily against one another. The juxtaposition of dream and reality, Originals and Duplicates, of melodrama, farce, and fantasy— all have a radically disjunctive impact, forcing the reader constantly to adjust to abrupt shifts in structural, thematic, and emotional terms. Along with the narrator, that is, we undergo a decentering experience that throws off balance any stable notions of the real, either literary or psychological or epistemological, and the individual's place in it. The tale's conclusion "in an empty and soundless world" circles back to the still solitude of the dreamy beginning, as it simultaneously reveals not only the solution to the mystery of 44's identity, but also the knowledge that we have had (or should have suspected) the solution all along. Structurally the tale is thus supposed to fold back on itself, as an earlier dream tale

Connecticut Yankee completes its circuit of time travel ("trans-position of epochs—and bodies") by ending at its beginning, the narrative frame, where the delirious Hank Morgan (our authority for "The Stranger's History" recording his stay in Camelot) is last heard raving about strange and awful dreams ("Dreams that were as real as reality—delirium, of course, but *so* real!"). *The Mysterious Stranger* ends similarly, inside the narrator's mind, in a self-enclosed mental world with no external referent and no reality apart from itself.

But just before the moment when all distinctions appear to have collapsed and the text is about to return to its dream origins, swallow its own tail, and self-destruct, history intrudes. A number of references to contemporary imperialist politics—a subject on which Mark Twain spoke and wrote frequently, and angrily, during these years—appear suddenly in a set of chapters actually written after the dream conclusion but which immediately precede it in the text itself. First, in a section written in 1905, 44 attacks Mary Baker Eddy and her "Christian Silence" as well as Imperial Russia's "prodigious war" (the Russo-Japanese War, which was coming to an end as Mark Twain wrote this section. And then, in the last bit written in 1908, 44's final effect: his "Assembly of the Dead," the procession of skeletons going backward in time, each labeled, "by the force of 44's magic," with name, date, and major accomplishments.[59]

This theatrical spectacle consisting of battles, blood, and the Missing Link, together with the contemporary references that precede it, remind us of a similar historical presence in the earlier manuscript, "Chronicle of Young Satan." Satan's theatrical "History of the Progress of the Human Race" from Cain and Abel to Queen Victoria tells the same sordid tale of public and private murder as 44's Assembly. Finally, near the end of "Chronicle," Twain's satiric impulses toward events occurring at the time he was writing again bring contemporary politics, rather incongruously, as in "No.44," into the medieval Austria of his text. Satan refers sardonically to various imperialist ventures of 1900, particularly to the struggle of the Chinese Boxers, and then, abruptly, the manuscript breaks off in the court of an Indian rajah, in the middle of a parable of British imperialism in India. Both first and last versions of *The Mysterious Stranger* thus in the end finally do acknowledge history, virtually in spite of themselves. Twain's self-enclosed dream structure, erected freestanding in the 1904 conclusion but never completely linked to any of the manuscripts, violates in some sense all of the manuscripts. They do not comply with the conclusion's movement inward to the self or outward to infinite space, but instead return us with characteristic satiric force to the world of the twentieth century.[60]

VI

During the years when Mark Twain was writing *The Mysterious Stranger*, a period of transatlantic voyages and European exile, he also wrote another fascinating series of dream tales, even more fragmented and entangled with one another than the three versions of *The Mysterious Stranger*. These are the writings that I have referred to earlier, stories of excursions not into the stranger's exhilarating "cosmic consciousness" but rather into a terrifyingly alien "cosmic environment." Whether a microscopic drop of water that becomes an ocean or the bloodstream of a tramp teeming with a world of cholera germs or a Hannibalesque village, these regions are defined by nightmarish reversals of fortune (family disaster, financial ruin), spatial and temporal distortion, and confusion of dream and reality. Unlike *The Mysterious Stranger*, with which they share many characteristics, none of these other tales comes even to the determinate conclusion that life is all a dream. Instead, the nightmare and simultaneous escape they court is total undecidability. That is, they do not resolve the question they pose as to "which was the dream"—the good fortune or the bad—but rather break off asserting that we just cannot tell. Ultimately, however, we will see, these putatively unlocated, ahistorical, and relativistic writings prove no more successful at evading painful historical realities than does *The Mysterious Stranger*.

The overt parallels between these writings and the agonies suffered by the Clemens family during these years have long been recognized as central to Mark Twain's virtual compulsion to write himself over and over again into (but never out of) the same dream/nightmare structure. But although Twain's dream writings are certainly in this respect highly personal and idiosyncratic, reflecting his need to retreat from the family tragedies of these years, the particular form of this retreat—dream voyages to unknown worlds and planets—owes much to the general findings of psychical research, specifically to the literature on out-of-body travel. Twain, we know, was drawn to the idea of mental telepathy, or telegraphy, the possibility of communication between minds over distances, as a possible explanation for how and why his writings so often seemed to have been produced by someone other than himself. But his late experimental tales go farther than purely *mental* telepathy to imagining psychic excursions in the flesh. The once-human narrator of "Three Thousand Years Among the Microbes," for example, travels into the germ world of a tramp's body and writes of his experiences as "a real cholera germ, not an imitation one." However absurd a scenario this might seem, similar cases of what were called "traveling clairvoyance" seemed to demonstrate that a part of the personality can leave the body, travel considerable distances, and radically change its own center of perception and action. And indeed, the microbe story insists comically on this kind of split perception. "I could observe the germs from their own point of view," the microbe-narrator begins. "At the same time, I was able to observe them from a human being's point of view . . . Another thing: my human measurements of time and my human span of life remained to me, right alongside of my full appreciation of the germ-measurements of time and the germ span of life" (*WWD*, 435).

This is how Twain begins his latest and most elaborate tale exploring the premise that Frederic Myers described as "obviously involving the hypothesis that we are living a life in two worlds at once" (a "planetary life" and a "cosmic life" in an "unseen world").[61] All of the tales play with the psychical notion of "unseen worlds" via the medium of the microscope and the unimaginably microscopic, even microbic, worlds it reveals. In order to cultivate such a doubled perspective and the disorientation, associated with authorship, it implied to Mark Twain, his dream tales are all structured as framed narratives, told in the first person in various ways to cast doubt on the validity of the frame, the inset story, and ultimately on the reliability, even the sanity, of the narrator himself. In all four of the pieces I will discuss, the frame consists of some type of a written manuscript providing the authority for the story that is about to be told. According to its title page, "Microbes" purports to be a "History" written by a microbe in his own tongue and "translated from the Original Microbic by Mark Twain." The other three stories— "Which Was the Dream?", "The Great Dark," and "Which Was It?"—all open in almost exactly the same way: a short statement by the narrator's wife, explaining that her husband is presently writing a family sketch and seems to be drowsing over the manuscript, is followed by the separately titled "husband's narrative" ("Major General X.'s Story," "Statement by Mr. Edwards"), which tells the tale of the dream of disaster. None of these inset dream tales is finished, nor does any of the three the dream dream-narrators ever awaken.

One of the earliest, "Which Was the Dream?" (1897), begins with "General X." smoking a cigar in a dreamy haze, falling asleep, and dreaming a seventeen-year sequence of disasters, starting with his own burning house and including being swindled by a close associate, charged with forgery, and going bankrupt—details that are recognized as roughly parallel to the agonizing Clemens family history during the later 1890s. The General and his family were to have gone on a voyage ending in "The Devil's Race-Track," a region of endless storms and swirling concentric currents with a deathly still center called "The Everlasting Sunday." Finally, the narrator would learn that all of this had been only a fifteen-second dream, but one so real that he would actually have aged by seventeen years, awakening unable to recognize his own children.

The related work that grew out of this one (which breaks off even before the sea voyage) the following year is "The Great Dark" (1898), in which another sea voyage takes place, this one in a cosmic-seeming ocean that is actually a drop of water magnified by a microscope. According to the wife's introductory statement, the narrator and his children are looking at the drop of water under the microscope just "before it happened." The husband's statement testifies that when his imagination is fired by the possibility of a voyage in that "unknown and uncharted" ocean, a figure called the Superintendent of Dreams appears to provide a ship and crew. On the ship the narrator and his wife share memories of their former life—bounded by the moment of their peering into the microscope—as the fading impressions of dream-visits to an unreal place in comparison to the often terrifying realities of shipboard life. Monstrous fish, bacteria in the drop of water magnified to gigantic proportions, attack the ship; when the ship enters the region directly beneath the light of the microscope, the sea dries up. Like "Which Was the Dream?", this story breaks off before its planned ending, when the narrator was supposed to have awakened from his nightmare, finding himself back at home.

This deliberately disorienting microscopic perspective— Twain's technology enlarges what Myers calls "unseen worlds," but also shrinks the viewer to microscopic size—is conjured even more bizarrely in "Three Thousand Years Among the Microbes" (1905), where as we have seen, the microbe-narrator constantly translates into human terms what he calls microbic life, history, and "orthography." Not only does he provide a table of "Time-Equivalents" (one human year is "roughly" equal to 52,416 microbe years), but he also asserts that to the microbe-eye, much as to the mediumistic or clairvoyant eye, whole worlds are visible, "alive and in energetic motion" down to the individual molecules and atoms, worlds which to the human eye exist "only in *theory*, not in demonstrated fact" (*WWD*, 447).

And finally, a story, by far the longest of all of these, that seems rather incongruous in the context of their exotic settings, yet is clearly related to "Which Was the Dream?" and "The Great Dark" in terms of structure and plot. "Which Was It?" (1899–1903), set in the Hannibalesque Indiantown, begins with another dream frame and features another unfinished nightmare from which the dreamer-narrator was supposed to have awakened: the respectable George Louisiana Purchase Harrison commits murder while trying to save his family from debt, unleashing a series of tragedies upon them and himself, culminating in his enforced servitude to a vengeful ex-slave who has evidence of the crime. ("Dey's a long bill agin de low-down ornery white race, en you's a-gwyneter *settle* it.") The story stops here, just when the greatest white nightmare of racial reversal—black over white—is about to begin: George Harrison, "slave of an ex-slave! it is the final degredation" (*WWD*, 415, 413).

What do these writings have in common, other than the fact that they are unfinished dream fantasies collected in one volume entitled *Mark Twain's "Which Was the Dream?" and Other Symbolic Writings of the Later Years?* They all rest, as we have seen in the above sketchy summaries, on deliberately destabilized narrative grounds, forcing the narrators to infer rather than know their own reality. The principal work of the narrators, and by extension, the principal burden of the tales themselves, is a process that might be called reality testing. That is, in various ways the narrators attempt to formulate methods of testing and verifying the validity and the foundations of the unstable worlds in which they find themselves. The primary method of ascertaining knowledge in all the tales is a comparative one in which reality is inferred, or even constructed, through an ongoing series of contrasts between seemingly opposed poles of experience: shipboard life and life on land, past success and present failure, dream and reality, microbic or microscopic and human or macrocosmic perspectives.[62] Underlying all of these, finally, is the fundamental structural opposition between the inset tale and the frame, between the dream within and the reality without.

The microbe-narrator, for example, describes the physical world of the tramp's body which he now inhabits by making reference to human geography: "Our tramp is mountainous, there are vast oceans in him, and lakes that are sea-like for size, there are many rivers (veins and arteries) which are fifteen miles across, and of a length so stupendous as to make the Mississippi and the Amazon trifling little Rhode Island brooks by comparison" (*WWD*, 437). In a similar comparative vein, the "Great Dark" narrator tries to locate himself definitively in the ocean he thought was a drop of water by measuring relative distance, climate, and time. In answer to his question of why, at one point in the voyage, it is always night, the Superintendent says that they are sailing in the shadow ("consequently in the dark") of one end of the lens-holder of the microscope. As to why it appears so huge, we get a kind of tall tale: "Because it is several thousand miles in diameter. For dimensions, that is nothing."

> The glass slide which it is pressing against, and which forms the bottom of the ocean we are sailing upon, is thirty thousand miles long, and the length of the microscope barrel is a hundred and twenty thousand . . . If you should thrust that glass slide through what you call the 'great' globe, eleven thousand miles of it would stand out on each side—it would be like impaling an orange on a table-knife. (*WWD*, 122)

The narrator's response to such unsettling relative measurements: "You make me dizzy . . . It gives me the head-ache." We see this dizzyingly relativized process of reality construction operate once more, in terms of comparative measurements of time, in "Which Was the Dream?" when General X. faints upon hearing that he is accused of forgery and revives an hour later, still in the dream section of the story, in disgraced exile in a California town called "Hell's Delight." Just before the narrative breaks off, X., who barely recognizes his own children, articulates his sense of total disorientation by explaining that he had been asleep only an hour—"by the clock—but in the *true* sense a whole year and a half" (*WWD*, 71). The irony here is that the narrative itself undermines the possibility of a "true" sense by breaking off before its dream structure has been completed, thereby leaving open the question of which was the dream, the frame or the inset tale.

As the above examples suggest, all of the dream writings move gradually toward undermining the very bipolar distinctions through which they are constructed. They reject their own epistemological project of locating an authoritative foundation for knowledge, and instead opt for a totally decentered, relativized vision of experience. The microbe-narrator admits the failure of his table of time equivalents: "I wanted to translate a microbe hour into its human equivalent, but it kept shrinking and diminishing and wasting away, and finally disappeared from under my pen, leaving nothing behind that I could find again when I wanted it" (*WWD*, 450). The "Great Dark" narrator is similarly frustrated by his futile efforts to gauge space and time in his microscopic dream-world: "Are these the fictitious proportions which we . . . have acquired by being reduced to microscopic objects?" Full of anger, he tells the Superintendent that he can end the dream whenever he likes; the Superintendent answers, "The dream? *Are you quite sure it is a dream?* . . . You have spent your whole life in this ship. And this is *real* life. Your other life was the dream!" (Twain's emphasis; *WWD*, 122–24). As the narrator's wife, who remembers their "land-life" only as a "dream-life," blows "another wind of doubt" upon his "wasting sand-edifice of certainty," the very foundations of his knowledge dissolve away. "Damnation! I said to myself, are we real creatures in a real world, all of a sudden, and have we been feeding on dreams in an imaginary one since nobody knows when—or how *is* it?" (*WWD*, 133, 127, 130).

As stable distinctions are thus unmade, the dream tales set themselves adrift in a relativized and unmoored universe. Here there is no omniscient mysterious stranger to function as authoritative guide. Instead, all possible sources of authority are undercut. By the same token, the tales themselves cannot come to formal closure—they do not conclude their own dream frames—because such conclusiveness is denied. This is Mark Twain's nightmare, indistinguishable, we must add, from what he must have seen as an escape from intolerable realities: that there are no definitive standards of judgment, no verifiable means of telling where or who we are, or even of deciding whether we are sane or insane. There can be no guilt, either, in such a world.

In an extreme and global version of the law's problems with proof in *Pudd'nhead Wilson*, "Wapping Alice," and the Harry Thaw trial, these writings blend victims with their victimizers, the devourers and the devoured, suggesting that ultimately, as the microbe-narrator remarks, "there is no moral difference between a germicide and a homicide" (WWD, 504). Everyone feeds off some-one else, cholera germs and humans alike, and some, the "Great Dark" narrator suspects, even consume their own dreams. "You is my meat," says the black ex-slave become master of the white ex-master. "Jasper contemplated his serf's misery . . . , his mind trav-eling back over bitter years and comparing it with the thousand instances wherein he himself had been the unoffending victim and had looked like that, suffered like that" (WWD, 410, 416). The implicit image of an amoral universe consisting of nothing but an infinite regress of persecutors who are themselves, unknowingly, victims to some larger persecutor becomes the explicit premise of the microbe story. To the microbe-narrator, the spectacle of bil-lions of cholera germs unsuspectingly feeding off of the body of the tramp they perceive as their planet and deity, himself a parasite living off of society, "hints at the possibility that the procession of known and listed devourers and persecutors is not complete . . . the possibility [exists] . . . that man is himself a microbe, and his globe a blood-corpuscle drifting with its shining brethren of the Milky Way down a vein of the Master and Maker of all things, Whose body, mayhap, . . is what men name the Universe" (WWD, 454).

If one impulse of this simultaneously "limitless and receding" view of man's place in the universe is to render him puny and destroy human pretension, it also ends by destroying the founda-tions of any belief in anything. "It doesn't make any difference who we are or what we are," the microbe-narrator concludes to-ward the end of his narrative. "There's always *somebody* to look down on!" It also follows, "according to the inexorable logic of the situation" that "below that infester there is yet another infester that infests *him*—and so on down and down and down till you strike the bottomest bottom of created life—if there is one, which is extremely doubtful" (WWD, 479, 526–527).

VII

Taking a cue from Mark Twain, we must ourselves beware of resting on any such definitive conclusion about his writing. Even in the midst of these apparently solipsistic fantasies, seemingly so different from the rest of his more historicized fiction, fleeing from the real world into nihilism, and seeming ultimately to assert, as one of the microbe's informants does, that there is "no such thing as substance—substance is a fiction of the Mortal Mind," we feel the pull of an equal and opposite counter-movement toward active engagement with historical realities. Not only are the tales, as we have seen, thoroughly saturated in the context of late-nineteenth-century psychology, but also, perhaps in spite of themselves, and only at their margins, they show signs of Mark Twain's characteristic satiric, often humorous, dialogue with contemporary social and political issues. Like *The Mysterious Stranger*, the microbe tale satirizes a wide variety of issues, ranging from Christian Science, evolutionary science, and scientific methods of deduction, to Tammany Hall, stock market manipulations, the Philippine annexation, and imperialism. The principal republic of the microbe planet, for example, is "Getrichquick," a microbic United States with vast imperialist appetites, whose noble policy of "Benevolent Assimilation," most recently exhibited in connection with an "archipelago" inhabited by "those harmless bacilli which are the food of the fierce *hispaniola sataniensis*," has earned the praise that "pus and civilization" are "substantially the same thing" (*WWD*, 492–93, 443, 439).

The related issue of American race relations at home is addressed even more searingly in "Which Was It?", the story that breaks off in the middle of its historically resonant vision of black supremacy. Here the racial, sexual, and legal tangle of *Pudd'nhead Wilson* returns in the form of a mulatto (named Jasper, like the black slave with whom Roxana banters) sired by a white man and then swindled by him, first freed and then sold back into "a second slavery" (as Roxana is by her son). But unlike *Pudd'nhead Wilson*, as we have seen, this story goes deep into the slave son's revenge. Having blackmailed George Harrison into his power ("You b'longs to me, now. You's my proppity, same as a nigger"), Jasper muses on the tortuous connections between himself and this white man, so broken that he seems "rather a spectre than a man":

> Jasper's mind slipped back over long years, and he saw the duplicate of this apparition: himself. It was when he went to his father to ask for a new bill of sale in place of the one which had burned up with his cabin, and his father mocked him. . . . The mulatto sat studying the meek apparition . . . This was a Harrison, *that* was a Harrison—the hated blood was in his own veins! (*WWD*, 320, 413, 423)

The vision of uncanny self-duplication here leads not to epistemological doubt, as it does, for instance, in the Duplicates plot of

The Mysterious Stranger, but instead to recognition of an identity that has been culturally denied.

Perhaps even more telling than these examples of historical grounding in the dream tales is their collective engagement with the issue of writing as a problem of power and its control. All the tales originate, we remember, in the acts of a writer writing and then somehow losing control over his own literary creation. The microbe-narrator is at the mercy first of his unsympathetic translator Mark Twain, who asserts at the start that he tried without success to "reform" the author's style, and second of his own constant efforts to translate microbic into English. In each of the three dream-of-disaster stories, the narrator drowses over his manuscript (intended as a record, on the occasion of a child's birthday, of familial happiness) and awakens to find himself in the midst of a burning house and other nightmarish disasters, foremost among them loss of personal reputation, family tragedy, and financial ruin. The association between writing and loss of control—psychological, social, and especially economic—is, we know, characteristic of Mark Twain's view of authorship. For him the process of literary creation is inseparable from the circumstances in which it is produced and consumed. And as we have already seen, the circumstances of the late-nineteenth-century literary marketplace tended to undermine the individual author's control over his work. As the struggle for an international copyright demonstrates, though the nexus of images in the dream tales (associating writing with dreaming and disaster) may have been unique to Mark Twain, the problem itself was not.

All of which is to say that even when he would prefer not to be, Mark Twain is a deeply historicized writer. Even when he would prefer, as he does in the other-worldly dream writings, to relegate the history of "the damned human race" to the margins of his text, his work takes distinct historical shape from its time, as we have seen in the context of psychological research. In none of his writings does he succeed completely in freeing himself from what he sees as the bonds of historical circumstance—"chains of training, custom, convention, association, disposition, environment—in a word, Circumstance" (*WWD*, 485). His work, from the journalistic hoaxes of the 1860s to the late dream writings, is always animated by and embedded in an intimate relationship to its own cultural context. This relationship may often be disguised or displaced (as it is in *Pudd'nhead Wilson*'s antebellum setting), submerged or suppressed (as it is in *Connecticut Yankee*'s apparent honoring of nineteenth-century technological "progress"), derided (as it is in "The Whittier Birthday Dinner Speech"), or simply silenced (as it is in the truncated transvestite tales). This evasion is especially potent in *Huckleberry Finn*, a book which gives vent to the writer's will to turn his back on civilization and light out for the territory, but always by circling back to and through the Mississippi River valley. Nothing in Mark Twain's fiction, however, attests more powerfully to the complex, often paradoxical historical embeddedness of his writing than the so-called dream tales, which return us again and again, in most minute detail, to the realities of Mark Twain's America.

CHAPTER SIX

DRESS REFORM AND COPYRIGHT

If Mark Twain's writings during the last phase of his career were increasingly eluding his control, tending more and more toward incompleteness, fragmentation, disintegration, as well as toward an irony that repressed humor, "Mark Twain" the public personality was not in any comparable way suffering what James Cox has called "the fate of humor."[1] After returning to America in 1900, following nearly a decade of exile in Europe, the writer was publishing fewer completed, longer works, instead devoting himself to ongoing projects (his autobiography, his "gospel" *What Is Man?*) not generally intended for the contemporary reading public; but during this same period, Mark Twain's *talk* and his personal participation in activities both public and private were extensively reported in the newspapers. So newsworthy, indeed, was the social celebrity of the so-called "Belle of New York" that, for example, his seventieth birthday dinner celebration on 5 December 1905 at Delmonico's was covered in a special supplement in *Harper's Weekly*; the awarding of his honorary Litt. D. at Oxford in June 1907, along with the scarlet robe it entitled him to wear, occasioned extended daily coverage in both American and British newspapers; and even his performance as one of a pair of Siamese twins at a private dinner party at his home at 21 Fifth Avenue on New Year's Eve, 1906, rated a report on the front page of the *New York Times*.

The paradoxical result of all this publicity: Mark Twain expressed himself more and more in the form and the mode of a fully public personage, "freeing himself into the kingdom of personality" (as James Cox puts it), even as he produced masses of apparently unusable manuscript that seemed to deny his identity as a writer.[2] Thus, though he may have run toward fragments in his writing and toward an impasse in his doubt about identity, he was at the same time emerging as the very strongest identity in his person. He was becoming a myth even as he entertained the chaotic possibilities and dubieties of identity.

Nowhere is this tension more apparent than in Twain's last lobbying expedition, what Howells, the newspapers, and others describe as the dramatic performance he gave in Washington in December 1906 when he testified before the Joint Committees on Patents of the Senate and the House of Representatives. The main thrust of Twain's testimony, both to the Committees and to the press, was his frustration at the copyright law, which he believed should protect the author's literary property in perpetuity, but which instead dictated a temporal limit, to be extended by the bill under consideration from the then-current limit of forty-two years to the term of the author's life and fifty years thereafter. Twain's argument was that he, like the few other American authors whose books outlive the forty-two year limit, had lost control not only of his own property during his lifetime, but also of his ability to care for his children after his death.[3] Yet all of this talk of pecuniary victimization and loss of control took place in the special aura of this moment, also the occasion of the first public unveiling of Mark Twain's new white suit. Howells's memory of this episode in *My Mark Twain* puts a finger on precisely the tension operating here between the putative issue of copyright and that of Twain's own performance in the authors' hearing before the Joint Committees. Of his appearance on the floor of the committee room in the Library of Congress, Howells says admiringly:

> Nothing could have been more dramatic than the gesture with which he flung off his long loose overcoat, and stood forth in white from his feet to the crown of his silvery head . . . ; but the magnificent speech which he made, tearing to shreds the venerable farrago of nonsense about non-property in ideas which had formed the basis of all copyright legislation, made you forget even his spectacularity.[4]

Twain is, in effect, competing with himself, his spectacular performance subverting his speech or vice versa. In the eyes of his audience, *either* the white dress *or* the copyright issue takes precedence, each "making you forget" the other; they are self-canceling opposites, inharmoniously joined together like Siamese twins. "Dress Reform and Copyright," the title afterwards given to one of the informal speeches he made to reporters on this occasion, should read: "Dress Reform or Copyright."[5]

A similar irony emerges from Twain's long and futile engagement with the issue of copyright itself—what he referred to in an Autobiographical Dictation of 1906 as "copyright-anguishes."[6] Despite a fundamental scepticism about the legal process, we know that throughout his life he brought numerous, generally unsuccessful suits against literary pirates and others using his writings and name without authorization. At the 1906 hearings, still convinced of the law's incomprehensibility ("I have read the bill," he says, "at least I have read such portions of it as I could understand. . . . Nobody can understand a legal paper, merely on account of the language that is in it."), he argued at length for a principle he knew was rarely supported in the courts, that of property in ideas. Referring to his earlier testimony in England in April 1900 before a copyright committee of the House of Lords, Twain recapitulates the argument he made—to no avail then—against the conventional legal distinction between intellectual property and real estate. *All* property derives from an idea or ideas, he insists, rejecting what he sees as the legal pretense that an author's property is not created, produced, and acquired in the same way as any real estate:

> Every improvement that is put upon real estate is the result of an idea in somebody's head. A skyscraper is another idea. The railway was another idea . . . The washtub was the result of an idea. There is no property on this earth that does not derive pecuniary value from ideas and associations of ideas applied . . . again and again . . . , as in the case of the steam engine.[7]

But as though anticipating the repeated failure of this argument, as early as 1873 Twain had started to push a trademark rather than copyright as a legal means of protecting his name and writings from piracy. In *Clemens v. Such* (1873), for example, the writer's lawyers asked for an injunction against Benjamin J. Such's publication of *Fun, Fact & Fancy: A Collection of/ Original Comic Sketches/ And Choice Selections of Wit and Humor*, a pamphlet that contained six sketches supposedly written by Twain (and, according to the front cover, "revised and selected for this work" by him as well), of which five had never been copyrighted (and for only one of these had Such been given permission to publish) and one was not his at all. The Plaintiff's Complaint rests on the theory of a trademark or trade name in the pseudonym "Mark Twain," claiming that his pen name bestowed extra-statutory blessings on his work, rights in addition to those allowed other authors under federal copyright law.[8]

This is an argument that recurs throughout Twain's litigations and correspondence through 1908, when he incorporated himself, registering his name, photograph, and autograph as trademarks for tobacco and whiskey—an effort to protect the trade value of the Mark Twain name rather than a venture for profit. Twain hoped that his pen name, converted to a legal trademark, would hold his copyright in perpetuity. One unidentified news clipping for January 1908 recognized that the Mark Twain Company was also a new way to perpetuate the self, commenting, "Mark Twain has had himself patented." But it did not succeed, at least as a means of securing "exclusive use of the name . . . and practically obtaining a continuing trade-mark protection for it," as the leading copyright authority R. R. Bowker noted. More broadly, American courts have maintained that trademarks and trade names cannot be substituted for copyright laws, which exert an exclusive statutory character. Even in the Such case, where Clemens was granted the injunction he sought, the court failed to articulate clearly its basis for granting relief, and therefore the decision could play no role in establishing precedent for trademark as transcending copyright laws. In 1906, therefore, we find Mark Twain still seeking protection via the copyright hearings, and again in 1908 via the trademark route. Reporting prophetically, it turned out, on the 1873 suit against Such, one New York Times headline read, "The 'Innocent' at Law."[9]

Yet in Twain's own construction of his role in the 1906 hearings, as well as in the reconstructions of the event by the newspapers and others, the apparently central issue of copyright was almost entirely obscured by the performance of the "Mark Twain" personality—in particular by his dress.[10] He himself chose the copyright hearings as the moment to make his public entrance into Cox's "kingdom of personality where he would wear his famous white suit," a kingdom that proved to be both liberating and imprisoning for the author (and copyright advocate) who was privately known to his sycophantish household as "the King." He not only appeared in white before the committee but drew attention to that costume, which we know he believed, perhaps hoped, would be censured, by giving an impromptu interview to reporters while waiting to testify. The subject of the interview: why he is "wearing such apparently unseasonable clothes" and their relation to conventions of male and female dress. Only near the end of his remarks does he revert, almost as an afterthought, to the matter at hand: "But I am not here to talk fashions, but copyright law."[11]

Not surprisingly, although the newspapers devoted extensive attention to Twain's testimony at the hearings, most of the coverage centered at least as much on what the *New York Times* called in a 10 December 1906 editorial the "star performance" given by "the star performer for the authors and publishers" as on his copyright arguments—which, the *Times* noted wryly, notwithstanding the "great achievement" of the performance, "are apt to be rather dull and to hurt us by revealing that the authors whom we so much revere do not write wholly for fame and a 'cause,' as we would like to believe." Reflecting this division between public performance and copyright argument, a *Times* headline on 8 December links together, as though perfect equals, the issues both of dress and of copyright. "Mark Twain In White Amuses Congressmen," reads the lead, followed by the trailers, "Advocates New Copyright Law and Dress Reform. Wears Light Flannel Suit. Says at 71 Dark Colors Depress Him—Talks Seriously of Authors' Right to Profits." Almost more of an afterthought than Twain's own return to the copyright issue at the end of his remarks on dress reform, that last "serious" phrase also reminds us of the distinction between humor and "serious" writing that plagued Twain from the beginning of his career to its end. More thoroughly enmeshed in this division than the *Times*, *The World* neglected even to mention the copyright issue in its front-page headlines on 8 December: "Mark Twain in Cream-Colored Summer Flannel. 'When a Man Reaches Seventy-one He May Dress as He Pleases,' He Says on Visit to Congress. Dark Garb Depresses Him; Would Dress As Women Do. Yes; Peekaboo Waists and All—Men's Clothing Absurd, Ungraceful, Uncomfortable."[12]

All of the direct quotation in these headlines comes from Twain's informal interview with reporters in the House gallery rather than from his copyright testimony itself. *The World* implicitly defends this odd balance at the opening of the article, stating apologetically that "Mr. Clemens apparently preferred to talk about clothes rather than copyrights, for he spent most of his time discussing what men should wear." And indeed, a brief look at the interview itself may seem to confirm this distinction. Beginning by drawing attention to himself ("I suppose everyone is wondering why I am wearing such apparently unseasonable clothes"), he argues that his advanced age gives him "a right to arrogate to himself many privileges to which younger men cannot aspire." And in this case the privilege is one that we have already seen him argue for, that of eschewing the traditional, conservative, dark-colored clothing of the male, which he finds "depressing," in favor of light-colored clothing. "Of course," he continues, underscoring the subversion of social custom he sees in this preference,

> before a man reaches my years, the fear of criticism might prevent him from indulging his fancy. I am not afraid of that. I prefer light clothing, colors like those worn by the ladies at the opera . . . Nothing is more absurd, ungraceful, and uncomfortable than modern man's clothing, day or night, and at night man wears the most ridiculous of all garbs—evening clothes.

And then in response to a reporter's question—"What would you suggest for men—peek-a-boo waists, with short, puffy sleeves?"— that dares Twain to be more explicit in his radical views of dress and gender roles, he answers in kind:

> Of course, I have ideas of dress reform. For one thing, why not adopt some of the women's styles? Goodness knows, they adopt enough of ours. Why should we not learn from them? They always have beautiful fabrics, splendid colors, and, moreover, women's clothes are always pretty. Take the peek-a-boo waist, for instance. It has the obvious advantages of being cool and comfortable, and in addition it is almost always made up in pleasing colors, which cheer and do not depress.

And finally, as if in response to the twin dangers of looking effeminate and of having gone too far in self-revelation, Twain harkens back comically to the Middle Ages, when "gorgeous, glorious, gaudy costumes" were considered manly. "Then we could wear colors . . . ; Back to the days of tights and helmet! Yes, I admit that it might be uncomfortable for a bald-headed man wearing a tightly screwed-on helmet, with a bee or fly imprisoned therein."[13]

This talk is reminiscent, of course, of the long confessional passage on Twain's white clothing that we have already seen, a passage in the middle of a chapter of the Paine biography on the 1906 copyright hearings and entitled "A Lobbying Expedition." For Paine the whole episode demonstrates his subject's "love for theatrical effect"—hence the passage on Twain's white clothing.[14] It was also during this lobbying expedition that Howells first saw Twain's white clothing, prompting him to remark that "the white serge was an inspiration which few men would have had the courage to act upon," and then to go on to praise the "magificent *coup*" of the performance in white on the committee floor.[15] But for all the attention to Twain's dress, neither Paine nor Howells— or the newspapers, for that matter—makes anything at all of the connection between the issue of copyright and the theatrical dress—other than to see it as entirely gratuitous.

For us, though, the juxtaposition is telling: it links a concern with male identity, and with gender roles, explicitly with the project of authorship, and more broadly with a number of related issues we have seen to be central to Twain's conception of himself as a writer. The copyright debate raised fundamental questions about the author's legal control, or lack thereof, over his literary property, an issue implicitly related to the broad problem of ownership of property of all kinds—material, ideal, human. For Twain, we know, the notion of self-ownership—control over one's ideas, one's art, over *oneself*—was also fraught with paradox: the creation of ideas, never being "original" with any one individual, entails unconscious plagiarism; the creation of art is disturbingly equated with illegitimate or otherwise culturally tainted procreation; and the "self" emerges as the most unstable phenomenon of all, a social creation trapped by its awareness of the reality of its own constructedness.[16] Fundamental to all of these issues is the law, which Twain recognized for what it was—an effort to determine individual identity and responsibility in a world where identity was unknowable. Thus Twain shows us how the institutions of American society, both law and science, are implicated in permanent American anxiety about freedom, race, and identity.

If, then, Twain's public performance in the 1906 copyright hearings ultimately subverted itself, making its actual legal goals appear irrelevant, still we must conclude that the strangely misfiring cultural dialogue it engendered in the newspapers and elsewhere is no failure, no silencing at all. Rather, shared but often unvoiced anxieties about the law, about the cultural role of the writer, especially the popular writer, and about gender roles—all sublimated parts of the copyright furor—emerge in the only way they can, not directly in the discourse of official testimony, but indirectly, in the various representations of Twain's star performance in Washington. So, too, do Mark Twain's own shared anxieties gain expression not despite but through the sheltering displacements of the "distracting" public personality. The kind of public performance typified by the 1906 copyright episode always was and came even more to be a basic mode of artistic expression for Mark Twain, not a repression of the self but a means of self-expression.[17] This is the "Mark Twain" for whom *talk* is essential, fundamental to the oral tradition of American humor in which the writer first conceived himself. The Barnum showman, with his art of deception, is the paradigmatic figure of Twain's creativity, both in literature and in business. The evasions and disguises almost inevitably suggested by the notion of "performance" are also essential to the subversive humor that animated most of Mark Twain's career. Finally it was the public personality, Mark Twain talking, that gave this writer a voice and enabled him to speak even when publishable writing became no longer possible.

NOTES

ABBREVIATIONS

DE	*The Writings of Mark Twain,* Definitive Edition
DV	Refers to cataloging system in the Mark Twain papers
ETS1	*Early Tales and Sketches,* volume 1
ETS2	*Early Tales and Sketches,* volume 2
FP	*Finger Prints*
GA	*The Gilded Age: A Tale of Today*
HF	*Adventures of Huckleberry Finn*
LL	*Literature and Life: Studies*
MPS	"My Platonic Sweetheart"
MS	*The Mysterious Stranger*
MTA	*Mark Twain's Autobiography*
MTB	*Mark Twain: A Biography*
MTDW	*Mark Twain: The Development of a Writer*
MTE	*Mark Twain in Eruption*
MTHL	*Mark Twain-Howells Letters*
MTL	*Mark Twain's Letters*
MTLP	*Mark Twain's Letters to His Publishers*
MTN	*Mark Twain's Notebook*
MTP	Mark Twain Papers, Bancroft Library, University of California, Berkeley
MTS	*Mark Twain Speaks for Himself*
MTSB	*Mark Twain's Satires and Burlesques*
PW	*Pudd'nhead Wilson*
SSW	*Selected Shorter Writings*
TS	Typescript of Holograph
WA	"Wapping Alice"
WIM	*What Is Man?*
WJ on EMS	*William James on Exceptional Mental States*
WJ on PR	*William James on Psychical Research*
WWD	*Which Was the Dream?*

CHAPTER ONE

1. William Dean Howells, *My Mark Twain: Reminiscences and Criticisms*, ed. Marilyn Austin Baldwin (Baton Rouge, La., 1967), p. 6.

2. James M. Cox, *Mark Twain: The Fate of Humor* (Princeton, 1966), p. 21, n.12.

3. For this last predicament, see the various versions of "Wapping Alice," ed. Hamlin Hill, number 29 of the "Keepsake" series, The Friends of the Bancroft Library, University of California (Berkeley, 1981). I discuss this story in detail in chapter 4.

4. Theodore Dreiser, "Mark the Double Twain," *The English Journal* 24 (1935): 615–27.

5. Justin Kaplan, *Mr. Clemens and Mark Twain* (New York, 1966), pp. 36, 18, 211.

6. See Twain's account of how he won his *nom de guerre* in *Life on the Mississippi*, vol. 12 of *The Writings of Mark Twain*, Definitive Edition, 37 vols. (New York, 1922–25), pp. 401–3; further references to works in this collection will be abbreviated *DE* and cited by volume and page numbers.

7. Leslie Fiedler, *Freaks: Myths and Images of the Secret Self* (New York, 1978), p. 270. Fiedler's source for this deathbed account is Albert Bigelow Paine, *Mark Twain: A Biography*, 3 vols. (New York, 1912), 3: 1575; further references to this work will be abbreviated *MTB* and cited by volume and page numbers.

8. On "duality" as a nineteenth-century term, see Karl Miller, *Doubles: Studies in Literary History* (Oxford, 1985), p. 38. Miller describes the eighties and nineties as "an age tormented by genders and pronouns and pen-names, by the identity of authors" (p. 209).

9. Jane Tompkins, *Sensational Designs: The Cultural Work of American Fiction, 1790–1860* (New York, 1985), pp. xv–xvii.

10. Peter Gay, *Education of the Senses*, vol. 1 of *The Bourgeois Experience: Victoria to Freud* (New York, 1984), pp. 3, 110, 67–68.

11. T. J. Jackson Lears, *No Place of Grace: Antimodernism and the Transformation of American Culture, 1880–1920* (New York, 1981), pp. 32, 41–47.

12. *MTB*, 2: 591–92. This comment was made in the context of a trip to Bermuda with a Clemens family friend and neighbor, the Reverend Joseph Twichell, in May 1877 (described in *A Tramp Abroad* [1880]). There Twain was dazzled by the whiteness of the houses, but was certain that this Eden too would be ruined by the "triple curse."

13. Gay, *Education of the Senses*, p. 8.

14. *Webster's Third New International Dictionary of the English Language Unabridged* (Springfield, Mass., 1976), s.v. "imposture."

15. P. T. Barnum, *The Humbugs of the World* (New York, 1865), p. 102.

16. The phrase is Judith Fetterly's in "Mark Twain and the Anxiety of Entertainment," *Georgia Review* 33 (1979): 388.

17. Kenneth Burke, *A Grammar of Motives* (New York, 1952), p. 514.

18. See epigraph, dated 4 September 1907, to *Mark Twain in Eruption*, ed. Bernard De Voto (1940; rpt. New York, 1968); further references to this work will be abbreviated *MTE*.

19. Clemens [hereafter SLC] to Howells, 8 December 1874, *Mark Twain-Howells Letters*, ed. Henry Nash Smith and William Gibson, 2 vols. (Cambridge, Mass., 1960), 1: 49–50; further references to this collection will be abbreviated *MTHL* and cited by volume and page numbers.

20. *Mark Twain's Notebook*, ed. Albert Bigelow Paine (New York, 1935), pp. 348–52; further references to this work will be abbreviated *MTN*.

21. On the unpublished material concerning sexuality that I refer to here, see Hamlin Hill's provocative treatment of the last ten years of Twain's life, *Mark Twain: God's Fool* (New York, 1973).

22. *MTHL*, 1: 133; *Mark Twain to Mrs. Fairbanks*, ed. Dixon Wecter (San Marino, Ca., 1949), pp. 18–21; "The Whittier Birthday Dinner Speech" in *Selected Shorter Writings of Mark Twain*, ed. Walter Blair (Boston, 1962), pp. 151–55; *DE*, 12: 375; *The Love Letters of Mark Twain*, ed. Dixon Wecter (New York, 1949), p. 26.

23. In a letter of appreciation from SLC to Yale President Timothy Dwight, 29 June 1888; quoted in *Mark Twain Speaking*, ed. Paul Fatout (Iowa City, 1976), p. 237.

CHAPTER TWO

1. Mark Twain, *Early Tales and Sketches*, ed. Edgar M. Branch and Robert H. Hirst, vol. 1, *1851–1864* (Berkeley and Los Angeles, 1979), p. 245; further references to this work will be abbreviated *ETS1*.

2. During the summer of 1835, the *New York Sun* ran a series of articles on a sensational fraud called the "moon hoax." The secrets of the moon were supposedly seen through a new telescope invented by the noted British astronomer Sir John Herschel. The *Sun* claimed the articles were reprinted from the *Edinburgh Journal of Science*, although they were actually written by Richard A. Locke, one of the *Sun*'s own journalists. In 1844 the *Sun* reported another hoax, a fraudulent balloon-crossing of the Atlantic. "The Balloon-Hoax" was perpetrated by Edgar Allan Poe, who also wrote "Diddling Considered as One of the Exact Sciences," a piece satirizing the prevalence of deception in business and social life.

3. Phineas T. Barnum to Moses Kimball, 2 September 1843, Barnum-Kimball Letters, Boston Athenaeum.

4. *Struggles and Triumphs: or, The Life of P. T. Barnum, Written By Himself*, ed. George S. Bryan, 2 vols. (New York and London, 1927).

5. Quoted in Neil Harris, *Humbug: The Art of P. T. Barnum* (Boston, 1973), p. 77.

6. David Brion Davis, *The Slave Power Conspiracy and the Paranoid Style* (Baton Rouge, La., 1969), p. 28.

7. The Roosevelt commentary is in *MTE*, 98; the "kindred swindles" line comes from a passage I quoted in the Introduction (see chapter one, n. 23).

8. See Louis J. Budd's comments on what he calls these "fake Mark Twains" in *Our Mark Twain: The Making of His Public Personality* (Philadelphia, 1983), pp. 43–76.

9. SLC to Jerome B. Stillson, 25 January 1875, MS owned jointly by Robert E. Atkinson and Mrs. Madeleine Edward, New York, photocopy in The Mark Twain Papers, Bancroft Library, University of California, Berkeley; hereafter abbreviated *MTP* (†).

10. SLC to Dr. John Brown, 27 April 1874, Charles Sachs (Scriptorium), Beverly Hills, photocopy in *MTP* (†).

11. SLC to Orion Clemens, 10 May 1874, *MTP* (†).

12. Between 1873 and 1886, Twain brought eight major litigations against various publishers over copyright infringement, none of which succeeded. See Herbert Feinstein, "Mark Twain's Lawsuits" (Ph.D. diss., University of California, Berkeley, 1968).

13. Albert M. Lee, *The Daily Newspaper in America: The Evolution of a Social Instrument* (New York, 1937), p. 430.

14. James Gordon Bennett, 1855; quoted in ibid., p. 608.

15. Barnum, *Humbugs of the World*, p. 102.

16. "The Whittier Birthday Dinner Speech," first published in the *Boston Evening Transcript* (18 December 1877); rpt. in Blair, *Selected Shorter Writings*; further references to this collection will be abbreviated *SSW*.

17. My reading of the speech and its background and aftermath is indebted to Henry Nash Smith's pioneering work, especially his newspaper research, in "The California Bull and the Gracious Singers," chap. 5 in *Mark Twain: The Development of a Writer* (New York, 1967), pp. 92–112; further references to this work will be abbreviated *MTDW*.

18. See Henry Nash Smith's analysis of how various writers used the word "reverent" in newspaper articles in ibid., 100–107.

19. SLC to Howells, 23 December 1877, *MTHL*, 1:212.

20. Howells to Charles Eliot Norton, 19 December 1877; quoted in *MTHL*, 1: 214.

21. Quoted in *MTDW*, 104.

22. Howells, *My Mark Twain*, p. 6.

23. *ETS1*, 79.

24. First printed in *The Saturday Press* (18 November 1865); rpt. as "Jim Smiley and His Jumping Frog," in Mark Twain, *Early Tales and Sketches*, ed. Edgar M. Branch and Robert H. Hirst, vol. 2, *1864–1865* (Berkeley and Los Angeles, 1981), pp. 282–88; further references to this work will be abbreviated *ETS2*.

25. Hooper's tales are collected along with selections from other humorists in Kenneth S. Lynn, ed., *The Comic Tradition in America: An Anthology of American Humor* (New York, 1958).

26. For a provocative article on the transforming effects of the new mass-market magazines on the reading process itself, see Christopher P. Wilson, "The Rhetoric of Consumption: Mass-Market Magazines and the Demise of the Gentle Reader, 1880–1920," in *The Culture of Consumption: Critical Essays in American History, 1880–1980,* ed. Richard W. Fox and T. J. Jackson Lears (New York, 1983), pp. 39–64. For more general information on the American book business, see William Charvat, *The Profession of Authorship in America, 1800–1870: The Papers of William Charvat,* ed. Matthew J. Bruccoli (Columbus, Oh., 1968); John Tebbel, *The Expansion of an Industry, 1865–1919,* vol. 2 of *A History of Book Publishing in the United States* (New York, 1975). On publishing in England, see Richard D. Altick, *The English Common Reader: A Social History of the Mass Reading Public, 1800–1900* (Chicago, 1957); Q. D. Leavis, *Fiction and the Reading Public* (1932; rpt. London, 1968).

27. William Dean Howells, *Literature and Life: Studies* (New York and London, 1902), p. 7; further references to this work will be abbreviated LL.

28. James Cox has taken this line of argument even further in seeing Mark Twain as "himself an embodiment of the twin activities of investment and invention . . . Art and business were for him a single creative enterprise." See *Fate of Humor,* pp. 185–86.

29. *Mark Twain's Letters,* ed. Albert Bigelow Paine, 2 vols. (New York, 1917), 2: 641; further references to this collection will be abbreviated MTL and cited by volume and page numbers.

30. SLC to Orion Clemens, 5 January 1889, MTL, 2: 508.

31. For a good summary of the situation, see Tebbel, *Expansion of an Industry,* pp. 130–49.

32. Walter Benjamin, "The Work of Art in the Age of Mechanical Reproduction," in *Illuminations,* ed. Hannah Arendt (New York, 1969), pp. 217–51. See especially pp. 220–23 on the concepts of authenticity, authority, uniqueness.

33. Howells, *My Mark Twain,* pp. 116–17.

34. In a review of Isak Dinesen, John Updike recounts how in a 1934 interview she accounted for her pen name "on the same grounds my father hid behind the pseudonym Boganis . . . so he could express himself freely, give his imagination a free rein." Quoted by Updike in " 'Seven Gothic Tales': The Divine Swank of Isak Dinesen," *New York Times Book Review,* 23 February 1986, p. 3.

35. Benjamin, "Work of Art," p. 231.

36. The "crucifying" line comes from MTL, 1: 172–73; the "robbing" and "pecuniary compulsions" comments are in MTE, 169.

37. Howells, *My Mark Twain,* p. 46.

38. SLC to Olivia Langdon [Clemens], 14 January 1870, MS in MTP (†).

39. My source for this quotation is Paine's account in MTB, 2: 786.

40. See Benjamin, "Work of Art," p. 218.

41. See Edgar M. Branch's summary of Twain's characterization of his

creative process, especially the comments on unconscious artistry, in "Mark Twain: Newspaper Reading and the Writer's Creativity," *Nineteenth-Century Fiction* 37 (March 1983): 591–600.

42. Susan Gubar alludes briefly but perceptively to male attitudes toward creativity in " 'The Blank Page' and the Issues of Female Creativity," *Critical Inquiry* 8 (Winter 1981); rpt. in *Writing and Sexual Difference*, ed. Elizabeth Abel (Chicago, 1982), pp. 73–93.

43. This passage and all of the others in this paragraph come from *MTE*, 196–99.

44. Kaplan, *Mr. Clemens and Mark Twain*, pp. 205, 73.

45. This account of the Holmes plagiarism is in *The Autobiography of Mark Twain*, ed. Charles Neider (New York, 1959), pp. 150–51. Twain also discusses various experiences with plagiarism in print in a piece entitled "Mark Twain on Thought-Transference," *Journal of the Society for Psychical Research* 1 (October 1884): 166–67.

46. Twain's emphasis; first printed in *The Art of Authorship*, ed. George Bainton (New York, 1890); rpt. in *SSW*, 225–26.

47. Bernard De Voto, *Mark Twain at Work* (Boston, 1967), p. 116.

48. Van Wyck Brooks, *The Ordeal of Mark Twain* (New York, 1920; rpt. New York, 1955), p. 193.

49. On the issue of Mark Twain as a public figure, see Budd, *Our Mark Twain*, and Sara de Saussure Davis and Philip D. Beidler, eds., *The Mythologizing of Mark Twain* (Tuscaloosa, Ala., 1984). In the latter volume, see especially Henry Nash Smith, "Mark Twain, 'Funniest Man in the World,' " pp. 56–76, on the distortions and contradictions in "the image evoked by the name Mark Twain . . . in American popular culture" (p. 56).

50. "A Glance at San Francisco Literature," *Grass Valley* (Calif.) *National*; rpt. in *Californian* 2 (11 February 1865): 5; quoted in Introduction, *ETS2*, 1–2.

51. "Mark Twain's Seventieth Birthday. Souvenir of Its Celebration," Supplement to *Harper's Weekly*, 45 (23 December 1905), p. 1886; quoted in Smith, " 'Funniest Man in the World,' " p. 62. My discussion in the preceding paragraph is much indebted to Smith's article.

52. Mark Twain, *Pudd'nhead Wilson and Those Extraordinary Twins*, ed. Sidney E. Berger (New York, 1980), p. 119; further references to this work will be abbreviated *PW*.

53. James Cox's insightful analysis of the "literary Caesarean operation" also centers on its genealogical confusions, noting that "the novel is curiously and strikingly figured not as the child of the farce but as the *mother* from whom the child—the farce—is forcibly extracted" (*Fate of Humor*, p. 227).

54. Quoted in *MTDW*, 99–100. Letter in *Harvard Library Bulletin* 9 (Spring 1955): 164.

55. Evan Carton has also recently discussed *Pudd'nhead Wilson* in

light of Twain's 1872 remark to Howells; he reads the novel, as I do, as "a narrative that itself radically involves problems of authorship, identity, and responsibility." See Carton, "*Pudd'nhead Wilson* and the Fiction of Law and Custom," in *American Realism: New Essays*, ed. Eric J. Sundquist (Baltimore, 1982), pp. 82–94.

56. William Faulkner, *Mosquitoes* (New York, 1927), p. 251.

57. My discussion, here and elsewhere, of the relationship between difference and control is much indebted to Sander L. Gilman, *Difference and Pathology: Stereotypes of Sexuality, Race, and Madness* (Ithaca, 1985). See especially the theoretical introduction (pp. 15–29), where Gilman makes a case for "how deep is the human disposition to structure perception in terms of binary difference," thereby "to preserve our illusion of control over the self and the world" (pp. 24, 18).

58. Abridged version of "My Platonic Sweetheart" first published in *Harper's Magazine* (December 1912); rpt. in *The Mysterious Stranger and Other Stories* (New York, 1923). The complete holograph manuscript, from which I quote, is in *MTP*, No. 3A, Box 16 (formerly Paine No. 111) (†); further references to this work will be abbreviated *MPS*.

59. SLC to Howells, 21 January 1879, *MTHL*, 1: 245–46.

60. *MTN*, 348–52. Paine heads the entry "London, Jan. 7, '97," but his accuracy has been questioned. Sholom J. Kahn argues that 1898 is the correct year (*Mark Twain's Mysterious Stranger: A Study of the Manuscript Texts* [Columbia, Mo., 1978], p. 41). Until the editors of the University of California Press edition of *Mark Twain's Notebooks and Journals*, vol. 4, date the entry, I will use 7 January 1898. A number of passages in the notebook entry parallel, nearly word for word, unpublished sections of "My Platonic Sweetheart," written in August 1898. Such striking similarity makes January 1898 the more convincing date for the entry. On the biographical and literary significance of this entry, see Kaplan, *Mr. Clemens and Mark Twain*, pp. 403–5, and John S. Tuckey, "Mark Twain's Later Dialogue: The 'Me' and the Machine," *American Literature* 41 (January 1970): 532–42.

61. Notebook #35 (1895), TS, p. 35, *MTP* (†). Written ten years after the publication of *Huckleberry Finn*, the entry describes the novel as "a book of mine where a sound heart and deformed conscience come into collision and conscience suffers defeat."

62. In addition to *Dr. Jekyll and Mr. Hyde*, Twain also mentions "Chamisso's striking tale of a century ago" (*MPS*, 9)—a reference to Adelbert Chamisso, *Peter Schlemihl's wundersame geschichte* (1835) [*The Shadowless Man; or, The Wonderful History of Peter Schlemihl*, (London, n.d.)]. On the copies (in German and English) that Twain owned, see Alan Gribben, *Mark Twain's Library: A Reconstruction*, 2 vols. (Boston, 1980), 1: 137–38.

63. The best general history of the development of psychology is Henri F. Ellenberger, *The Discovery of the Unconscious: The History and Evolu-*

tion of Dynamic Psychiatry (New York, 1970); on the particular period I refer to here, see "The Emergence of Dynamic Psychiatry," pp. 53–102. I will return to this subject in much greater detail in the last chapter.

64. Paine described Mark Twain's dictating his autobiographical reminiscences in his later years: "He went drifting among episodes, incidents, and periods in his irresponsible fashion; the fashion of table-conversation, as he said, the methodless method of the human mind" (*MTB*, 3: 1268).

CHAPTER THREE

1. Hjalmar Hjorth Boyesen, "In the World of Arts and Letters," *Cosmopolitan* 18 (January 1895): 379.

2. Hershel Parker, *Flawed Texts and Verbal Icons: Literary Authority in American Fiction* (Chicago, 1984), pp. 115–36. While Parker is patently wrong when he dismisses *Pudd'nhead Wilson* as "patently unreadable," he does pose a number of provocative questions about authorial intention and racial issues in the manuscript (see pp. 142–44).

3. The frontispiece of the first American edition (Hartford, Conn.: American Publishing Co., 1894) pictures Mark Twain looking at an advertisement for the "Wonderful Twins."

4. The terms in which I discuss these developments derive largely from George M. Fredrickson, *White Supremacy: A Comparative Study in American and South African History* (New York, 1981).

5. For two critical arguments that (briefly) try, as I do, to read *Pudd'nhead Wilson* in the context of the Siamese twins novel, see James Cox, who concludes that "the book does not reveal so much as it implies the ligature connecting the two figures" of the "*real* twins," Tom Driscoll and David Wilson (*Fate of Humor*, p. 236); and Henry Nash Smith, who argues that Tom Driscoll himself is "the psychological equivalent of the twins" (*MTDW*, 173–74).

6. *New York Herald* (31 August 1868).

7. On the Siamese twins, see Irving and Amy Wallace, *The Two: A Biography* (New York, 1978) and Fiedler, *Freaks*.

8. "The Siamese Twins," *Philadelphia Public Ledger*, 28 February 1854, p. 1; Untitled, *Alta California*, 24 July 1864, p. 3. I am indebted to Richard Bucci of the Mark Twain Papers for drawing my attention to the newspaper material on twins.

9. "The Siamese Twins," San Jose *Mercury*, 21 July 1864, p. 1, rpt. from Macon (Georgia) *Telegraph*. (The last two sentences come from the *Telegraph* piece; rpt. in San Francisco *Evening Bulletin*, 9 July 1864, p. 1.)

10. "The Siamese Twins—Chang and Eng," Downieville (Calif.) *Mountain Messenger*, 28 April 1866, p. 1.

11. Mark Twain, "People and Things," *Buffalo Express*, 2 September 1869.

12. First published in *Packard's Monthly* (August 1869); rpt. in *DE*, 7: 248–53.

13. "The Tocci Twins," *Scientific American* 65 (12 December 1891): 374.

14. Quoted on p. 75 in Stephen Jay Gould, "Living With Connections," in *The Flamingo's Smile: Reflections in Natural History* (New York, 1985), pp. 65–75.

15. Sigmund Freud, "The Uncanny," in *Collected Papers*, ed. Ernest Jones, trans. Joan Rivière (New York, 1959), 4: 368–407.

16. Joel Williamson, *New People: Miscegenation and Mulattoes in the United States* (New York, 1980), p. 63.

17. See, for example, Parker, *Flawed Texts*, on the "serious anomalies involving vestigial functions for characters" (pp. 129–35); I would disagree, however, with his conclusion that the "surviving vestiges of [the twins'] status as Siamese twins" are "a distracting embarrassment."

18. SLC to Fred J. Hall, 30 July 1893, *Mark Twain's Letters to His Publishers, 1867–1894*, ed. Hamlin Hill (Berkeley, 1967), pp. 354–55; further references to this work will be abbreviated *MTLP*.

19. On the sequence of changes in chronology, see Parker, *Flawed Texts*, p. 126.

20. Williamson, *New People*, pp. 24, 57–59.

21. On the legal issue of the slave's humanity, see Eugene D. Genovese, *Roll, Jordan, Roll: The World the Slaves Made* (New York, 1976), pp. 28–37.

22. Fredrickson, *White Supremacy*, p. 133; see section entitled "Race Mixture and the Color Line," pp. 94–135.

23. Williamson, *New People*, p. 47.

24. Genovese, *Roll, Jordan, Roll*, p. 30. Genovese is referring to overt and visible action, such as slave insurrection, but the analogy still seems pertinent. Roxana's apparently willful exchange does expose the "notion that in fact, not merely in one's fantasy life, some human beings become mere extensions of the will of another" (p. 30).

25. Mark Twain, *Adventures of Huckleberry Finn*, The Mark Twain Library Edition, ed. Walter Blair and Victor Fischer (Berkeley, 1985), pp. 228, 254; further references to this work will be abbreviated *HF*. See Lee Mitchell's discussion of adapting selves and creating identities in " 'Nobody but Our Gang Warn't Around': The Authority of Language in *Huckleberry Finn*," in *New Essays on Adventures of Huckleberry Finn*, ed. Louis J. Budd (Cambridge, 1985), pp. 83–106; the section relevant to my argument is pp. 88–97.

26. Horace W. Fuller, *Noted French Trials. Impostors and Adventurers* (Boston, 1882), p. 100.

27. Morgan manuscript, chap. 6, p. 113 (interpolated typescript page), Morgan Library, New York.

28. Genovese, *Roll, Jordan, Roll*, pp. 445–46.

29. This part of the manuscript is in the Berg Collection, New York Public Library. On the dating, see Parker, *Flawed Texts*, p. 121.

30. Twain, *HF*, 95–96.

31. The argument is made by Marvin Fisher and Michael Elliott in "*Pudd'nhead Wilson:* Half a Dog Is Worse than None," *Southern Review* 8 (1972): 533–47.

32. On the "descent rule" or "rigorous ancestry principle," see Fredrickson, *White Supremacy,* pp. 95–99, 129–30; see also pp. 101–8 on the antebellum history of the legal color line. On "statutory homogenization," see Winthrop D. Jordan, *White Over Black: American Attitudes Toward the Negro, 1550–1812* (Chapel Hill, 1968; Baltimore, 1969), p. 169.

33. Fredrickson, *White Supremacy,* p. 96; Jordan, *White Over Black,* p. 175, n. 84.

34. Leon Litwack argues that despite such legal erasure, on a more informal level, both before and after the Civil War, "whites made no attempt to deny the presence of a substantial mulatto population." The distorting combination of acknowledgment and denial is precisely what *Pudd'nhead Wilson* registers. See Litwack, *Been in the Storm So Long: The Aftermath of Slavery* (New York, 1980), pp. 265–66.

35. John C. Hurd, *The Law of Freedom and Bondage in the United States,* 2 vols. (New York, 1858), 1: 236.

36. Quoted in Williamson, *New People,* p. 66.

37. On Southern "muleology" and religious arguments about the South's defeat (including this passage in a letter from William Heyward to James Gregorie, 12 January 1868), see Williamson, *New People,* pp. 73, 92, 96; on the etymology of "mulatto" and its cultural meanings, see Jordan, *White Over Black,* p. 168.

38. Jordan, *White Over Black,* p. 178.

39. George Washington Cable, "The Freedman's Case in Equity" and "The Silent South," in *The Negro Question: A Selection of Writings on Civil Rights in the South,* ed. Arlin Turner (New York, 1958), pp. 71, 85.

40. Edward S. Abdy, *Journal of a Residence and Tour in the United States,* 3 vols. (London, 1835), quoted in Leonard L. Richards, *Gentlemen of Property and Standing: Anti-Abolition Mobs in Jacksonian America* (New York, 1970), p. 42; Jefferson quoted in Ronald T. Takaki, *Iron Cages: Race and Culture in Nineteenth-Century America* (Seattle, 1979), pp. 46, 49–50; Lincoln quoted in Henry Louis Gates, Jr., "Editor's Introduction: Writing Race and the Difference It Makes," *Critical Inquiry* 12, no. 1 (Autumn 1985): 3.

41. Richards, *Gentlemen,* pp. 45, 166.

42. Mary Boykin Chestnut, *A Diary From Dixie,* ed. Ben Ames (Boston, 1949), pp. 21–22.

43. On race classification in Louisiana, see Virginia R. Dominguez, *White By Definition: Social Classification in Creole Louisiana* (New Brunswick, N.J., 1986). On the "one-drop rule" in general, see Fredrickson, *White Supremacy,* p. 130.

44. Francis Galton, *Finger Prints* (New York, 1892), p. 12; further references to this work will be abbreviated *FP.*

45. SLC to Howells, 21 January 1879, *MTHL*, 1: 246.

46. Arthur Conan Doyle, *The Complete Sherlock Holmes* (Garden City, N.Y., 1930), p. 17.

47. SLC to Fred J. Hall, 30 July 1893, *MTLP*, p. 355. This is the same letter in which the author also expressed enthusiasm for the murder and trial aspects of his newly revised novel (see n. 18).

48. SLC to Miss Darrell, 23 February 1897, typescript in *MTP* (†).

49. Leslie Fiedler, "As Free as Any Cretur . . .," *The New Republic*, 15 & 22 August 1955; rpt. in *Mark Twain: A Collection of Critical Essays*, ed. Henry Nash Smith (Englewood Cliffs, N.J., 1963), p. 138; Cox, *Fate of Humor*, p. 323.

50. I am indebted to Leslie Fiedler's reading of the final Calendar entry as "a disconcerting ending for a detective story, which should have faith in all disclosure" ("As Free as Any Cretur . . ." in *Critical Essays*, p. 138).

51. On the history of developments in anti-civil rights legislation following the Civil War, see Richard Bardolph, ed., *The Civil Rights Record: Black Americans and the Law, 1849–1970* (New York, 1970), pp. 58–72, 144–54.

CHAPTER FOUR

1. William Dean Howells made the "rehabilitation" statement in a letter to Mark Twain dated 9 January 1898, *MTHL*, 2: 668. *Following the Equator* sold 30,000 copies soon after its publication as a subscription book in September 1897.

2. SLC to Howells, 2 April 1899, *MTHL*, 2: 690.

3. Cox, *Fate of Humor*, pp. 245–46 (note).

4. My thinking on *Following the Equator* has been significantly influenced by conversations with Richard Bridgman; see his discussion of sexuality in the novel, especially his analysis of what he calls "a blurring of genders," in his *Traveling in Mark Twain* (Berkeley, 1987), pp. 135–45.

5. Mark Twain *Following the Equator*, 2 vols., in *DE*, 21: 13.

6. Native skin and voices are similarly characterized as fluid: "Indian brown," for example, is "afraid of no color, harmonizing with all colors and adding a grace to them all"; African language "seemed to have no angles or corners, no roughness, no vile *s's* or other hissing sounds, but was very, very mellow and rounded and flowing" (*DE*, 21: 52, 363).

7. See Gilman, *Difference and Pathology*, p. 11.

8. Ibid., 21, 25, 35.

9. On how medical language affected women's roles in Victorian America, see Carroll Smith-Rosenberg's broad-ranging analysis of what she calls "the politicization of the body" ("the transformation of expressive medical metaphors into agencies for social control") in *Disorderly Conduct: Visions of Gender in Victorian America* (New York, 1985), pp. 167–296; see p. 180 for the phrases that I quote.

10. Joel Prentiss Bishop, *New Commentaries on Marriage, Divorce,*

and Separation, 2 vols. (Chicago, 1891), vol. 1, 124–25. Age-of-consent statutes were altered individually, state by state, during the late nineteenth century. A contemporary legal authority, William L. Snyder, explained the variations in age of consent: "This period is not the result of a mere arbitrary rule, but is dictated on account of reasons which spring from physical causes, . . . although this period of development may be reached earlier or later, owing to climactic influences and physical temperament." See Snyder, *The Geography of Marriage; or Legal Perplexities of Wedlock in the United States* (New York and London, 1889), pp. 3–4.

11. Since Twain's time, modern statutes have taken into account the age of the male offender by making penalties less severe if he is a minor. However, if both parties are minors, the male is charged with rape but the female is not, even though she may have been the seducer. Below the age of fourteen, a boy is considered physiologically incapable of rape. See Frederick J. Ludwig, *Rape and the Law: The Crime and Its Proof* (New York, 1977), pp. 7–9.

12. This dictation is catalogued as an independent piece entitled "Imaginary Interview with the President," DV #250, *MTP* (†).

13. *Mark Twain Speaks for Himself*, ed. Paul Fatout (West Lafayette, Ind., 1978), pp. 180–85; further references to this work will be abbreviated *MTS*.

14. *Mark Twain's Autobiography*, ed. Albert Bigelow Paine, 2 vols. (New York, 1924), 2: 146; further references to this work will be abbreviated *MTA* and cited by volume and page number.

15. See Mark Twain and Charles Dudley Warner, *The Gilded Age: A Tale of Today*, ed. Bryant Morey French (Indianapolis and New York, 1972), pp. 417–29; further references to this work will be abbreviated *GA*. Since *The Gilded Age* satirizes what Twain viewed as the abuse of the insanity plea (as well as of the jury system) during the Tweed Ring's control of the New York courts, it is only fair to say that in this case his sympathies are not entirely with the woman. Indeed, though Twain's Laura Hawkins, like Laura Fair, is acquitted after a spectacular court trial, he finally kills her off: she dies of a heart attack when her career as a lecturer fails. See Bryant M. French, "Mark Twain, Laura D. Fair, and the New York Criminal Courts," *American Quarterly* (1964): 545–61.

16. Roger Smith, *Trial By Medicine: Insanity and Responsibility in Victorian Trials* (Edinburgh, 1981), p. 144. My discussion of this issue, here and in the following paragraph, draws heavily on the chapter "Medico-Legal Views of Women," pp. 143–60.

17. *MTB*, 2: 1034; "St. Joan of Arc," in *DE*, 22: 376.

18. Both stories are published in *Mark Twain's Satires and Burlesques*, ed. Franklin R. Rogers (Berkeley and Los Angeles, 1967); further references to this collection will be abbreviated *MTSB*. A newly edited text of "Hellfire Hotchkiss" is to be included in the forthcoming Mark Twain Library volume *Huck Finn and Tom Sawyer Among the Indians*, ed. Dahlia Armon.

19. Here Twain associates the need for verbal affection—praise and encouragement—with women, just as he describes victims of rape as vulnerable to "persuasion"—his euphemism for the verbal (and physical) foreplay leading to seduction.

20. *Personal Recollections of Joan of Arc,* 2 vols., in *DE,* 18: 203.

21. James Cox quotes George Bernard Shaw's preface to *Saint Joan:* "Mark Twain's Joan, skirted to the ground, and with as many petticoats as Noah's wife in a toy ark, is an attempt to combine Bayard with Esther Summerson from *Bleak House* into an unimpeachable American school-teacher in armor." See Cox, *Fate of Humor,* p. 261, n.19.

22. Quoted in Kaplan, *Mr. Clemens and Mark Twain,* p. 315 (note).

23. See "The Aquarium Manuscript," dated "Summertime 1908," DV #375, *MTP* (†).

24. I use the text of "A Medieval Romance" in *DE,* 7: 198–208.

25. Mark Twain, "Feud Story and the Girl Who Was Ostensibly a Man," ca. 1902, DV #325, *MTP* (†). On the top of the first page of the manuscript, Albert Bigelow Paine (Twain's first literary executor) notes, "Unfinished & not usable." While I was completing the draft of this book, the story was published for the first time, edited and with an introduction by Robert Sattelmeyer, in *Missouri Review* 10 (1987): 97–112.

26. Transcript of the trial in F. A. Mackenzie, ed., *The Trial of Harry Thaw* (London, 1928), pp. 191–92. The "Dementia Americana" speech was probably the single most widely quoted and discussed moment of the trial. In a pattern characteristic of the news media's self-consciousness about its own coverage of the trial, many newspaper articles and editorials not only covered the daily courtroom proceedings, but also reported on the various journalistic responses to the trial, especially in out-of-town and foreign papers. (See notes 48 and 49 below for two different examples of how the newspapers quoted each other, particularly in post-trial analysis.) By commenting on media coverage of the Thaw trial—reporting on their own reporting—the newspapers acknowledged, explicitly or implicitly, their own participation as audience in shaping this legal performance and attempted to clarify the meaning of the legal discourse and their own relationship to it.

27. This phrase comes from the first of the three letters written by Clemens to his wife Livy, all dated 17 July 1877, and all of which provide the most "factual" eyewitness account of the original incident as it was happening. See Wecter, *Love Letters,* pp. 197–202.

28. All of this material—the 1877 letters, the original holograph manuscript and an 1898 typescript, and the Autobiographical Dictations of 9 and 10 April 1907—is in *MTP.* So, too, is a letter from Clemens to James J. Tuohy, dated 10 November 1898, offering the story for $1,600.

29. This edition of "Wapping Alice," edited and with an introduction and afterword by Hamlin Hill, is number 29 of the "Keepsake" series (Berkeley, 1981); further references to this work will be abbreviated *WA.*

30. These phrases come from the last two of the 17 July 1877 letters.

See Wecter, *Love Letters*, pp. 199–200. The name "Simon Wheeler" refers to the title character of a play that Mark Twain was composing during that summer, "Cap'n Simon Wheeler, The Amateur Detective, A Light Tragedy." The play, a burlesque of detective fiction, suggests how conjoined were Mark Twain's interests in theatricality and the law.

31. Although it is not clear why Mark Twain should have waited over twenty years to write a story based on the Wapping Alice incident, it is clear that during the summer of 1897, at Weggis, Switzerland, he was working on several pieces that explore sexual identity. Over that summer, in addition to "Wapping Alice," he also wrote "Hellfire Hotchkiss."

32. Quoted in Hill, *Mark Twain: God's Fool*, p. 83.

33. Walter Oettel, *Walter's Sketch Book* (New York, 1943), pp. 54ff.

34. Mark Twain wrote several versions of the last lines, changing the original ("The couple never lived together. There are no heirs.") to "The couple never lived together. They have no family." He then canceled both lines from the typescript that he prepared for publication, restoring the line as I have quoted it in the text only when he revised the holograph for his autobiography. See Hill, Afterword, to *WA*, 78–79.

35. The phrase "phallic woman" is used by Robert J. Stoller in his clinical study of cases of transvestism and fetishistic cross-dressing. See Stoller, *Sex and Gender: On the Development of Masculinity and Femininity*, 2 vols. (New York, 1975), 1: 177.

36. My interpretation of the response to that innovative social phenomenon, the emergence of the New Woman, and how often it was imaged in terms of breakdown and social disorder, derives from the following: Nina Auerbach, *Woman and the Demon: The Life of a Victorian Myth* (Cambridge, Mass., 1982); Gay, *Bourgeois Experience*, vol. 1; Sandra M. Gilbert, "Costumes of the Mind: Transvestism as Metaphor in Modern Literature," in *Writing and Sexual Difference*, ed. Elizabeth Abel (Chicago, 1982), pp. 193–219; Smith-Rosenberg, "The New Woman as Androgyne: Social Order and Gender Crisis, 1870–1936," in *Disorderly Conduct*, pp. 245–96.

37. Howells, *My Mark Twain*, p. 80.

38. Wecter, *Love Letters*, p. 198.

39. These phrases come from an earlier dictation than the rest of Mark Twain's Thaw references, this one the Autobiographical Dictation of 28 February 1907, *MTP* (†).

40. Transcript of William T. Jerome's summing-up for the prosecution, in Gerald Langford, *The Murder of Stanford White* (Indianapolis, 1962), p. 204.

41. All of the newspaper quotations in this paragraph are taken from the *New York Times*, 8 and 9 February 1907.

42. Irvin S. Cobb, *Evening World*, 8 February 1907; quoted in Langford, *Murder of Stanford White*, p. 118.

43. Ibid., 148, 154.

44. Ibid., 203.

45. Transcript, in Langford, *Murder of Stanford White*, p. 103.

46. *New York Times*, 13 April 1907.

47. *New York Tribune*, 13 April 1907.

48. *Morning Leader*, quoted in *New York Times*, 14 April 1907.

49. *Evening Mail*, quoted in *New York Times*, 14 April 1907. (Another instance of the newspapers analyzing and quoting their own coverage of the trial, in this case a British paper. See notes 26 and 48 above.)

50. Thaw's second trial, a year after the first, ended in his being found not guilty by reason of temporary insanity. He was committed to the Mattewean (New York) State Prison for the criminally insane; a sanity trial in 1915 set him free and thus the Harry K. Thaw episode finally came to an end.

51. Howells, *My Mark Twain*, p. 6. (See my earlier discussion of this passage in chapter two.)

52. See Laurence B. Holland, "A 'Raft of Trouble': Word and Deed in *Huckleberry Finn*, *Glyph 5: Johns Hopkins Textual Studies* (Baltimore, 1979); rpt. in Sundquist, *American Realism*, pp. 66–81.

CHAPTER FIVE

1. This statement comes from a passage not included in the abridged version of "My Platonic Sweetheart" published in 1912; see the type script, No. 3A, Box 16, *MTP* (†).

2. For the history of this extraordinary period of development in psychology, see Ellenberger, *Discovery of the Unconscious*; Robert C. Fuller, *Americans and the Unconscious* (New York, 1986); Alan Gauld, *The Founders of Psychical Research* (New York, 1968); Renée Haynes, *The Society for Psychical Research, 1882–1982: A History* (London and Sydney, 1982); Janet Oppenheim, *The Other World: Spiritualism and Psychical Research in England, 1850–1914* (Cambridge, 1985).

3. Quoted and discussed in Gauld, *Founders*, pp. 182–85. For a more openly partisan treatment than Gauld's, see Haynes, *Society for Psychical Research*, pp. 40–43.

4. "What Psychical Research Has Accomplished" was published in parts in various magazines, beginning with *Scribner's* (March 1890), and then in its entirety in *The Will to Believe and Other Essays* (1897); rpt. in *William James on Psychical Research*, ed. Gardner Murphy and Robert Ballou (New York, 1960), pp. 25–47; further references to this collection will be abbreviated *WJ on PR*. James discusses the Census of Hallucinations on pp. 35–36.

5. The most illuminating biographical accounts are Hill, *Mark Twain: God's Fool* (which focuses entirely on the last decade of Twain's life) and Kaplan, *Mr. Clemens and Mark Twain*, pp. 336–88. For John S. Tuckey's pioneering efforts in identifying the background of psychological develop-

ments essential to Twain's late writing, see his *Mark Twain and Little Satan: The Writing of "The Mysterious Stranger"* (Lafayette, Ind., 1963), p. 27; Introduction to *Mark Twain's "Which Was the Dream?" and Other Symbolic Writings of the Later Years* (Berkeley and Los Angeles, 1966), pp. 1–29; further references to this volume will be abbreviated *WWD;* Introduction to *Mark Twain's Fables of Man* (Berkeley and Los Angeles, 1972), pp. 1–29; "Mark Twain's Later Dialogue: The 'Me' and the Machine," *American Literature* 41 (January 1970): 535–37. See also William M. Gibson, ed., Introduction to *The Mysterious Stranger* (Berkeley and Los Angeles, 1969), pp. 26–29; further references to this volume will be abbreviated *MS.*

6. See Howard H. Kerr, *Mediums, Spirit-Rappers, and Roaring Radicals: Spiritualism in American Literature, 1850–1890* (Urbana, Ill., 1972), pp. 22–54, 155–89; Alan Gribben, "Mark Twain, Phrenology, and the 'Temperaments': A Study of Pseudoscientific Influence," *American Quarterly* 24 (1972): 45–68; and Gribben, "Those Other Thematic Patterns in Mark Twain's Writings," *Studies in American Fiction* 13 (1985): 185–200.

7. Kaplan, *Mr. Clemens and Mark Twain,* p. 343.

8. "Not only psychic research," James concludes in "The Last Report," "but metaphysical philosophy and speculative biology are led in their own ways to look with favor on some such 'panpsychic' view of the universe as this" (*The American Magazine* [October 1909]; rpt. *WJ on PR,* 324).

9. Paul Baender, ed., *What Is Man? and Other Philosophical Writings* (Berkeley and Los Angeles, 1973), p. 182; further references to this volume will be abbreviated *WIM.*

10. The letter, dated 4 October 1884, was published under the title "Mark Twain on Thought-Transference" in the *Journal of the Society for Psychical Research* 1 (October 1884): 166–67.

11. See, for example, Cesare Lombroso, *Man of Genius,* trans. from German, *Entartung und Genie* (London, 1891); Max Nordau, *Degeneration* (Berlin, 1892); Frederic W. H. Myers, "The Subliminal Consciousness; The Mechanism of Genius," *Proceedings of the Society for Psychical Research* 8 (1892): 333–61, and his "Genius," chap. 3 in *Human Personality and Its Survival of Bodily Death,* 2 vols. (New York and London, 1903), vol. 1, 70–120. Ellenberger discusses the question of how literary creation in particular was viewed in *Discovery of the Unconscious,* pp. 168–70.

12. Quoted in Haynes, *Society for Psychical Research,* p. 6.

13. C. S. Peirce, "Criticism of *Phantasms of the Living,*" *Proceedings of the American Society for Psychical Research* 1 (December 1887): 150–57. The two-volume study (written by Edmund Gurney, Frederic Myers, and Frank Podmore) and Peirce's response to it are discussed in Gauld, *Founders,* pp. 173–74.

14. G. Stanley Hall, "Review of Some Literature in Psychic Research,"

American Journal of Psychology 7 (1894–95): 135–142, quoted in R. Laurence Moore, *In Search of White Crows: Spiritualism, Parapsychology, and American Culture* (New York, 1977), p. 144. See also Hall's Introduction to *Studies in Spiritism* by Amy M. Tanner (New York, 1910), p. xvi; quoted in Moore, *White Crows*, p. 153.

15. The central passage in the M'Naghten rule holds that an accused is not criminally responsible if, "at the time of committing the act, . . . [he] was labouring under such a defect of reason, from disease of the mind, as not to know the nature and quality of the act he was doing, or, if he did know it, that he did not know he was doing what was wrong" (M'Naghten's Case, 8 Eng. Rep. 718 [1843]). See Roger Smith, *Trial by Medicine: The Insanity Defense in Victorian England* (Edinburgh, 1981), pp. 14–19.

16. H. Maudsley and C. L. Robertson, *Insanity and Crime: A Medicolegal Commentary on the Case of George Victor Townley* (London, 1864), p. 39, quoted in Smith, *Trial By Medicine*, p. 52.

17. Myers reports discussions, in French, German, and even Australian sources, of the "question of 'hypnotic crimes'" and concludes that there is no evidence for such crimes, in *Human Personality*, 1: 198, 513–17. See also Ellenberger, *Discovery of the Unconscious*, pp. 151–58, 763, 768.

18. *GA*, 403. On the subject of the insanity defense and the Laura Fair case, Twain once proposed the following reference to Cain as a dedication for *Roughing It* (1872): "It was his misfortune to live in a dark age that knew not the beneficent Insanity Plea." See *MTL*, 1: 188; *MTB*, 2: 439–40.

19. John Charles Bucknill, *Unsoundness of Mind in Relation to Criminal Acts* (London, 1854), quoted in Charles E. Rosenberg, *The Trial of the Assassin Guiteau: Psychiatry and the Law in the Gilded Age* (Chicago, 1968), p. 56.

20. *William James on Exceptional Mental States: The 1896 Lowell Lectures*, ed. Eugene Taylor (Amherst, Mass., 1984), pp. 131, 147–48; further references to this work will be abbreviated *WJ on EMS*. James's lecture notes quote from Lombroso, who uses Longfellow, Bellamy, Tennyson, Coleridge, George Eliot, and Bulwer as examples of degenerative anomalies in geniuses; James also notes that Max Nordau cites symptoms of morbidity in Ruskin, Ibsen, Tolstoy, Zola, and the pre-Raphaelites— among others (see p. 156).

21. Regarding exactly what we know of Twain's reading of William James, according to Alan Gribben, he probably read *Principles of Psychology* in London during 1896. See Gribben, *Mark Twain's Library*, vol. 1, 351.

22. SLC to Sir John Adams, 5 December 1898, quoted in Lawrence Clark Powell, "An Unpublished Mark Twain Letter," *American Literature* 13 (January 1942): 405–7. Sir John Adams, a professor in Glasgow, had just sent Clemens a copy of his new book *The Herbartian Psychology Applied to Education, Being a Series of Essays Applying the Psychology of*

Johann Friedrich Herbart (Boston, 1897). See Tuckey, Introduction to *WWD*, p. 17, for a discussion of the possible influence of *Herbartian Psychology* on one of Twain's late dream tales, "The Great Dark."

23. Myers, *Human Personality*, 2: 117–18.

24. Théodore Flournoy, *Des Indes à la Planète Mars. Etude sur un cas de Somnambulisme avec glossolalie* (Paris and Geneva, 1900); an English translation was published by *Harper* in 1900 as *From India to the Planet Mars. A Study of a Case of Somnambulism with Glossolalia* (New York and London, 1900).

25. Mark Twain, "Mental Telegraphy," in *DE*, 22: 111–12.

26. SLC to Sir John Adams, 5 December 1898 (see note 22).

27. De Voto, *Mark Twain at Work*, p. 116; Kaplan, *Mr. Clemens and Mark Twain*, p. 340.

28. Twain jotted this idea for a play in a note dated January 1898, Unpublished Notebook, TS #32B, p. 54, *MTP* (†).

29. Mark Twain, *The American Claimant*, in *DE*, 15: 12, 27.

30. The whole Lambton discussion occurs in "Mental Telegraphy," *DE*, 22: 127–28. This account is a slightly revised version of an entry Twain made in his notebook, 1 August 1880, in *Mark Twain's Notebooks and Journals*, ed. Frederick Anderson, Lin Salamo, and Bernard L. Stein (Berkeley and Los Angeles, 1975), vol. 2, *1877–1883*, p. 367.

31. *MTN*, 72–73. See Kaplan, *Mr. Clemens and Mark Twain*, pp. 332–33, on the connection between Paige as an inventor and the poet or artist.

32. On several occasions during April 1900, SLC corresponded with William James on the efficacy of Jonas Kellgren's treatment; he highly recommended the osteopathic treatment in conjunction with Plasmon. These letters, dated 17 and 23 April 1900, are in Houghton Library, Harvard University.

33. SLC to Richard Watson Gilder, 23 July 1899, quoted in Kaplan, *Mr. Clemens and Mark Twain*, p. 353.

34. SLC to Olivia Langdon Clemens, 27–30 January 1894, *MTP* (†).

35. SLC to Susy Clemens, 7 February 1896, *MTP* (†).

36. SLC to Laura Fitch McQuiston, 26 March 1901, MS Cyril Clemens, Kirkwood, Missouri.

37. Gribben notes that on 30 September 1896 Twain included the James book in a list of works he wished to obtain; see *Mark Twain's Library*, p. 351.

38. See Notebook 39, TS p. 36, *MTP* (†).

39. F. W. H. Myers, Introduction to *Phantasms of the Living*, 2 vols. (London, 1886), vol. 1, xlii–xliii. See Tuckey, Introduction, to *WWD*, p. 26, for speculation on how Twain's reading during the winter of 1897 may have influenced his long, January 1898 notebook entry on the dream-self.

40. Mark Twain, "Shackleford's Ghost," DV #318, *MTP* (†). The manuscript is dated, by Albert Bigelow Paine, "90s." David Ketterer conjectures that these notes were probably written in the year following the

publication of H. G. Wells's *The Invisible Man* (1897), a conjecture supported by Twain's reference in the first draft of *What Is Man?* (written in 1898) to "Mr. Wells's man who invented a drug that made him invisible" (*WIM*, p. 179). See Ketterer's Introduction to *The Science Fiction of Mark Twain* (Hamden, Conn., 1984), pp. xxvii–xxviii.

41. See Ellenberger, *Discovery of the Unconscious*, p. 118; and for an ethnographic account of how the particular phenomenon of multiple personality was linked to the cultural situation of women in the late nineteenth century, see Michael G. Kenny, *The Passion of Ansel Bourne: Multiple Personality in American Culture* (Washington, D.C., 1986), pp. 129–59.

42. Moore, *White Crows*, pp. 112–13, 118; see Moore's penetrating discussion of what he calls "female professionalism" in "The Medium and Her Message," pp. 102–29.

43. Cox, *Fate of Humor*, pp. 271–72. "Paine's edition," Cox concludes, "was clearly a brilliant performance, . . . the closest thing to Twain's intention that we shall ever have." Albert Bigelow Paine, together with Frederick Duneka of Harper & Brothers, edited the 1916 *Mysterious Stranger*, using the second of Twain's four attempts to write this story, and grafting onto this "Eseldorf" manuscript a separate six-page conclusion that Twain intended for the last ("Print Shop") version and which Paine discovered among Twain's papers after his death. (See Gibson, Introduction to *MS*, pp. 1–4.)

44. See Gribben, *Mark Twain's Library*, p. 495.

45. James's obituary for Myers credits him with taking "a lot of scattered phenomena, some of them recognized as reputable, others outlawed from science, or treated as isolated curiosities; he made series of them, . . . and bound them together in a system by his bold inclusive conception of the Subliminal Self." The obituary was published under the title "Frederic Myers's Service to Psychology," *Proceedings of the Society for Psychical Research* 17 (May 1901): 13–23; rpt. *WJ on PR*, 217. Théodore Flournoy's review of Myers's *Human Personality* similarly comments on the way in which the theory of the subliminal self drew together "une foule de théories analogues mais moins élaborées," in *Proceedings of the Society for Psychical Research* 18 (June 1903): 46.

46. F. W. H. Myers, "Multiplex Personality," *Proceedings of the Society for Psychical Research* 4 (1886–87): 496–514; for a definition of Myers's basic terminology, see his *Human Personality*, 1: 12–18.

47. F. W. H. Myers, "The Subliminal Consciousness. Chap. 1—General Characteristics of Subliminal Messages," *Proceedings of the Society for Psychical Research* 7 (1891–92): 305. Freud's connection to Myers's theories is primarily through Freud's early work with Breuer on hysteria and on the use of hypnosis as a therapeutic tool. Myers publicized their *Studien uber Hysterie* (1895) in England, and cites it in *Human Personality* as a "valuable contribution," particularly to the understanding of the "idée

fixe." Symptoms which to others would have seemed "merely baffling and capricious," Myers says, draw from "Dr. Freud a psychological lesson which illustrates with curious delicacy the superposition of strata more and more segregated from waking consciousness" (*Human Personality*, 1: 50–52). Freud himself became a member of the SPR in 1911, though Ellenberger and others agree that he remained sceptical about parapsychological phenomena. On the Freud connection to psychical research, see Ellenberger, *Discovery of the Unconscious*, pp. 534, 771–76; Fuller, *Americans and the Unconscious*, pp. 97–108; Kenny, *Passion of Ansel Bourne*, pp. 85–94; Oppenheim, *Other World*, pp. 245, 454–55.

48. Myers, "Subliminal Consciousness," p. 301.

49. Meyers, *Human Personality*, 1: 13–18.

50. "Frederic Myers's Service to Psychology," in *WJ on PR*, 218–19.

51. Meyers, *Human Personality*, 1: 71.

52. Ibid., 1: 150. In this chapter on "Sleep," Myers emphasizes the importance of reversing the "negative" way sleep has "generally been treated": "We cannot be content merely to dwell, with the common textbooks, on the mere *absence* of waking faculties; . . . we must treat sleep *positively*" (p. 122).

53. On the importance of play to "No.44," see Bruce Michelson, "*Deus Ludens:* The Shaping of Mark Twain's *Mysterious Stranger*," *Novel* 14 (Fall 1980): 44–56.

54. William James, Review of *Human Personality*, *Proceedings of the Society for Psychical Research* 18 (1903); rpt. in *WJ on PR*, 237; *MS*, 376.

55. See Gibson, Introduction to *MS*, p. 10, for both Gibson's and Twain's own critique of this part of the plot (Twain's assessment: it is "too diffusive").

56. Gibson also notes the Colonel Sellers connection in ibid., 10, 26.

57. On the dating of this part of the manuscript, see ibid., 10–11.

58. See Pascal Covici's discussion of "the hoax as cosmology" in *Mark Twain's Humor: The Image of a World* (Dallas, 1962), pp. 213–50.

59. *MS*, 383; see also Gibson, Introduction, p. 24, and his Explanatory Notes, p. 482 (n. 383.29).

60. In this sense, James Cox is right to say not only that the dream ending is "a goal to be reached" *and* a beginning, but also that "the ending gives the lie to the identity of the book" (*Fate of Humor*, pp. 282–84).

61. Myers, *Human Personality*, 1: 151.

62. I am indebted to John Tuckey, who coined the phrase "micromacrocosmic" to describe the perspective of the dream writings; see his Introduction to *The Devil's Race-Track: Mark Twain's Great Dark Writings* (Berkeley and Los Angeles, 1980), pp. ix–xvii.

CHAPTER SIX

1. Cox, *Fate of Humor*; see especially pp. 222–24.

2. See Cox's extended analysis of this last phase of Twain's career,

beginning with the "kingdom of personality" and focusing on the Auto-biographical Dictations, in ibid., 297–310; for a whole work devoted to the "making of Twain's public personality" and his status as a "culture-hero," see Budd, *Our Mark Twain;* for two biographical works that address the late period of Twain's celebrity and its costs, see Kaplan, *Mr. Clemens and Mark Twain*, pp. 361–63, and Hill, *Mark Twain: God's Fool*, pp. 118–77.

3. Not until the U.S. Copyright Code of 1909 was the maximum copyright of authors and heirs extended from 42 to 56 years. There are several, slightly different versions of Twain's 1906 testimony. The earliest text is Copyright Hearings, 7 to 11 December 1906; *Statements Before the Committees on Patents of the Senate and House of Representatives, Conjointly, on the Bills S. 6330 and H.R. 19853* (Washington, 1906). The most readily available text, and the one from which I will quote, is "Remarks on Copyright," in Fatout, *Mark Twain Speaking*, pp. 533–40.

4. Howells, *My Mark Twain*, p. 80.

5. See *Mark Twain's Speeches*, compiled by F. A. Nast, with an Introduction by William Dean Howells (New York, 1910), pp. 85–89.

6. Autobiographical Dictation, 23 November 1906, *MTP* (†).

7. Twain's point about the law is taken from *Statements Before the Committees on Patents of the Senate and House of Representatives;* the quotation on property in ideas comes from Fatout, *Mark Twain Speaking*, p. 537.

8. My discussion of the *Such* case and of the legal issue of trademark relies upon Feinstein, "Mark Twain's Lawsuits," pp. 15–68.

9. The remark on Twain's patenting himself is quoted in ibid., 23; for a brief discussion of incorporation as self-perpetuation, see Budd, *Our Mark Twain*, p. 225. The remaining two quotations in the paragraph come from Feinstein, "Mark Twain's Lawsuits," pp. 23, 41.

10. On Twain's white dress at the copyright hearings, see Kaplan, *Mr. Clemens and Mark Twain*, pp. 379–81; Hill, *Mark Twain: God's Fool*, pp. 157–58; Budd, *Our Mark Twain*, pp. 207–12.

11. See "Interview," 7 December 1906, in Fatout, *Mark Twain Speaking*, p. 532.

12. *New York Times*, 10 December 1906, 8 December 1906; *The World*, 8 December 1906.

13. All of the quotation in this paragraph comes from "Interview," in Fatout, *Mark Twain Speaking*, pp. 530–31, with the exception of the reporter's question, which is quoted in *The World*, 8 December 1906.

14. See *MTB*, 3: 1340–48.

15. Howells, *My Mark Twain*, p. 80.

16. A strikingly similar conjunction of virtually all of these issues appears in the Autobiographical Dictation of 26 December 1906, *MTP* (†). Dictated only a few weeks after the copyright hearings, this piece covers the following subjects: Twain's experiments in phrenology with Fowler, in which Twain presented himself to the phrenologist twice, once under

an assumed name and then under both his own name and his *nom de guerre*, all in an effort to test phrenological claims of reading the personality through "bumps" in the skull; Twain's experiments in palmistry and its claim to read character in the palm of the hand; and, finally, the copyright speech itself. As with the "Wapping Alice" Autobiographical Dictations of 9 and 10 April 1907, the apparent randomness of Twain's thoughts speaks tellingly once the particular juxtapositions he makes are contextualized.

17. James Cox takes a similar view of the Autobiographical Dictations, arguing that Twain's "public personality and art were his forms of genuine expression," less censored and more revealing than his "private writings"; see *Fate of Humor*, pp. 303–5. Budd, too, argues for the centrality of the public personality in Twain's art; see Introduction, *Our Mark Twain*, pp. xiii–xiv.

INDEX